Quality

OR ELSE

Quality
OR ELSE

THE REVOLUTION IN
WORLD BUSINESS

Lloyd Dobyns and
Clare Crawford-Mason

Houghton Mifflin Company
BOSTON / NEW YORK

For information about permission to reproduce selections from
this book, write to Permissions, Houghton Mifflin Company,
215 Park Avenue South, New York, New York 10003.

Library of Congress Cataloguing-in-Publication Data

Dobyns, Lloyd.
Quality or else : the revolution in world business /
Lloyd Dodyns and Clare Crawford-Mason.
p.   cm.
Includes bibliographical references.
ISBN 0-395-57439-0
ISBN 0-395-63749-X (pbk.)
1. Total quality management.   I. Crawford-Mason, Clare
II. Title
HD62.15.D63   1991   91-24378
658.5 — dc20   CIP

Printed in the United States of America

BP 10 9 8 7 6 5 4 3 2 1

To Reuven Frank
who always made it possible for us to do our best
and made it enjoyable.

CONTENTS

Quality

OR ELSE

Introduction

Quality is a system, and it is the one system that can solve America's economic problems. Quality can also improve education, streamline federal and state bureaucracies, help with growing social problems, and maybe even make airlines run on time. We are not economists but journalists who try to explain complicated subjects in straightforward terms. Statisticians understand how a quality system works better than we do, but they explain it in statistical terms, and that doesn't help unless you have a strong mathematical background. We stumbled onto the economy and its problems on assignment when we worked on a television documentary called *If Japan Can, Why Can't We?*, which appeared in the summer of 1980.

The program examined industrial productivity, a subject that may make your eyes glaze over, but this will interest you: productivity controls our future. Because industrial productivity in the United States was essentially flat from 1973 into the 1990s, median family income was also essentially flat. Adjusted for inflation, the average American worker actually lost money. Figures from the Bureau of Labor Statistics show that the average American worker in private industry made $187 a week in 1970. By 1989 the same worker made about $167, a loss of $20 a week in twenty years. The only way a worker can make more money and live better is for productivity to go up. Productivity is simply how much you can make and how much it costs to make it. The more you can make for less, the higher your productivity. It's that simple.

The documentary ended with this statement: "Unless we solve the problem of productivity, our children will be the first generation in the history of the United States to live *worse* than their parents." Since then the problem has gotten worse, not better. Judith Waldrop, the research editor of *American Demographics* magazine, writes that Americans will know it's the twenty-first century when "parents no longer dream of better lives for their children." She is off a little. Fifty-six percent of young Americans, from sixteen to twenty-four years old, said in late 1990 that the world would be a worse place for their children, and 70 percent said the world had been a better place for their parents. Pessimistic as that sounds, it could be right. At current rates of productivity growth, our children will live no better than we do, nor will our grandchildren. As other people in more productive countries catch up to, then exceed, the American standard of living, our grandchildren will not thank us for having made them citizens of what will seem a Third World country, backward and nonindustrial.

That is not carved in stone, however. We believe that there is a way out and that quality is the answer. We aren't talking about quality as if it were decency, nobility, truth, and true justice. We're talking about quality as a better way of producing goods and services, a way that eliminates waste, gives employees pride in their work, and keeps the customer coming back for more. Quality starts in research and development and involves every part of the company (school, hospital, office), including suppliers and customers. It is the first and last thing you think of, and you keep it in mind in between.

As you produce quality, productivity automatically goes up and costs automatically go down. People have been taught by economists that quality costs more, but a good deal of what is taught about the economy is outdated. In fact, quality costs less, which helps to explain why the Japanese could sell a better car for less money in the 1980s, why a Japanese stereo system in the 1970s would produce better sound for a longer time with less trouble than a more expensive American model. Except for outrageously expensive components, the Japanese all but own the stereo business because they learned a better way to build quality products for less money. Understanding that is part of a subtle but important distinction. What Americans have done is *not wrong*, but what the Japanese do now is *better*. To understand how that happened, we decided to take a historical approach because, to the best of our knowledge, no one has ever written the history of the quality movement. Once you understand its history, understanding what happened and why becomes much easier.

Essentially, American economic problems are in four broad areas: money, machines, management, and manpower. These are the four elements of a classic capitalist economy, but economists usually refer to them as capital, technology, management, and labor, proving that economists know more about economics than they do about alliteration.

Of the four, money is the easiest to explain. The United States now owes more money than any other country on earth. As a nation, the United States has been badly in debt before, but it spent the borrowed money then to build railroads and harbors and bridges; the country invested in ways that would help it prosper, and it prospered. This time the United States is in debt because people, companies, and the government all decided that they wanted what they wanted, they wanted it yesterday, and they borrowed to get it. They didn't invest a dime; they consumed it all in an orgy of borrowing and spending. As a result, the United States has a $3 trillion–plus national debt, a figure that makes no sense because no one can comprehend a trillion. (The oldest known written record is 6,000 years old; if you convert years to seconds, 6,000 years is right at 189 billion seconds. One trillion seconds is 30,000 years and then some. That many years ago was about the time prehistoric man was learning to make sound by drumming on a hollow log with a stick.)

The harm caused by owing that much money is not that debt is somehow immoral or indecent but that interest must be paid on it, and that interest payment is already the third largest item in the federal budget and going up. In 1990 the federal government spent not quite $265 billion in interest — not to pay off the debt, just to pay that year's interest — and that's more than $1,000 for every man, woman, and child in the country in just one year. Money being spent on interest cannot be spent on schools, bridges, social programs, defense, agriculture, research, or anything else even remotely useful.

There's another way to try to comprehend the U.S. national debt. How long does it take you to earn $30,000? In early 1990, the U.S. government borrowed that much *every five seconds*. Still, despite this huge federal debt, Americans were told by their political leaders not to worry about the federal budget deficit because it was coming down. It was, in fact, going up. Congress was simply playing games with the social security and other federal trust funds.

In 1981, for the first time, the United States owed a trillion dollars. By 1988, that figure had tripled. In eight years the government had borrowed twice as much as it had in its entire history, from George Washington through Jimmy Carter. However, no one seemed to care. Ronald Reagan had criticized President Carter in the 1980 presidential campaign because Carter had had a $20 billion deficit the year before. Reagan said that if he were elected, he'd do something about it. The voters elected him, and he did something about it: he made it ten times worse. In 1983 the deficit was $200 billion. Congress, of course, helped with the spending; Congress is dependable that way.

What would really do something about the debt — something positive, for a change — would be for the federal and state governments and private businesses to adopt quality programs. Of course, were it as simple as that, everyone could get it done by Tuesday. A quality program, however, is extremely difficult and time-consuming to implement; there is no easy way. Worse, what is required is a change in an organization's entire philosophy. It isn't a matter of an adjustment here, a bit of fine tuning there; quality is a change in the structure and purpose of an organization, whether it's a manufacturing plant, an insurance office, or a public school. The only reason to do it is because it works. Private industry profits would increase, meaning more tax revenue. Government efficiency would increase, meaning that services would cost less. Tax revenue goes up, government costs go down, the deficit shrinks, and no one necessarily has to pay higher tax rates or get fewer services. It would be the exact opposite of what is happening now and has been happening for ten years or more. Very simply, Americans must change to survive.

Individuals can make their own contributions by saving more, which almost always means spending less. The more money people put away, the more money there is to finance long-term improvements in business and industry. Because of the massive debt on all levels, it has cost more for American businesses to borrow than it has their foreign rivals. Every increase in costs makes it harder to compete.

The two of us watched the United States slip farther and farther into the hole, partly because working on the documentary had made us curious about what would happen and partly because we had learned that the economy was not nearly so mysterious as we had been led to believe. It can be understood; it can even be fun. After all, what we're talking about is the money in your pocket and what you can do with it. Economic theories can get a bit thick; our advice is to ignore them in favor of what you can see for yourself or accept as logical. Unless you're working on your doctorate in economics, theories won't help much anyway.

We have used as little theory as possible in putting together this book. It's based more on what we've seen, who we've interviewed, where we've been. We've worked for several years with W. Edwards Deming, the man who helped teach the Japanese how to produce quality goods after World War II. We introduced him to the American public in our documentary, and in recent years we've helped him with his videocassette series. In 1989 Florida Power and Light became the first American company to win the Deming Prize, *Japan's* highest award for industrial productivity and quality.

It seems ironic that Japan's prize is named for an American, particularly one who was all but unknown in his own country outside the rarefied worlds of statistics and academia. He was not a major figure nor even an important minor one in American industry before 1980. By contrast, Robert C. Christopher in *Second to None* says, "The Deming awards are pursued by Japanese-based corporations with almost the intensity of Sir Gawain pursuing the Holy Grail." Christopher calls Deming "one of the most revered figures in Japan's business pantheon." David Halberstam in *The Reckoning* agreed: "With the possible exception of Douglas MacArthur, he [Deming] was the most famous and most revered American in Japan during the postwar years."

We've been around the world, literally, looking for examples of companies that produce quality, not only in manufacturing but in services and education as well. The single worst problem Americans now face is education. We went to a high school in Sitka, Alaska, that has taken the Deming quality method, now widely used in industry, and adapted it to education. It's working, and imagine what that could mean — better schools at less cost, students who can read, write, do simple mathematics, and hold a job.

We've talked with some of the best-known executives in Fortune 500 companies and with some people you never heard of in companies that aren't even big enough to qualify as small. We've talked to economists, production workers, teachers, line foremen, office workers, truck drivers, mechanics, students, telephone installers and operators, auto workers, steelworkers, chemical workers. We've talked to economists, middle-level managers, government officials, industrial consultants, and military personnel as well as professors, psychiatrists, psychologists, and public opinion experts. We've studied industrial history and read economic and social forecasts, and we've listened to people's dreams and fears. We believe this is the first time that all these viewpoints on quality have been gathered in one place, and we were surprised to find that, taken together, all that information paints a new picture of the world, everything from international competition to how people feel about their jobs.

We've also added our own experience. Clare started her own production company, made a profit, and learned personally the meaning of government regulations, tax reports, marketing, public relations, and a lot of other things she had previously reported but now experienced. One temporary early lesson was that *undercapitalized* means the same thing as *broke;* it's a trade-off — the former sounds nicer, but it's harder to spell.

Lloyd lived in Japan for two years, reporting from Asia, often about international trade and national economies in China, Vietnam, the Philippines, Korea, and Thailand as well as Japan. He learned that in almost all circumstances, Deep Throat was absolutely right — follow the money.

We did the research and interviews for this book in eight countries in Asia and Europe because this is not an "us" against "them" polemic. We aren't wrapped in the flag, dashing for the ramparts. That's not the problem. No one has questioned America's patriotism, only its products. We are reporters, and for this assignment we've tried to stand back and look at the world to find out what works and what doesn't, to see who is doing what to whom and why. In the end, of course, we talk mostly about American business and industry and what quality can do to ensure the country's future, but you could change the names, and the discussion would apply just as well to any other industrial country.

We'll start with history, because without that background, what follows would be like starting a motion picture in the middle —

you can vaguely puzzle out who the players are and what the plot is, but you're guessing. We don't want you to guess. We had the best experts we could find explain what's happening in the global economy, and we'll introduce the best-known American and Japanese quality teachers. All of these experts were studied by an American company that then developed its own quality system. We'll take you through it. We get into the role of government in quality; that is, what Washington, D.C., is doing that it probably shouldn't, and what it probably should do but isn't — at least, not yet. One thing the government did do that *may* prove to be useful is create the Malcolm Baldrige National Quality Award. We'll talk about the award and the winners. There's a chapter on America's economic problems, and they're not just money and interest and global competition. How about increasing violent crime and jammed prisons, hospitals that seem sicker than their patients, and public schools that don't satisfy anyone, least of all the students? They could all be helped by quality programs.

All the quality experts agree that if any quality program is going to succeed, it must involve the top. Without the commitment of senior management, nothing gets better. "The job of management," Deming writes, "is not supervision, but leadership." Leadership requires a long-term outlook, but American business and industry is organized on a short-term basis, where the quarterly profit-and-loss statement controls the price of the stock, and the price of the stock is widely and wrongly believed to show the health of the company. Management, therefore, concentrates on the paper value of the company — the stock price — to the detriment of the product, the customer, the community, and the work force.

The workers also have a key role to play. In the 1970s and early '80s in the United States, senior management of the major corporations routinely said that American workers were the problem. They aren't and never have been. In a quality program, workers are recognized as part of the solution. We'll look at the new roles for workers and leaders in a company using a quality program. Finally, we try to tie it all together to explain what needs to be done or what we believe the consequences of not doing it will be.

T. J. Blackhurst, from the class of 1991 at Mount Edgecumbe High School in Sitka, said that all the nation's schools "are going to have to get in gear if we're going to make it." That is as good an analysis of what we face in education, government, service, and manufacturing as you are likely to find. If we are going to make it, we are going to have to get in gear.

The gear is quality. Or else.

Lloyd Dobyns
Garner, North Carolina

Clare Crawford-Mason
Washington, D.C.
June 1991

1

Building Good Ships

For most of the last fifty years, the United States was the agricultural and industrial supplier to the world. At one point after World War II, the United States controlled a third of the total world economy and made half of all the manufactured goods sold anywhere in the world. Now Americans buy more from other countries than they can sell to them; no one particularly wants the products that used to be the envy of the world. If there is one single person who caused that turnabout, it is General of the Army Douglas MacArthur, Supreme Commander of the Allied Powers in Japan after World War II. He did not do it on purpose; Japan's economic success is the unintended consequence of a logical decision. MacArthur wanted reliable radios, a lot of them, so that the occupation forces' orders and propaganda programs could be heard in every town and village in occupied Japan, and when Japanese manufacturers in the 1940s couldn't give the general what he wanted, he sent for Americans to teach them how.

Think of that: one man wanted a radio that worked, and the world economic order changed.

Among the Americans MacArthur sent for was twenty-nine-year-old Homer M. Sarasohn, a systems and electronics engineer with experience in physics, radio, and radar. He agreed to go to Japan for nine months to survey its communications problems. He stayed more than five years and learned to speak Japanese so that he could teach more effectively. Charles W. Protzman, a forty-eight-year-old engineer from Western Electric, joined him in 1948. A year later, those two got a new and sympathetic boss, Frank Polkinghorn from Bell Laboratories in New Jersey. With his blessing, Protzman and Sarasohn started teaching the Japanese how to manage modern manufacturing firms. It was not a general, theoretical course; it was, according to Kenneth Hopper, who studied what happened, "a concentration of how to manage technology, and in particular, how to manage a factory." Sarasohn and Protzman quoted on the first page of their instruction manual an American industrialist named Collis P. Huntington. He was one of the tycoons who built the transcontinental railroad in the 1860s, and at an age when most men retire, he built the Newport News Shipbuilding and Drydock Company along the James River in Virginia. Huntington wrote the company motto that Sarasohn and Protzman quoted to help the Japanese understand what quality meant: "We shall build good ships here; at a profit if we can, at a loss if we must, but always good ships."

When the war ended, it's doubtful the Japanese could have built ships at all, good or bad. American bombing raids had reduced Japan to rubble. No port city was less than 70 percent destroyed, no industrial city less than 40 percent destroyed, and many were much worse than that. Tokyo had been all but burned to the ground by an American incendiary air raid in March 1945, and in August atomic bombs were dropped on Hiroshima and Nagasaki.

Paul Connolly, a Washington attorney, was the first American into Hiroshima after the bombing. A young naval officer on the destroyer *John Pierce*, Connolly led a landing party into the city to assess the damage. In an interview in 1976 he said, "We weren't prepared for the devastation that we saw en route. The countryside was almost deserted. I don't know what the weather was, but I have an abiding impression everything seemed gray. . . . We were appalled at the final scene. We saw a desert stretching maybe three, four miles in diameter where there was literally nothing above your shoe tops."

A Japanese businessman writing of that postwar period said that Japan's industrial capacity had been reduced to "piles of ashes and skeletons of scrap." It was no better in February 1946, when Sarasohn arrived: "Factories no longer existed, and people were starving. They had no food. There was no public transportation. The Japanese economy did not exist any longer." MacArthur himself wrote later, "Never in history had a nation and its people been more completely crushed."

Sarasohn's orders were to build reliable radios so that the Japanese could listen to American "information and education programs," to take care of the communications needs of the occupation forces, and to use the communications industry as an example of how the Japanese economy could be revived.

The economic revival of Japan was not a universally popular idea in the late 1940s. Senator William P. Knowland, a conservative from California, demanded a congressional investigation of MacArthur's economic policies, which conservatives saw as socialistic, or worse. Henry Morgenthau, Jr., Truman's secretary of the treasury, resigned when his plans to totally dismantle German industry and occupy Japan for twenty *generations* were rejected. The idea of punishing the former enemy also existed on MacArthur's staff. The Economic and Scientific Section (ESS), which was essentially responsible for all Japanese industry except communications, opposed Sarasohn's and Protzman's plan to reeducate the communications industry. The ESS was larger than the Civil Communication Section (CCS), which Sarasohn worked for, but neither side would back down. MacArthur had to decide.

Each section had twenty minutes, no more, to persuade the general. Sarasohn argued for the CCS, and he remembers the ESS man saying that "we would create a monster . . . that we didn't know what would be the end result of all this, but we should not give them any more to work with to improve their status than we absolutely had to." Did the ESS man see the future Japanese economic competition with the United States? Sarasohn says no. "We did not look down the road that far. . . . My own faith, my own belief in the American system was that we could meet any competition. . . . That same confidence in America is what buoyed my argument." Sarasohn's argument was pragmatic: the United States couldn't stay in Japan forever, so the Japanese economy had to be put back on its feet. "I finished, and during all of this time on both arguments, MacArthur sat in back of his desk, smoking his pipe, no reaction whatsoever. I had no idea how well I was getting, if indeed I was getting over to him. Finally, a minute or so after I had finished and sat down, he got up and started walking out of the office, and I thought, 'Oh, boy, I've blown it.' Just as he about reached the door, he turned around, and he stared at me, and all he said was, 'All right, go do it!' And he walked out."

Sarasohn and Protzman, sitting in separate hotel rooms in Osaka for thirty days, wrote their own textbook, then Polkinghorn added a foreword praising democracy, equality, and cooperation and condemning "greed, selfishness and other antisocial characteristics." A few copies of *The CCS Management Seminar* manual, four hundred typewritten pages, still exist. Later Sarasohn wrote a textbook in Japanese titled *The Industrial Application of Statistical Quality Control*, although when the Union of Japanese Scientists and Engineers (JUSE) first asked for a course in statistical quality control, Sarasohn refused. He said JUSE believed that statistical quality control was "the real secret" that had let America win the war. "Now, if they could get hold of statistical quality control, then — and this is a quote — they could regain their 'place in the sun.' I put a squash to that movement." Sarasohn wanted to get factories operating before he taught the Japanese any theory. In fact, what he taught them was a complex theory, but to his engineer's mind it seemed simple, practical, and straightforward: "My conception of all of this is that what exists is a system. . . . You're not looking at one factory . . . you're looking at a *system*, the input of which is your design, the purpose for which you want this item to exist, and everything that it takes to get to the customer and place that item in his hands to his satisfaction."

The idea that making products or performing services was part of a system had been catching on slowly in the United States since the 1920s and was essentially the second step in the search for quality. The first step had been inspection — the master checking his apprentice's work, the buyer checking the craftsman's product. Inspection works well on an individual basis, but in mass production it is expensive and wasteful. An inspector can only separate good from bad *after* it's already made, and it costs just as much to make it wrong as it does to make it right. That's why typically, the experts say, 20 to 40 percent of a manufacturing plant's budget is spent to build, find, and fix mistakes. If, however, mass production is viewed as a system, then statistics can analyze what the system is doing, then be used to get it under control. By eliminating waste, you drive costs down; at a very minimum you save the money you don't spend fixing mistakes. That was being taught to some American engineers during World War II, but the idea was not widespread.

Sarasohn is not sure where he heard it before he taught it to the Japanese. "It just seemed natural to me," he says. "It was the way things should go, and from an engineering point of view, it made sense." Myron Tribus, the former director of the MIT Center for Advanced Engineering Study and a director of Exergy, Inc., asked Sarasohn later how he had known all that at his age. Sarasohn still doesn't know how he knew, he just knew. Other experts agree that he was right: producing anything from a ton of steel to a megawatt of electricity to a bank loan to an insurance policy to a restaurant meal is a system, and unless you look at the whole system simultaneously and find out what it can do, you can't improve it. The CCS management seminar lasted eight hours a day, four days a week, for eight weeks. "And the people who attended were the

14

senior executives, a president, a chief executive. . . . They were required to attend; they could not send deputies." American occupation forces could require what they liked, and while Sarasohn says he believes in democracy and individual rights, "at that time, in that position, with our charge to revive the Japanese economy, I became a dictator." Those he wanted to attend were simply ordered to be there. Some of Japan's leading industrialists now were Sarasohn's and Protzman's students then — whether they wanted to be or not.

Sarasohn's first question to the students was, "Why is your company in business?" No one had an answer. "And that was the starting point for my argument that there has to be a purpose, there has to be a reason for a company to be in business. A company cannot be merely a money-making machine; it had to have a purpose that went beyond mere profit." Like building good ships.

When Japanese plants first started working again after the war, it was a good day when ten out of one hundred radio vacuum tubes were made well enough to use, a 90 percent failure rate. However, quality was not the American team's first concern. The plan was to get factories running with Americans in charge, then find competent Japanese who had not been managers of war industries to take over, and then get them trained at a CCS seminar. The final phase was to wind down American supervision and get the Japanese managers trained in quality control. Sarasohn wanted quality control to be taught by Walter A. Shewhart, the man who had developed the theory of statistical control of quality while working at Western Electric, but he wasn't available.

Sarasohn remembers that the ESS then turned to Deming, a friend of Shewhart's and a former statistician with the U.S. Census Bureau who had helped the American occupation forces with statistical sampling techniques to get reliable Japanese population figures. MacArthur's headquarters arranged for Deming to be invited to lecture in Japan by Kenichi Koyanagi, the managing director of JUSE, the same group Sarasohn had originally turned down when it asked for statistical quality control training. JUSE members started studying some of Shewhart's material on their own in 1949, but Koyanagi wrote later that he believed "a lecture course by a famous statistician like Dr. Deming could bring about epochal results." Deming agreed to give lectures to the Japanese.

What Deming would teach was a new philosophy of quality that had evolved from techniques he and others had developed for the War Production Board to help improve American war matériel. During the war, urged by Deming and with his help, thirty-five thousand U.S. industrial engineers and technicians were taught to use statistics to find out how to get better results in manufacturing.

For a week in July 1950, three months before his fiftieth birthday and one month after the Korean War began, Deming, through a translator, taught "Elementary Principles of the Statistical Control of Quality" to 230 Japanese engineers and technicians. In his privately published travel diary, *Japan 1950,* Deming said, "I've never had better students. I'd describe them as the top five percent of all the classes that I ever taught." The lectures tired him; summer in Tokyo can be broiling, and consumer air conditioning was still in the future. His shirt was sweat-soaked by midmorning. What made Deming's lectures a success was not his willingness to work hard under difficult conditions but his ability to persuade senior Japanese that he was right. On Thursday, July 13, Deming met for dinner at the Industry Club in Tokyo with the presidents and senior officials of Japan's twenty-one leading industries to talk about quality. He noted in his diary, "I talked to them an hour. There was a lot of wealth represented in that room, and a lot of power. I think they were impressed, because before the evening was over they asked me to meet with them again, and they talked about having a conference in the mountains around Hakone."

Within five years of the end of World War II, which had for any practical purpose destroyed Japan's industrial capacity, managers were being taught management of quality, engineers were learning statistical quality control, and the most senior industrialists were being impressed by the importance of quality.

Americans were teaching all of that in Japan while, in the United States, other Americans were busy ignoring it. Tribus remembers that "at about the time Sarasohn and Protzman were lecturing to the Japanese, I was studying some of the same material, though not very seriously. I can report that the common wisdom in the USA was that quality had to be balanced against the cost of attaining it." That common wisdom prevailed, and the idea that higher quality led to lower cost — what Deming would teach the Japanese — was unknown in the United States. "The sad thing for me," Sarasohn says, "is that in my cockiness when we went up in front of MacArthur to argue for this CCS management seminar, I had full confidence in the American capability to keep on growing, to keep on going, and as I look back, I see that did not happen."

Sarasohn and Protzman returned to the United States in 1950, Protzman going back to his work at Western Electric (now AT&T). He was still fired up by his work in Japan, and he tried to teach those same principles of quality management to his American colleagues. For his efforts, his son says, he was demoted.

Deming has said, "Export anything to a friendly country, except American management." He says the greatest mistake he ever made was in teaching quality to American engineers and technicians, but not to their bosses, during the war. Engineers and technicians make products, bosses make policy, and the decision to produce quality is a policy decision. The people who made policy in American business in 1945 decided that quantity was more important. That decision was neither callous nor venal; as badly as it has turned out, at that time quantity made sense. Other industrial nations had been damaged or destroyed, so America had to supply much of the world's needs and, equally important, buy the goods other nations could produce. Daniel Yankelovich, president of the Public Agenda Foundation, says, "In the postwar period, the United States was the engine of world growth. It wasn't simply that our economy was growing, but we provided a market for the economies of other countries to sell their goods. If it weren't for the U.S. market, there would be no Japanese miracle." At the same time, U.S. industries had to satisfy the domestic demand, which was incredible.

The Great Depression had led into World War II, so in the late 1940s and early '50s, people finally had money to buy what they had done without for more than twenty years. During the war, Americans had saved $100 billion to help finance the war effort. Later, that money financed the pent-up demand for houses and cars and appliances that politicians and industrialists could not ignore. So quantity was the key. John Patrick Diggins in *The Proud Decades* says that 54 percent of American families owned autos in 1948. By 1956, 73 percent did. Make it in mass, get it out the door, and if something's wrong, someone else will fix it. Cars couldn't be made fast enough. Diggins writes, "But really to fulfill the American dream one needed a Cadillac, or so advertisers informed the arriviste of new wealth with such effectiveness that one had to wait a year for delivery." A year! The concern for quality that had grown during the war all but disappeared as American and world consumers demanded more, and more is what America had learned to make better than anyone in the twentieth century.

It was the American economy as much as the Allied fighting forces that won World War II. Both Japan and Germany made superior weapons, but not enough of them. When President Franklin Roosevelt announced during the war how many bombers were rolling off American assembly lines, neither the Allies nor the enemy believed him. Accepted wisdom was that no nation could produce that much, and, in fact, no *other* nation could.

To understand how different quality management is, you have

to understand quantity management and mass production. To mass-produce anything you need the parts, a way to put them together, and an efficient way to organize the work. Americans had discovered how to do all three.

The first machine-made, interchangeable parts were introduced at an industrial exhibition at London's Crystal Palace in 1851. An American gunsmith took ten working rifles, disassembled them, put the parts in a box, mixed them up, and then reassembled them. It would be so ordinary now as to border on the ho-hum, but then it was almost shocking, an achievement so stunning that Europeans referred to machine-made, interchangeable parts as "the American system of manufactures."

Once you have parts that are alike, or enough alike that it doesn't matter, you need an efficient way to put them together. Henry Ford could sell every Model T he could make, and it occurred to him that he could build a lot more cars if he could keep the workers in one place and move the parts past them. His engineers built the first modern assembly line in 1914.

Once you've got interchangeable parts and a fast way to put them together, you have to organize the people who will do the work.

Frederick Winslow Taylor published what became a classic book in 1911, *Principles of Scientific Management.* (Deming says Taylor did not like the title, but his publisher insisted on it.) More than thirty-five years after its publication, Sarasohn was still teaching parts of it in Japan, but with substantial modification. "Taylor," Sarasohn says, "neglected the personal quotient much too much. He was more mechanistic." Taylor suggested a precise, scientific method of organizing a factory to get the most out of it, but he also dealt with organizing the work force, reducing each job to its smallest parts and assigning each worker to one repetitive task. In a way, that was determined by America's immigrant work force: men standing side by side on the assembly line often spoke different languages. As necessary as Taylor's method may have been, it meant that craftsmanship gave way to efficiency.

Interchangeable parts, the assembly line, and scientific management were the basis of modern industrial production; they were also the basis for Charlie Chaplin's classic film *Modern Times* and for Aldous Huxley's novel *Brave New World* (which was set in the year 632 AF, meaning After Ford). Both condemned the dehumanizing effects of modern technology.

Where Chaplin and Huxley saw social costs, others saw economic benefits. In 1908, before the assembly line or Taylor, a Model T Ford cost $850. In 1925, after the assembly line and Taylor, the least expensive Tin Lizzie cost only $290. Adjusted to 1990 dollars the difference is even more dramatic — nearly $12,000 for a Model T in 1908, less than $2,100 in 1925. In 1916 there were 3.4 million cars registered in the United States; there were 23 million by 1930. Whatever else mass production may have done, it turned out modern goods for less money, vastly increased the standard of living in the United States and the industrial world, and completely changed how the world made its money. That first major change in the modern world — the ability to mass-produce — happened in only sixty-four years.

The United States stayed with that system through World War II. Then, when the Japanese were learning how to use quality systems to build better goods for less money, the country was distracted. There were other, more urgent problems — the civil rights movement, the Vietnam War, the war on poverty, the sexual revolution, women's liberation, and concern for the environment. It's worth remembering that while the American economy was growing worse, the country's social system was changing and the environment improving. The country's rivers and air, to name only two, are markedly cleaner today than they were twenty years ago. In the United States, however, which was hard at work on other i˞ ˞es, the new economic order remained a stunning surprise.

The Japanese had learned how to produce quality from Sarasohn, Protzman, Polkinghorn, Deming, Joseph Juran, Armand Feigenbaum, and others. Kaoru Ishikawa and Genichi Taguchi would add their own quality wrinkles in Japan over the years, just as Philip Crosby would in the United States beginning in 1979. What is interesting years later is that no two of those men — indeed, no two people we've talked to anywhere — agree precisely on how to define quality.

John Stewart, a director of McKinsey and Company, says, "There is no one definition of quality. . . . Quality is a sense of appreciation that something is better than something else. It changes in a lifetime, and it changes generation to generation, and it varies by facets of human activity." Michael Maccoby, a psychologist and consultant, says the difficulty with defining quality is that the definition changes as industry does. Quality in silversmith Paul Revere's day had nothing to do with what it was in Henry Ford's day, and neither has anything to do with what the definition is today. Globally, industrial nations have gone from a craft definition to an industrial definition to what Maccoby calls a postmodern definition, and each step gets more complicated.

But however quality is defined, Americans seem to find more of it at less cost more often in foreign products. That has hurt their national economy, created unemployment and underemployment, and given their nation an enormous trade deficit. The only way to change that trend is to begin to produce quality goods and services that other people in other places can't do without. The United States has to do that fairly soon because international trade is beginning to get surly. For instance, in Clive Cussler's popular novel *Dragon*, set in 1993, the villain is not the KGB or the Mafia or a group of international terrorists but a secretive, right-wing Japanese industrialist who is intent on putting Japan on top of the world's nations. In popular fiction, the Japanese haven't been the bad guys since World War II. Until now.

The change in relative economic wealth between the United States and Japan has changed more than just a few figures in some government functionary's accounts book. In a recent public opinion poll, Japanese high school students said that if their country went to war again, the likely enemy would be the United States. In the United States, even before Eastern Europe came unglued for the communists, a majority of Americans said that Japan was more of a threat than the Soviet Union. Sarasohn thinks that goes too far. He says the Japanese have been restrictive in some trade policies and have taken advantage of some situations; "on the other hand, you have to recognize that the Japanese are not responsible for our failures." In the United States, that sort of self-analysis is not popular. It is so much easier to blame the Japanese.

Not a few members of Congress talk about "economic war," and Russell Braddon argues in *The Other 100 Years War* that what is happening now is only the economic extension of Japan's military acts in World War II. Braddon says Japan put up propaganda posters when things started going badly during the war, urging the Japanese people to "rally round the Imperial Throne and fight on, for this is a HUNDRED YEAR WAR." Braddon, an Australian, was imprisoned by the Japanese, and he recounts this scene when he was released.

"As I walked toward the convoy of jeeps that would transport us to the docks, I passed one of the Imperial Japanese Army's few English-speaking officers who was being escorted into the gaol [jail]. In a spirit half of elation and half of spite, I turned and shouted, 'This war last one hundred years?'

" 'Ninety-six years to go,' he called back; and neither of us bothered to bow."

In one sense, at least, the hundred years' war seems true. Part of Japan's war strategy was to free the colonies of Asia from, essentially, white rule — except for Formosa (Taiwan) and Korea, Japan's own colonies — and bond them in the Greater East Asia Co-Prosperity Sphere. What Japan could not do militarily then, it seems to be doing economically now. Anyone who has been in

Asia lately knows that Japanese yen mean a great deal more than American dollars in Thailand, China, the Philippines, and other nations of the region. Traveling in Asia, it's easy to believe that Japan won World War II. (L.D.: In 1982, I covered the fortieth anniversary of the fall of Bataan and Corregidor. At one point along the route of the Bataan Death March, I stood in just the right spot in the road and made the sign marking the route of the march appear to be the picture on the Japanese television set advertised on a roadside billboard. The Japanese soldier had been thrown out; the Japanese salesman came back.)

In 1989 Japan surpassed the United States as the principal donor of foreign aid to underdeveloped nations, and the same year a plurality of Japanese said they thought their country would surpass the United States as the world's political and economic leader someday. Deming says he doesn't think the Japanese planned it that way and that, if it happens, it will be only an incidental consequence of their industrial excellence. Others, like Braddon, think it's the result of the same attitude of superiority that caused Japan to invade Manchuria in 1931 and spread war in the Pacific. Because of the war and what Japanese soldiers did to other Asians during the war, there is still distrust and dislike of Japan in Asia, but those feelings are fading as the men and women who lived through the war are succeeded by their sons and daughters, born after 1945.

Paul Kreisberg of the Carnegie Endowment for Peace spends a lot of time in Asia. He says the attitude of, for instance, a young professor in Indonesia or the Philippines would be, "This is another generation. If you talk to my grandfather, he is very anti-Japanese. If you talk to my father, he is uneasy about Japan. If you talk to my students, they don't care." After so many years, personal dislike rarely overcomes economic reality, and even Koreans, whose feelings toward the Japanese can often be described as all-consuming hatred, now find it convenient to cooperate economically. It's easy to believe that at about the turn of the century, an Asian economic bloc led by Japan will be one of the world economy's three key players.

The other two could be a united European Community, led by a united Germany, and an American economy, led by the United States and including Canada and Mexico. The technocrats who run the European Community from its headquarters in Brussels already believe that their competition will come from Asia, not America. That is, in part, because none of the five advantages the United States had at the end of World War II still exists.

The MIT Commission on Productivity says in its report *Made in America* that the American advantages after the war were a huge domestic market, the world's best technology, the best educated work force, enormous wealth, and the world's best managers.

- America in 1945 was eight times larger than the next largest domestic market. It is now only twice as large as Japan, and if the European Community merges, as it eventually will, perhaps by the end of 1992, it will be almost one-third larger than the United States. But domestic market size no longer makes that much difference because there is no longer any such thing as a purely domestic market. A plant in Knightdale, North Carolina, is as likely to have a competitor in Korea as in Kentucky.
- American facilities and equipment are no longer the world's best, and Americans have not invested in new technology as they should have. The first industrial robot in a factory was installed in a GM assembly plant in New Jersey in the 1960s. It was built by Unimation, Inc., of Danbury, Connecticut. For a variety of reasons, most of them shortsighted, American industry did not much care about that new technology, so Unimation sold a license to manufacture its industrial robot to Kawasaki of Japan. Today, Japan has four times as many industrial robots as the United States. Worse, the United States is out of the robotics business. Cincinnati Milacron, the last U.S. robot manufacturer, was sold to the Swiss in 1990. Robotics is one more technology,

like the VCR, that Americans invented, then failed to exploit.

- America no longer has the best-educated work force; indeed, it's not even close. There is an argument about how many youngsters drop out of high school, but whether it's 5 or 30 percent is only a difference in numbers. Given the demands of the job market, any student who doesn't get at least a high school diploma is bound to be a drain on the economy. There is another argument about how many American adults are functionally illiterate, but no one is willing to argue that adult illiteracy doesn't matter. It matters deeply. In 1950, roughly a third of all industrial jobs could be done perfectly well by people who did not have a high school education. If even one of those jobs still exists, we can't find it.

- The wealth the United States amassed after World War II has been squandered, wasted, thrown away. Consumers borrowed to buy what they could not afford, and corporations hocked all they had to buy one another out for no discernible reason. Yankelovich says, "Junk bonds and leveraged buyouts were the curse of the 1980s. They were taking what Americans had built for over two hundred years and exploiting it for the advantage of a handful of people. It was despicable from a moral point of view and destructive from an economic point of view." Deming says that junk bonds and leveraged buyouts are only another example of American management wrecking the country by focusing on short-term profit rather than long-term product. But it is not fair to blame greed and debt entirely on business management. The government proved its moral courage by putting the next two or three generations of Americans into debt rather than face voters angered by higher taxes or fewer services. The government can continue to function only because the newly wealthy Japanese continue to buy U.S. Treasury bonds by the billions. What happens if they stop?

- The MIT commission wrote, "Finally, American managers were the best in the world." We respectfully suggest that that was more appearance than reality. All the other industrial nations, except for relatively small Canada and Switzerland, had been damaged or destroyed by the war. Their plants had been bombed, their equipment burned. American managers could sell everything they could make because no one else could make enough of anything, so American success was guaranteed by world circumstance. Deming tells his seminars that you have to work especially hard not to succeed in a booming economy. But whether the commission was right or we are no longer matters, because American managers now are not the world's best, nor do they appear to be.

More important than the loss of any one of those advantages — or even the loss of all of them — is that while the United States was playing one game, its competitors started a new game, and America didn't notice. While the country remained devoted to producing the quantity that the world had *needed*, competitors decided to produce the quality that the world now *wanted*. Brian Joiner, of Joiner Associates in Madison, Wisconsin, explains what happened with a sports analogy.

At the turn of the century, no high jumper could hope to be a world-class competitor unless he used the scissors method, the style still used in some secondary schools to get young athletes started. Then, a few years later, someone developed the roll-over method, in eastern and western versions, and if you couldn't do one of the two, you could forget a gold medal. Roll-over was king until a high school senior named Dick Fosbury found he could get a lot higher if he went over the bar backward; now, if you can't master the Fosbury Flop, you can just as well get off the field and avoid embarrassment.

Does that mean the scissors method and the roll-over were wrong? They couldn't have been wrong; they produced world champions. Both were the best until someone found something better. What American industry had done since the gunsmith reassembled ten working rifles at the Crystal Palace was to create the strongest, most vibrant economy the world has ever known by producing quantity. Therefore, what Americans did couldn't possibly have been wrong, but in today's world it is no longer right. Immediately before, during, and immediately after World War II, Deming and Sarasohn and others found something better and wanted American industry to change, to do things differently. They taught the Japanese instead because American managers wanted to stay with what they knew, producing quantity, selling everything they could make.

In the global market today, it isn't how many you can make, it's how well you can make them. The new game has new rules.

2

New Rules

As the rules for industrial success have changed, so has the way that nations calculate theoretical wealth. Natural resources mattered most under the old rules and matter least under the new ones. What matters now is the production of quality with the only natural resource that counts — people.

The rules in the old game were that those countries with abundant natural resources would do better than those without adequate natural resources. Wealth was more or less based on how well you did with what you had. (If you didn't have anything, you were a poor country until you became an undeveloped, then an underdeveloped, then a developing country, moving up the ladder of linguistic acceptability while remaining a hardscrabble economy.) Different countries had different levels of resources; in economics that is called comparative advantage. According to Herbert Striner, professor emeritus of American University's Kogod College of Business, comparative advantage underlies "the whole body of economic theory."

The United States has always had a virtual treasure chest of natural resources, and for a hundred years or longer, those resources have given the country an enormous comparative advantage in the world economy. However, there is some evidence that those natural resources that always have been an asset may have become a liability. The easiest way to see that is to compare the United States and Japan. The United States is rich in resources while Japan has few worth mentioning, yet, economically, Japan is outperforming the United States and other resource-rich industrial nations. What happened to comparative advantage?

"The problem," wrote Striner, "is that what we always thought were the critical variables or factors when discussing comparative advantage are no longer as critical as others have become." American reserves of coal and iron ore and other natural assets may not be as important as they once were. Howard Samuel, the president of the Industrial Union Department of the AFL-CIO, says, "Sometime about twenty years ago, a number of countries, led by Japan but including countries in Europe and also the newly industrialized countries, began to realize that these advantages don't have to be natural. They can be acquired; they can be bought; they can be manufactured."

Kenichi Ohmae of McKinsey and Company argues that an abundance of natural resources slows a country's current development because these resources are no longer a critical national asset, but most governments and some people still act as if they were. For instance, Gavin Wright, an economics historian at Stanford University, ties the economic decline in the United States to its having used up its inexpensive and abundant natural resources. In his view, no more natural resources equals no more economic superiority. W. Edwards Deming thinks the abundant natural resources in the United States helped put it into economic decline because it depended on resources for profit rather than finding a way to make superior products. Unlike Wright, however, Deming thinks the game is not over. "North America can surge up," he says, "be a model for the world instead of being an object of pity, living on borrowed money, living on natural resources, which have ruined us." As Striner suggests, the natural resources Americans have traditionally used may not be the ones they now need.

Ohmae points out that Switzerland, Singapore, Taiwan, South

Korea, and Japan are small and all but devoid of natural resources, but each has a well-educated, hard-working, ambitious population, and each is prosperous. "In a truly interlinked, global economy," he writes, "the key success factor shifts from resources to the marketplace, in which you have to participate in order to prosper. It also means *people* are the only true means to create wealth." Striner says the key to modern success is "human resources." How well you educate, train, and treat people in your society becomes more important than the coal you dig, trees you fell, or rivers you dam.

In 1980 Joji Arai, then the director of the Japan Productivity Center in Washington, D.C., told an American manufacturing group in New Orleans, "The only abundant natural resource Japan has is people." John Stepp, the former Labor Department deputy undersecretary, agrees that people are the critical difference. "Japan has essentially the same technology that we [Americans] have; Europe has essentially the same technology that we have. . . . What's making a difference in those societies, I think, is the way in which they capitalize on their human resources." Robert Reich, a professor of political economy at Harvard, writes, "As every advanced economy becomes global, a nation's most important competitive asset becomes the skills and cumulative learning of its work force. . . . Every factor of production other than work force skills can be duplicated anywhere around the world. . . . It is fungible: capital, technology, raw materials, information — all, except for one thing, the most critical part, the one element that is unique about a nation: its work force." The MIT Commission on Industrial Productivity says America's business and political leaders seem to ignore that fact. "There seems to be a systematic undervaluation in this country [the United States] of how much difference it can make when people are well educated and their skills are continuously developed and challenged."

The CCS manual that Japanese industrialists used after World War II hammers at both the need for training and the need for treating the work force with dignity and respect. All of the modern quality experts insist that everyone in a quality company must be trained, educated, and made to understand what is being done and why. At world-class companies, training is considered an attractive investment. Robert Galvin, Motorola's chairman of the Executive Committee, says that to produce quality you must have extensive training, "and you must have an act of faith that training is never going to cost you any money. You will indeed rotate some dollars to a line item called 'training' in your budget, but you'll get your benefits back far greater than the cost that you put in." Training is essential, but there is more to it than how-to instruction.

In 1988 the U.S. Department of Labor produced a documentary about six American businesses that had dramatically improved after each of them adopted some form of worker participation program; it wasn't just training, the employees helped to decide how the company would run and how work would be organized. The six companies were in different businesses in different states, and all of them had organized labor unions. There was Preston Trucking on the Eastern Shore of Maryland; U.S. West, the baby Bell in Denver; the New York City Sanitation Department central repair facility; the joint GM-Toyota assembly plant in California called New United Motors; American Velvet in Connecticut; and the Great Lakes division of National Steel.

A more recent example of breaking away from the traditional American system of managers manage, workers work, is GM's new Saturn auto line. The innovation is not so much in the car, the product, as it is in the process of building it. The new plant is organized so unlike its parent headquarters that the Saturn president and the UAW coordinator share the executive suite, and the union contract provides for consensus decision-making. A *Time* magazine article says what is important at the Saturn plant is GM's acknowledgment that "the secret [of Japan's success] is not advanced technology or low wages or some mystical Asian work ethic. Japan's most important advantage is its management system: the way it deals with employees, suppliers, dealers and customers."

In the old game, American management accepted that investments had to be made in plants and equipment, but it did not accept that human investments were equally important. Michael Maccoby, the consultant, says there's a new logic that is critical to quality management. "It's a whole new way of thinking, and human beings are the key to it. You can't stay in the old logic of hierarchy and control and contempt and ever get there. As a matter of fact, maybe the most important thing is to have real respect for human capabilities and understand that all economies are people doing things. . . . if people are still thought of as appendages to the machines, as costs rather than resources, we'll never get there." If "human beings are the key" to quality, as Maccoby suggests, and if Ohmae is correct and "*people* are the only true means to create wealth," then the only true means to get people capable of creating wealth is quality management.

That requires training, but it also requires something that many American managers may find far more difficult to consider. It requires long-term thinking, long-term planning, and long-term investment. The bible of American business, the quarterly profit-and-loss statement, loses its significance. Few other nations' businesses and industries pay as much attention to short-term financial results as do those in the United States. In many if not most major American firms, the item that gets and holds management's attention is not the quality of the product that's being made, it's the paper value of the company, its stock price. That is the indicator used by investors, shareholders, and boards of directors to judge the company and its management. If the stock price goes down, senior management may go out, or the company may be taken over, or both. For that reason, what the top manager needs to know for his own survival is not how to make better products but how to fiddle the figures.

That has produced a phenomenon that exists, so far as we can find, only in the English-speaking world. It was first reported in America in 1980 by Robert H. Hayes and William J. Abernathy, professors of business administration at Harvard Business School, who wondered why American companies seemed to be losing their competitive edge. They found more and more financial people and lawyers in executive suites, often hired from outside the company, who focused on short-term gains and financial management. The financial-legal types hadn't a clue to what was being made at the factory, nor did they much care. "What has developed, in the business community as in academia," the professors reported, "is a preoccupation with a false and shallow concept of the professional manager, a 'pseudo-professional' really — an individual having no special expertise in any particular industry or technology who nevertheless can step into an unfamiliar company and run it successfully through strict application of financial controls, portfolio concepts, and a market-driven strategy." By and large, American managers had been taught that management equals finance in America's advanced business schools.

That same phenomenon had been reported in 1977 in Great Britain in a sometimes bitter and wickedly funny book, *The Rise and Fall of the British Manager* by Alistair Mant, an educator and industrial consultant. "The cynical may even posit a direct correlation," he wrote, "between the amount of money spent on management education and development in Britain and the rate of decline in industrial performance." He reported that engineers were far more likely to head manufacturing companies on the European continent and in Scandinavia, that Germans did not even have words to express the concept of "professional manager," and that Britain had imported the silly idea from America and made it even sillier. The result was that "there are simply too many accountants in high places in British industry and business and their preponderance says something about a collective perception of industry in general and manufacturing in particular. It is as if the primary task of industry was laundering money, with production as an irksome constraint on that primary task."

In truth, the manipulation of money in the United States is not entirely because of too many financial-legal managers; it is, at least in part, *required*. Legally, a company pension fund manager, for instance, must seek the quickest, highest profit, and if the fund doesn't grow quickly enough through investment, the company is required to put more of its own profit into it. The law, the companies, and Wall Street apparently believe that enormous quarterly profits are good for the country and the economy, although, demonstrably, that is not necessarily true.

The columnist Hobart Rowen says American auto makers in the last decade had two opportunities to increase the domestic sales of their cars: first, when the so-called voluntary quotas were established for Japanese imports, and again when the value of the yen went up, making those imports more expensive for American car buyers. However, to improve their sales and take some of the market away from the Japanese car companies, American companies would have had to hold down prices. In both cases, the companies *raised* prices to increase their short-term profits at the expense of their own best long-term outlook.

Under what has come to be called the American management system, instead of being able to concentrate on a long-term quality improvement program that would increase sales, lower costs, improve profits, and create jobs, managers must concentrate on the quarterly manipulation of money. It's one of the reasons Deming tells his American audiences, "I see very little evidence that anybody gives a hoot about profit." Manipulating a profit is not the same as making one.

"One of the biggest obstacles to producing quality goods in America," the consultant Brian Joiner says, "is the failure to really understand the impact of the need to make each and every quarter's profit look just right." To do that, he says, toward the end of the quarter, companies work incredible overtime, ship everything whether it's ready or not — one company shipped empty boxes — keep the books open a day or two longer, and move parts around the company to get them out of one set of books and into another. All of that is done "to produce profits quarter after quarter after quarter. Nature just doesn't work that way. We're destroying the companies."

If American business and industry are to survive in the global market, that short-term financial concern with manipulating money will have to be replaced with a management system that is driven by the customer, involves all its people, continually improves, and concentrates on the long term.

None of that is a wholly new idea. Adam Smith talked about the importance of labor to a country's well-being in *The Wealth of Nations*, first published in 1776, and certainly the need to manage for quality has been known for years. Andrew Carnegie, the American industrialist and philanthropist whose autobiography was published in 1920, the year after he died, wrote, "This policy is the true secret of success. . . . I have never known a concern to make a decided success that did not do good, honest work, and even in these days of the fiercest competition, when everything would seem to be a matter of price, there lies still at the root of great business success the very much more important factor of quality. The effect of attention to quality, upon every man in the service, from the President of the concern down to the humblest laborer, cannot be overestimated. . . . The surest foundation of a business concern is quality. And after that, a long way after, comes cost." Homer Sarasohn and Charles Protzman quoted Carnegie in their manual for the same reason they quoted Collis Huntington, to show the Japanese how strong was the American respect for quality.

What has changed since the 1940s is that there is increasingly less of a Japanese or Scandinavian or American economy and increasingly more of a global economy, not because any nation or group of nations particularly wants it, but because technology allows it. A recent report by the (American) National Center on Education and the Economy says, "High speed communication and transportation make it possible to produce most products and services anywhere in the world. Modern machinery and production methods can be combined with low wage workers to drive costs down. High wage nations like the United States can succeed only by producing higher quality products, providing customers with greater product variety, introducing new products more frequently and creating automated systems which are more complex than those that can be operated in low wage countries."

Ohmae describes the global market in *The Borderless World*. "An isle is emerging," he writes, "that is bigger than a continent — the Interlinked Economy (ILE) of the Triad (the United States, Europe, and Japan), joined by aggressive economies such as Taiwan, Hong Kong, and Singapore. It is becoming so powerful that it has swallowed most consumers and corporations, made traditional national borders almost disappear, and pushed bureaucrats, politicians, and the military toward the status of declining industries."

Samuel says the global marketplace is not one place at all because there are still too many differences among nations, even within those groups of nations that are supposed to be economically alike, such as the United States, Europe, and Japan. "So it is really an omelet of many, many different countries around the world desperately competing with each other, sometimes using methods which we feel are below the belt, all of them trying to win some competitive advantage for themselves in some way. Now, one of the ways in which some countries try to gain competitive advantage is through emphasizing the quality of their products, and this is all to the good. The United States should be doing more of it to match what other countries are doing."

Whether the world is the seamless market of Ohmae's vision or the fragmented mix that Samuel sees, the global economy does exist across national borders. Philip B. Crosby says, "We live in a boundaryless economy now. . . . where we're headed for is a place where you can compete with anybody." Yankelovich thinks some of that has already happened. "Ten years ago," he says, "the world economy was nothing more than the sum of individual economies. There was no global economy. . . . Now, the integration, the cross-fertilization, the joint ventures, and the breakdown of lines of culture are creating a truly global marketplace. . . . You don't have a German market and a Japanese market and an American market," he continues. "If you have upper-middle-class people in the United States and in West Germany and in Japan and in France, they are more like each other, the counterparts of each other in the different countries, than they are like some of their fellow countrypeople."

Walter Kunerth, the president of Siemens automotive group, a German multinational firm, says that wherever you go in the world, the desire for quality is the same, and that universal desire drives a universal standard. "Being a global company, we can't design and produce one product with a different quality for Japan, for instance, or for Europe, or for the U.S.A. It has to be all the same quality standard," he says, and "the standard of quality is improving. Years ago, in electronics, for instance, we had a thousand [bad] parts per million as a quality standard. Today it's under a hundred parts per million, and it will improve more and more."

American industry, by and large, isn't meeting that ever-improving global standard for the ever-increasing global market. Officials of fifty-three American and Canadian companies that make automobile parts were told by Toyota Motor Company that if they wanted to continue doing business, they would have to get their quality up and their costs down. In October 1990, at a meeting in Nagoya, Japan, Toyota officials told its most promising North American suppliers that they had a thousand defects per million parts, which is an impressive-sounding one-tenth of 1 percent. Japanese parts suppliers were a hundred times more impressive — with a defect rate of ten parts per million. Those rates have been achieved only with quality management.

David Garvin, an assistant professor of business administration at Harvard Business School, studied the quality of American and Japanese room air conditioners over several years in the early 1980s. He picked room air conditioners because they aren't high tech, they are all produced more or less the same way, and the companies in both countries ranged from small to large. (As a general rule, different-size companies have different-size problems.) Nine of America's ten manufacturers took part in the quality survey, as did all seven of Japan's.

Garvin's general conclusion, published in the *Harvard Business Review*, was, "Japanese companies were far superior to their U.S. counterparts: their average assembly-line defect rate was almost 70 times lower and their average first-year service call rate nearly 17 times better." The *best* American manufacturer was about 10 percent worse than the *worst* Japanese manufacturer, and the Japanese spent less to produce quality than the Americans spent to produce something less. "In fact," Garvin wrote, "the total costs of quality incurred by Japanese producers were less than one-half the failure costs incurred by the best U.S. companies." Garvin also found a strong association between quality and productivity and between quality and cost: the more quality, the higher the productivity, the lower the cost.

The editors of the magazine added their own comment, which said in part, "His findings document a bitter but inescapable truth. The competitively significant variation in levels of quality performance is immense." The editors said the study showed that there was nothing magical about quality, it was the result of good management. "If nothing else," they wrote in 1983, "the data reported here should force American executives to rethink their approaches to product quality." That conclusion is like drawing to an inside straight or getting married for the fourth time: it's a triumph of expectation over experience. Equally impressive data had been ignored before and were again. Sarasohn remembers the chief executive officer of an American air conditioning firm, having listened to a report on the study, getting up from his seat, saying "I don't believe it!" and stalking angrily from the room. No fact can overcome a prejudice, and the explosive has not been invented that can blow a totally wrong-headed idea out of a believer's mind.

Members of the United Auto Workers smashed Japanese cars with sledgehammers, and senior managers of American auto companies talked about the "price advantage" Japanese auto makers had because of their lower wages, but both groups ignored another statistic. When Japanese imports caught on in the United States because of the 1979 oil shock, the person who bought a new American car would have to take it back to the dealer to get something fixed, on average, more than four times in the first year. The person who bought a new Japanese car would have to go back, on average, not quite once. Japanese cars in those days were less expensive, but they were also better built. Senior American auto executives focused on their foreign competitors' lower costs but ignored their higher quality.

Their narrow approach may be explained by what social psychologists call the theory of cognitive dissonance. It says that people try to make what they believe consistent with what they do, and one way to be consistent is to ignore facts that don't fit what they believe. (Remember the American air conditioning executive saying, "I don't believe it!" Cognitive dissonance in the cooling business.) The fact that the Japanese knew how to build better cars did not fit what American auto makers believed, so they ignored it, even though they had had ample warning. As early as June 1966, Joseph M. Juran told a European conference on quality control that "the Japanese are headed for world quality leadership and will attain it in the next two decades because no one else is moving there at the same pace."

Striner quotes Daniel Goleman, a Harvard psychologist: "We

do not see what we prefer not to see and do not see that we do not see." Striner says that the American auto industry "for years took the position that the reason the Japanese cars were competitive was as a result of the role of the Japanese government in aiding the Japanese car industry. They also took the position that the low cost of labor was such that the Japanese were able to produce cars for far lower prices. They preferred not to look at the problem of quality, because once they started looking at the quality problem — the fit of the doors, the sense of the ride, the lower maintenance costs — then they were confronted with the problem of 'What do we do if it's obvious that we're not meeting these standards?' "

Cognitive dissonance gradually led to competitive decline. By not seeing what they preferred not to see in 1980, senior American automotive managers found in 1990 that the ten most reliable cars sold in America, the ones that gave new car owners the fewest problems, according to J. D. Power and Associates, included seven from Japan, two from Germany, and only one from the United States. Japan's share of the U.S. auto market went from not quite 20 percent in 1980 to more than 30 percent in 1990.

It's not as though American auto makers had done nothing; they had made excellent progress, but they were still playing catch-up. Whereas once Ford, General Motors, and Chrysler had a defect rate that was 300 percent higher than that of the Japanese manufacturers, by early 1990 it had been cut to 25 percent. As Maryann Keller, an auto industry analyst for Furman Selz Mager Dietz & Birney, says, "We [Americans] move ahead three steps, but in the meantime, the Japanese have moved ahead two and a half. So in relative terms, we have closed the gap a little bit, but the gap is still there. . . . The customer today expects perfection in his car. . . . Once you get to perfection, though, something else causes you to select a car. Today, quality is just the ticket into the game." Kees van Ham, the secretary-general of the new European Foundation for Quality Management at Eindhoven, The Netherlands, has noticed that "the meaning of quality has changed from a focus on technical aspects, product aspects, to a focus on the complete interface between a company or a business and its customers. Today quality is everything which is valued by customers." Furthermore, what the customer values keeps expanding. "Just as U.S. car makers are getting their quality up to par," *Business Week* reported, "the Japanese are redefining and expanding the term." No longer are Japanese auto makers content to make cars that are essentially free of defects, now those cars must "fascinate, bewitch, and delight."

Howard D. Wilson, the director of Quality Management Systems at IBM, talks about "delight factors" as being an essential part of quality. Customers expect a certain level of quality, and if they don't get that, they won't be back, period. If they get the quality they expect, they're satisfied, but only that, and satisfaction is often not enough. The next time they have to buy, they may be back, or they may give a competitor a chance. However, the more customers get that they did not expect, the more there is that makes their life better or easier or more pleasant; in short, after basic quality, the more "delight factors" there are, the more likely that customers will come back and bring their friends. Wilson says the net to hold bags upright in the trunk of the Ford Taurus has absolutely nothing to do with making the engine perform properly or making the interior functionally comfortable, and if there were no net, the auto industry would not consider it a defect or a lack of quality, but it would make a difference. Taurus owners often mention that net as one of the things they like about the car. It's a "delight factor."

The Japanese manufacturers have gone beyond quality to load their export goods with "delight factors," which have helped make them successful. But that is not how other people see it.

People in the United States and Europe have been told or believe or just know *for sure* that Japan got ahead by (1) paying low wages, (2) cheating at international trade, (3) collusion between government and industry, (4) invisible trade barriers, and (5) a closed domestic market. It's all partially true. Steven Schlossstein cites these points in *Trade Wars,* at the beginning of the chapter "How on Earth Did Japan Do It?" He credits "industrial policy" for Japan's extraordinary success. Industrial policy, under which the government phases out failing industries and helps rising ones, did help Japan, but so did each of the other five items. Until about 1973 Japanese industry did pay lower wages, a lot lower; Japan does cheat at international trade (almost every nation does, we find upon inspection, but Japan seems best at it); government and industry do collude and have been caught at it; there are invisible trade barriers, especially in a wholesale distribution system that is maddeningly archaic; and the domestic market, while more open than it used to be, remains substantially closed. Even Shintaro Ishihara, a Japanese politician and critic of the United States, says, "Japan must open its market fully to foreign goods and services and our complex distribution system must be streamlined. We should make these changes because they benefit Japanese consumers, not because U.S. trade negotiators demand them."

If Pat Choate is correct, there is an extra advantage that Americans have given or, more correctly, sold to Japan in international trade. Choate, a political economist, says in *Agents of Influence* that Japan has hired so many American lobbyists and lawyers, that it funds so many think tanks and study programs in U.S. universities, and that it finances so much of the federal government's budget deficit that "it can, in effect, veto much legislation that it dislikes. It can ignore almost any U.S. law or policy that it finds inconvenient. It can politically overwhelm virtually any combination of American companies, unions, or other interests that it opposes." Choate is quick to add that none of this is illegal, so it is not a criticism of Japan but of the American system that allows it to happen. Many of the American lobbyists for Japan are former U.S. government officials or employees who learn what's going on inside the government, then leave the government and sell that knowledge to foreign firms. Roger Milliken, the chairman and CEO of Milliken & Company, says a foreigner could come to the United States and "could hire Americans — and our [former] government people sell their services to the foreigners like crazy — to help them change our government rules and everything else, which is one of the great scandals of our time. . . . Now, the rest of the world doesn't work that way. You couldn't conceivably hire people from foreign governments to try to help you get into their countries. They'd be ostracized immediately for doing that."

Low wages, closed markets, cheating, industrial policy, Americans for hire, and all the rest have made a difference, but less of a difference than most Americans and Europeans believe. Two specific reasons matter more, first for Japan and now for Korea and other Asian nations. First, remember Daniel Yankelovich's remark, "If it weren't for the U.S. market, there would be no Japanese miracle." Japan's economy now exists because the American economy was and is open and enormous, and other countries count on it. Mangi Paik of the Korean Ministry of Trade and Industry credits two factors for at least part of Korea's recent industrial success: "One is we depended much on the U.S. market, and at the same time, we depended much on Japanese production technology." That production technology is also the second specific reason for Japan's success. In the modern world, Japan produces higher-quality goods with more "delight factors" for less cost than anyone else. The nations of Europe and North America, while marvelously competitive in selected areas, don't come close overall; the high-quality, low-cost combination is the key to international trade figures. Ishihara says bluntly, "The [American] trade deficit with Japan will fall when U.S. products regain their reputation around the world for quality and design."

Edwin L. Artzt, the chairman and chief executive of Procter & Gamble, recognizes a lack of global competition in American business: "The standard of quality for products and services —

and it's a tough thing to say — but the standard of quality has not been as high here [in the United States]. . . . The thing that American companies have got to do is create products and services that would be competitive in all of the world's markets." He says the system at P&G has helped make it successful around the world. "We have been extolling the doctrine of globalization to our employees," he says, "and we define it for them as making sure that our products and our operations are competitive with anybody, anywhere, at any time, whether we're in direct competition with them or not." He calls that "a very pragmatic thing," because he believes that wherever the best is, you'll have to compete with it somewhere in the world sooner or later.

"The average American pays twenty cents of every dollar for goods or services produced outside the United States," Reich says. "Seventy percent of the goods produced in the United States right now are competing actively with goods produced in other countries, so that a world market has enormous political and social implications. What happens around the world affects our standard of living." That is a new phenomenon for the United States. America has always been a huge market, large enough that American companies have not had to go outside the country to sell profitably. Anand Panyarachun, a Thai businessman, says, "I think that the Americans in particular have not felt the need to go beyond their borders. There was a saying in the past that to an average American, export is the transfer of goods from one state to another."

In the 1960s, less than 10 percent of the total American economy involved export, but in Europe, where the domestic markets were too small to sustain industry, export accounted for 30 to 50 percent of those nations' economies. They had to export to survive, so they did; American companies could survive in their own market, so export didn't matter. Paul Kreisberg of the Carnegie Endowment says, "That's one of our problems in trade. Most American businesses have nothing whatsoever to do with foreign trade." Thomas T. Niles, the U.S. ambassador to the European Community in Brussels, says that American companies are not doing what they should do or could do to export. "We need as a country to take a look at some of the real success stories in exporting, such as the Federal Republic of Germany," he says, "and then ask ourselves why is it that you have thousands and thousands of small and medium-sized German companies successfully involved in exporting," while American companies of the same size are not.

Armand V. Feigenbaum, an American quality consultant, says his company made a survey of American executives and found that they believe their competition is with other American companies, not with companies in Japan, Europe, or South America. Feigenbaum believes this perception is, at best, shortsighted. In a global economy, there is no exclusive domestic market. "Murphy's Law internationalized says that if you can get an international competitor," Feigenbaum says, "you will get one."

Some American companies have changed. Len DeBarras of Motorola recalls that when he began working there, the market ran between Chicago and Fort Lauderdale. In the last ten years, he says, Motorola went into Europe and now "we have included Asia, China, Australia, Taiwan, Canada — you name it. The entire world is the arena, and we have to learn how to play in all areas of the world."

C. Jackson Grayson, Jr., the chairman of the American Productivity and Quality Center, believes national companies will have to be involved in international trade. "I think always there will be national headquarters and national characteristics of the firm that drive its values and direction," Grayson says, "but those companies that make a mistake are the ones that think they can stay within their own borders. They'll die." He says the new challenge for American firms is to make the quality necessary to compete effectively in the global marketplace. "Toynbee, when looking at civilization, said, 'Challenge and response is the key.' If you give the old response to a new challenge, you're probably going to fail. The new response is quality."

Official Washington and some U.S. industrial leaders are still giving the old response. Essentially they say that if American companies are still doing what they did when they owned half the world market and if they don't still own half the world market, clearly it must be the other guy's fault. Yankelovich, having listened to official Washington talk about economics and trade, says, "I wish that President [George] Bush were as skillful at mobilizing the country for the economy as he has been in mobilizing the other countries in the world for common security. *We need to have a good economy.* We *need* it for our social and political stability and health." Yankelovich doesn't think America has the leadership it needs on economic issues. "I don't think," he says, "that the people in Washington understand the public role in this issue and understand the importance of mobilizing the public and understand how to do it, because they're focused on things like the level playing field and monetary rates and all kinds of technical factors of that sort. That's not where the problem is."

Milliken, like Yankelovich, wishes the discussion of quality were more public, more widespread. "I don't know what the perfect answer is," he says, "but I do wish our government would recognize that this is a hell of a serious issue. . . . We're in deep, deep trouble, and I think if we can get this up to a high level for national debate, American people are sensible, over time, and we'll see the right answer come out." Deming, asked at one of his seminars why the political leadership in Washington had not done something to improve America's economy, answered simply, "Because not one of them has any idea what to do."

One of the reasons Americans have less money for social and rebuilding programs is the country's enormous national debt. Isabel V. Sawhill, a senior fellow at the Urban Institute, calculates that fifteen cents of every U.S. tax dollar goes to pay interest on the national debt. "Taxes that used to buy real benefits or real government services," she writes, "have been diverted to paying our creditors, many of them from other countries." Even if the United States stopped borrowing immediately, interest on the more than $3 trillion debt would continue to be high and continue to reduce the government's ability to spend for social or economic programs.

Myron Tribus says official Washington simply does not understand. "I watch the debate on the budget," he says, "and I see the Congress and the president trying to figure out how to do something that will be acceptable to the American people, but no matter what they do, it's painful. They do not seem to recognize the origin of this problem. We do not have enough money. . . . And the reason we don't have enough money is our economy is weak, and our economy is weak because we don't compete, and we don't compete because our managers don't know how to manage." In short, they don't know how to produce higher quality at lower costs.

And they haven't much time left to learn. Grayson and his colleague Carla O'Dell wrote *A Two Minute Warning* in 1988 "in the hope of awakening Americans to action before the end of the century. By then it will be too late." They included a bit of history to try to get American management's attention: "America now stands, at the end of the twentieth century, where England stood at the end of the nineteenth — the strongest economic power on the face of the earth, yet facing strong challengers from abroad. Britain did not respond to warnings, and it began its descent into the ranks of also-ran economies in the last decade of the nineteenth century."

So American management — and that includes political as well as industrial leadership — doesn't know what to do and has little time left to learn in a period when management is becoming increasingly more difficult. Not only is time running out, it's speeding up as well.

"Because new technologies become generally available more

47

quickly," Ohmae says, "time has become even more of a critical element in strategy." Neil Dial, a manager at Motorola, has a simple way to make that clear. "Ten years ago," he says, "it used to take two weeks to get your film developed. Today it takes two hours. The same mechanics, the same principles, apply in manufacturing."

Striner says, "The computer has changed the nature of markets and has radically shortened the development and the production cycles. With computers, and especially supercomputers, you can test out all sorts of parts of the process, and you can design much more rapidly, so that everything is now happening much more quickly than it ever did before." Through the use of computers, robotics, and advanced assembly techniques, Motorola has dramatically cut the time it needs to assemble an electronic pager on its Bandit Line at the plant in Boynton Beach, Florida. George Fisher, the chief executive of Motorola, says the Bandit Line "reflects a model of production that the United States is uniquely qualified to perfect. We're talking about lot-size-of-one manufacturing with cycle times on the order of two hours. That process used to take us two weeks." Within seventeen minutes of an order's being placed, production starts, and every single pager in production at any moment will be different in some way. Lot sizes of one. "But the real excitement," Fisher says, "is serving customers better with that capability. The manufacturing systems of the future will have brains that go right from the customer to the production line."

(It's worth noting that Boynton Beach's Bandit Line was named in corporate honesty; it was designed with ideas "borrowed" from successful manufacturing operations around the world. Actually, the whole project from the beginning was code-named Bandit, but that takes the fun out of the story. Also, for both of you who don't know, an electronic pager is one of those things that doctors years ago used to wear on their belts that would "beep" when they were needed in surgery or on the golf course. Beepers, as they're known, are now carried by almost everyone who is important or insecure or both. Doctors still wear them on their belts. Or their purse straps.)

What, exactly, is quality?

The problem is one of definition. Quantity is easy to define; it has a finite number. If you say six, everyone who understands the language and can count knows that six is one more than five, one less than seven, an even half dozen. In industrial jargon, the number six therefore has an "operational definition," which simply means that everyone who uses the word agrees on what it means. However, there's no operational definition of quality. That's one part of the difficulty of trying to understand what the quality experts are saying. Another is that they all believe Humpty Dumpty was absolutely correct when he told Alice scornfully, "When I use a word, it means just what I choose it to mean — neither more nor less."

Some of the linguistic confusion arises as the experts learn more and try to distinguish it from what they already know. Armand Feigenbaum, at General Electric, observed that quality doesn't work in bits and pieces; it's either all part of a single, defined effort or it fails. He calls that single, defined effort Total Quality Control. Kaoru Ishikawa noticed something similar in Japan and also called it Total Quality Control, but it isn't the same TQC. "Japan's QC [quality control] came from the West," Ishikawa observed. "If it had been adopted without modification, it would not have succeeded. We have sprinkled this QC with Japanese seasoning and made it more palatable to the Japanese taste." With or without Japanese seasoning, Crosby doesn't see the point of new names, that quality is quality and adding the word *total* doesn't change the result. He may be right about that, but words and their connotations are important.

Talking with Chairman Philip Caldwell at Ford in 1981, Deming kept saying "never-ending improvement." Caldwell didn't like it; "never-ending" sounded like too long a time. Deming changed it to "continual improvement," which didn't sound nearly as long. Clearly, "continual" and "never-ending" sound different but mean the same thing. Quality sounds the same no matter who says it, but no two people agree on what the word *quality* means, although they are talking about the same result.

John Stepp, asked to define quality, said, "I know it when I see it." That idea is also present in Robert Pirsig's *Zen and the Art of Motorcycle Maintenance,* which is more about quality than Zen or motorcycles. Pirsig wrote, "Even though quality cannot be defined, *you know what quality is.*" (The book was turned down 121 times before it was bought and published. It went on to sell two million copies.)

The problem is putting that knowledge into words. To Sarasohn, quality is "a fitness of a process, a product, or a service relative to its intended purpose," which is close to Juran's definition of "fitness for use" but nowhere near Crosby's definition of "conformance to requirements." Yankelovich likes "the German concept" that "quality is not just what you see on the surface, but what is underneath the surface," but he also likes the "American tradition," that "something is quality if you get really excellent value for the money that you put into it." Ishikawa says a quality product is "most economical, most useful, and always satisfactory to the consumer."

Peter Scholtes, a senior consultant for Joiner Associates, says, "I don't know any definition of quality, and I've listened to groups of managers spend endless hours trying to come up with a definition of quality. I suspect the first prehistoric humans discovered quality when they found out that they could do some things to make their lives better, to make their lives drier, to make their lives safer. They learned along the way to improve what they were doing, and they discovered quality."

If it was discovered by accident then, it has to be adopted on purpose now. Quality is what made the Japanese economically powerful. But it is a mistake to think of quality as a Japanese trait, an outgrowth of an Asian culture that cannot be transplanted to a Western one. Japan's economic success resulted from the adoption of the quality production philosophy and techniques that were taught by Americans after World War II, enthusiastically adopted by senior management, and improved and adapted by Japanese and other experts. It is true that the Japanese are hard and willing workers, but so are a good many other people in this world. Mant observed that British workers were superb when they worked for foreign managers, and that must be true of American workers as well. One of the most productive Honda plants on earth is in Marysville, Ohio.

Tim Leuliette, an American and a member of the Siemens Management Board, says, "No single country, in my mind, today controls quality. . . . Not all Japanese companies are perfect. Not all American companies are bad. Not all European companies are wondering what's going on. It's all now a global market with different companies acting in different ways." Feigenbaum agrees, saying, "Quality travels under no exclusive national passport, has no geographic entity, no particular cultural determinant. Quality depends entirely on the way a company operates, on the way a company management leads, on the way the company's men and women do their jobs. It is as true in the United States, or in Japan, or in Europe as it is in any other part of the world."

The most successful companies we could find around the world are acting in ways designed to improve their quality. As good fortune would have it, if quality cannot be defined, it can be taught.

3

Teachers and Sensei

Prehistoric man may have invented quality by accident, as Peter Scholtes suggests, but its beginning in modern times was not an accident and can be dated, at least by those who think that statistics led to quality in mass production — and among the experts, almost everyone does. Blanton Godfrey, at one time head of theory and technology at AT&T's Quality Assurance Center, says the quality movement started on May 16, 1924, the day Walter A. Shewhart gave his boss at Bell Labs at 63 West Street in New York a one-page memo, including a drawing of what may have been the first control chart. The memo suggested a way of using statistics to improve quality in telephones, which the company was all but desperate to do. Western Electric used "as alike as two telephones" in its ads, hoping to replace "as alike as two peas in a pod" in common usage.

The telephone company was growing, people demanded reliable phones, and the technical problems were severe. Of the 40,000 employees making telephone equipment at Western Electric's Hawthorne Works in Chicago, about 5,200 were in the inspection department. Shewhart, the company's leading theoretician, taught his statistical methods at Hawthorne and other plants. Within a few years, Western Electric put out a handbook of quality control methods that became an industrial bible. Two of the four Americans now recognized as quality experts were at

Hawthorne. Joseph M. Juran worked in inspection and knew Shewhart; W. Edwards Deming was in research and development but did not work with Shewhart until later, in New York and Washington.

Juran and Deming both come from backgrounds of poverty, where education was the key to improvement. Each spent part of his childhood living in a tarpaper shack, Deming in Wyoming when his family moved to the frontier from Iowa, Juran in Minnesota when his family emigrated when he was eight from what was then the Austro-Hungarian Empire and is now northern Romania. Deming, born in 1900, the last year of the nineteenth century, had his first job at a hotel when he was eight or nine (he can't remember exactly) and kept working odd jobs to make enough money to get his education. Juran, born on Christmas Eve, 1904, did the same thing, taking any job he could get, even shining shoes in Minneapolis.

The other two recognized American experts, Philip B. Crosby and Armand V. Feigenbaum, did not work for the telephone company. Feigenbaum met Shewhart on several occasions, but Crosby did not. Feigenbaum, born in 1920, worked at GE in Schenectady, New York, in the summers during college, then joined the company full time when he graduated in 1942. He stayed for twenty-six years. Crosby, the youngest of the four, was born in 1926; he still resents that, when he was already in his sixties, Juran once called him "a young whippersnapper," which Juran denies. Crosby worked in industry for twenty-seven years. Both men started at the bottom — Feigenbaum as an apprentice toolmaker, Crosby as a junior technician — and worked their way up.

Outside their work, the four men seem to have only two things in common.

The first is that each of the four thinks the other three are not quite right, yet some similarities in the four methods are striking; the obvious conclusion is that over the years, they have learned from one another and others. What they teach today is more evolved and more sophisticated than what any one of them taught originally. While there is broad conceptual agreement among them, there are differences, obviously, but many of them seem, well, obscure. The easiest way to explain this phenomenon is with a scene near the end of the film *Zorba the Greek*. Zorba (Anthony Quinn) explains to a timid Englishman why a recently deceased widow they knew will not have a local funeral. She was, Zorba said, "a Frank," who crossed herself with four fingers, which Zorba demonstrates with his thumb carefully tucked in his palm. The village natives cross themselves with three fingers, so no local funeral for the widow. In itself, the distinction is real enough, but its long-term relevance to Christianity seems highly suspect. While the four experts have basic differences — Deming's approach is philosophical, Crosby's is more technical, for example — when studying what they want as a result and the specific details of what they teach, we sometimes feel that we are dealing with three- and four-finger crosses. Anyone can recognize the differences, but anyone may also wonder at their long-term relevance to quality.

The second thing that all four have in common is that not one of them originally intended to work in quality. Asked why he was attracted to the quality field, Juran said, "I wasn't. I was a young fellow out of engineering school. I'm an immigrant. Like many impoverished immigrant families, the big goal was to find a steady job at steady pay." Western Electric hired him at the Hawthorne Works in 1924 and assigned him to the inspection branch and "that's how I got into this field. I didn't choose it. I didn't really care." When Deming went to the University of Wyoming in 1917, he didn't know what he wanted to do. "I studied engineering, but I really didn't know what engineers did," he says. He eventually decided to do research in mathematics.

Crosby, who comes from a medical family, got his degree in podiatry, then realized he didn't want to do that with his life, so he went to work in manufacturing, first for the Crosley Corporation in 1952, then Martin Marietta, and finally ITT. Assigned as a "reliability engineer," he essentially worked his way up through the quality field, first believing what the quality control professionals told him, then deciding they were wrong and making up his own rules. When he left ITT in 1979, after fourteen years, he was the corporate vice-president for quality, the first one in the country.

Feigenbaum learned the importance of quality as a young engineer at GE during World War II, helping to develop early jet airplane engines. Sometimes they worked, at other times they blew up, and Feigenbaum used statistical techniques to find out quickly what was going wrong. He says, "I realized that here was a body of knowledge that needed to be developed. It was as important as electronics." GE made him head of its quality in manufacturing program.

After the war, American industry returned to quantity production. In truth, it was only during the war, when America was desperate for reliable war production, that quality control was considered important, and its importance was more with the U.S. government than with private industry. Both before the war and after, American industry considered quality a secondary issue at best. If Americans wanted quality in the 1950s, they bought German cameras, Swiss watches, or European cars — and paid more for them.

If Shewhart's leading role in quality is recognized by some now, it was not before World War II. Deming told a seminar, "In his [Shewhart's] heart, it must have been a great disappointment to him that his own organization did not recognize him." The same could be said of Deming, whose own *country* did not recognize him until 1980, thirty years after Japan, but by 1990, four books about him were published in one year. Juran was not instantly recognized in the United States, either. His book on quality management was turned down by several publishers before McGraw-

Hill printed it in 1951. Juran says of the period from the end of the war until his book was published, "It was a time of real troubles. I wouldn't wish that on anyone." The book, *Quality Control Handbook,* got him his first invitation to Japan in 1954.

Deming and Juran both became freelance quality consultants after the war, but Feigenbaum stayed with GE until 1968, when he founded General Systems Company, his consultancy in Pittsfield, Massachusetts. Crosby didn't become a quality consultant until 1979.

Deming is the philosopher; the others are more pragmatic, telling managers what to do — specifically, to make things better. Deming does not. People who believe in his method have been known to compare it to religion because, they say, it not only improves quality in manufacturing, service, government, and education, but it also makes their lives better. Donald Petersen, the retired chairman of Ford Motor Company, describes himself as "a disciple of Dr. Deming's." William Scherkenbach, the statistician who became the director of Statistical Methods at Ford, then General Motors, has noticed that "people talk about their relationship or experience with Dr. Deming in a religious connotation. People describe themselves as disciples of Dr. Deming's; they are going to spread the gospel according to Dr. Deming, going to convert management. It's amazing. Without any prompting, people put it in that kind of context. And I think it's true, because he really reaches your soul. Dr. Deming reaches people through the heart." It is hard to imagine any of the other quality experts hammering away, as Deming does at his seminars, at the right of all people to have "joy in their work."

He hammers equally hard at the need of companies to make money, and he says repeatedly that quality produces greater profits. Deming will not say with which companies he consults, but he doesn't care if the companies say, so it's known that both Ford and General Motors are among his clients and seem to be pleased.

Petersen, in January of 1987, six years after Deming started, told an interviewer, "Ford Motor Company progress in total is even more than I dared hope we could achieve when I was first thinking about these issues . . . back in 1980. We are running well over 50 percent better levels of quality in our products today, and I dare say that I would not have predicted that much improvement in this short time."

If you have to date Deming's decision to work in quality control permanently, 1938 is as good a year as any. Deming had met and become friendly with Walter Shewhart; they remained friends until Shewhart's death in 1967. In the '30s Deming had used Shewhart's statistical approach to train clerks at the U.S. Census Bureau and to establish sampling techniques for census work. In March 1938, at Deming's request and after a full year of preparation, Shewhart gave four lectures at the Graduate School in the Agriculture Department, where Deming was in charge of courses in advanced mathematics and statistics. Statistics in those days was so esoteric that American universities did not regard it as a separate subject. Deming's doctorate, for example, is not in statistics, as one would expect, but in mathematical physics. There weren't any books on statistics then, so Shewhart's four lectures were published as *Statistical Method from the Viewpoint of Quality Control* in 1939 (and reprinted in 1986). Deming, who spent a year studying, editing, and clarifying the lectures for publication, wrote in 1988, "Another half century will pass before people in industry and in science begin to appreciate the contents" of Shewhart's lectures.

However, even Deming didn't claim that the lectures were models of clarity and simplicity. In *The World of W. Edwards Deming*, Ceil Kilian, his secretary for many years, tells one of Deming's stories about the lectures.

It's 1938. Deming is in Shewhart's room in the Hotel Washington on the third day of the lectures, and Shewhart carefully but casually explains a point in the fourth lecture that Deming doesn't understand. "I remarked," Deming said, "that if he wrote up these lectures as he had just explained them to me, they would be clearer. He said his writing had to be foolproof. I thereupon let go the comment that he had written his thoughts so damned foolproof that no one could understand them." Nothing much changed in the next fifty years. At a quality seminar in Dallas in 1988, one participant said he couldn't understand the first chapter of *Out of the Crisis,* Deming's book on quality, until he finished the book; then, having figured out what all the words and phrases actually meant, he started over. Deming, like Shewhart, is so insistent on getting everything precisely as he wants it that he uses words like *suboptimization,* whose meaning most people can only imagine.

Along with being philosophical, Deming's method is revolutionary in that nothing stays the same. Ben Carlson, the executive vice-president of Vernay Laboratories at Yellow Springs, Ohio, which adopted the Deming method in 1983, says it "changes the relationship with your customers; it changes the relationship with your suppliers; it changes the relationship you have with your employees." The Deming method has fourteen points but three key ingredients: continual improvement, constancy of purpose, and profound knowledge. Deming doesn't even pretend that his method is going to be anything but difficult and time-consuming.

Constancy of purpose is the first of fourteen points, the linch-pin to Deming's method. It is part of what Homer Sarasohn told the Japanese, that you have to have some reason to be in business other than to make money. But you also have to know what business you are in and how to stay ahead of the customer's needs in that business. Most companies don't. Buggy whip makers undoubtedly thought they were in the business of making buggy whips, which explains why they are no longer in business. Buggy whip makers were in the business of vehicle acceleration; had they known that, the coming of the internal combustion engine would not have put them out of business. They could have, for instance, switched over and made quality carburetors. Carburetor makers thought that making carburetors was their business, which explains why fuel injector companies took over so much of the market; and if fuel injector companies think making injectors is their business, they'll join the buggy whip people in the industrial trash. As Scherkenbach observed, one of these days someone may really say, "Beam me up, Scotty," and a fuel injector or a carburetor isn't going to do it. So constancy of purpose requires that you know what business you are in and how to *stay* in that business.

Continual improvement is the fifth of the fourteen points and is, perhaps, the most easily understood. Nothing is ever good enough, the job is never over, and the day you decide you can't make it any better, someone else somewhere else will and drive you out of business. That nothing is ever good enough is not a moral judgment; it simply means the system in which you work must be continually improved. It's another point that is accepted by most of the experts: the pursuit of quality can never stop even though it is as indefinable as love and as unattainable as justice. Quality is, therefore, rather like one of the precepts of Zen: "There is no answer; search for it lovingly."

Profound knowledge is not one of the fourteen points; it is what managers need to apply the fourteen points effectively to each situation. "There is no substitute," Deming says, "for what I call profound knowledge." He tells his seminars that people in management don't have to be experts, but they have to understand that profound knowledge exists and will help transform a company for the benefit of customers, workers, managers, stockholders, suppliers, the environment, and the community. Although Deming has used the phrase for years, he did not define precisely what profound knowledge meant until late 1988, and he has refined the definition since. There are now four broad categories: "appreciation for a system, theory of variation, theory of knowledge, psychology. . . . The various segments of the system of profound knowledge cannot be separated. They interact with each other. Thus, knowledge of psychology is incomplete without knowledge of variation."

Deming defines a system as "a series of functions or activities . . . within an organization that work together for the aim of the organization. . . . The aim of the system must be clear to everyone in the system. Without an aim, there is no system. The aim is a value judgment." The aim he proposes is that everyone works together so that everyone can benefit; his example is "a good orchestra. The players are not there to play solos as prima donnas, to catch the ear of the listener, they are there to support each other. They need not be the best players in the country. . . . A business is not merely an organization chart, all departments striving for individual goals. . . . It is a network of people, materials, methods, equipment, all working in support of each other for the common aim." When that happens, when every part of a system is working in support of every other part, Deming calls it "optimization." To achieve it, he says that internal competition between, for instance, divisions of a company or workers in a group has to be eliminated. That means numerical ratings, rankings, rewards, and punishments have to be eliminated. Deming is unalterably opposed, for instance, to grades being given to children in school, and in his classes at New York University, he does not grade his students. He believes that anytime you introduce competition between people, you automatically diminish cooperation.

The second part of profound knowledge is knowledge for the study of variation, or statistical theory. When Shewhart drew his control chart in 1924, he was addressing the problem of variation, which statisticians say exists in every system. Essentially, Deming teaches, there are two reasons for "a fault, complaint, mistake, defect, accident," and because "variation will always be," those two mistakes can never be completely eliminated — "You cannot have zero mistakes in both. . . . Impossible, impossible! Cannot be done!" The two mistakes are treating anything that goes wrong as if it were caused by something special when it was caused by random variation, and the reverse, treating anything that goes wrong as if it were caused by random variation when it was caused by something special. Either mistake is expensive because it all but guarantees more mistakes as you blunder about, trying to guess which one it is and how to fix it. The way to tell one from the other and minimize your loss is the Shewhart control chart.

It sounds more complicated than it is. To demonstrate its simplicity, Deming uses a control chart done by the ten-year-old son of a statistician friend of his. The boy wanted to track what time the school bus picked him up each morning, so he marked the time with a dot on a simple chart; the dots were reasonably close together. One day the dot was marked about twenty minutes later than usual. It had a note, "new driver," clearly as special a special cause in the school bus business as ever there was. The other dots were not all at the same time, but they were close enough that the daily differences could be accounted for by the flow of traffic, kids being marginally faster or slower getting on, and a varying number of traffic lights turning red — nothing special, just the everyday bumps and elbows of life, random variation.

The theory of knowledge teaches, Deming says, that "there's no true value of anything." If you're counting something, for instance, the result you get depends on how you count. If you change the way you count, the result also changes. The two figures are neither right nor wrong. "Both are the results of procedures, and, of course, they disagree," Deming says. "Change the procedure, get a new number." Deming says people accept that the speed of light is a true value, but it isn't; there were ten different published values of the speed of light between 1874 and 1932, and he quotes Galileo as saying, "If the speed of light is not infinite, then it's awful damned fast."

Knowledge, Deming says, is prediction, and knowledge comes from theory. "Experience teaches nothing without theory," he tells a seminar. It is for that reason that he warns people not to copy someone else's success. Unless you understand the theory behind it, trying to copy it can lead to complete chaos.

Then there's knowledge about psychology, which is the most difficult of all the issues because it deals with people. People are born, he says, with "intrinsic motivation. . . . People are born with a need for relationships with other people and with a need to be loved and esteemed by others. . . . One is born with a natural inclination to learn and to be innovative. One inherits a right to enjoy his work." Deming says that management grinds that intrinsic motivation out of people with rankings, ratings, personnel appraisals, bonuses, merit pay, and anything else that sets up a competition. Over a lifetime of playground games, school grades, and adult rewards and punishments, extrinsic motivation destroys intrinsic motivation, Deming says, and it is wrong. Do you go to school to get a grade or to learn?

Management must also realize that people learn in different ways at different rates, which is an example combining psychology and the theory of variation. It illustrates why Deming says the four parts of profound knowledge interact and must be considered together.

There's a great deal more. When Deming first defined profound knowledge, it had seven parts and was written on half a page of paper. The definition dated October 5, 1990, is fourteen double-spaced typewritten pages. But no matter how many pages it takes, to anyone looking for some clear, immediate rules on how to improve quality on a production line right now, a philosophical discussion of profound knowledge seems beside the point. An admirer of Deming's disagrees, saying that Deming with his philosophical approach is solving the quality problem forever, not just for the moment. Once you understand the philosophy, it can be applied to any situation, in business or out, in professional life or personal. It is the difference, she says, between giving a hungry man a fish or teaching him how to fish. Does he eat well for one meal or for a lifetime?

Deming's method is a system of logic that is quite different from the accepted standards of management, and learning that logic is something like learning a foreign language — you have to study and practice, again and again, until you get it. "I think one of the difficulties of learning what Dr. Deming is talking about," Michael Maccoby, the consultant, says, "is the fact that people have to unlearn so much that they've been taught that really isn't true. . . . They even have to question their own experience." James Gleick, writing about the new and controversial science of chaos, said, "Shallow ideas can be assimilated; ideas that require people to reorganize their picture of the world provoke hostility."

Deming is unusually blunt, which can also provoke hostility. When an interviewer asks what positive signs he sees in the United States economy, he answers, "I don't see any." One writer said, "Deming's style is confrontative (sic), and he tends to lose patience with those who resist the learning. . . . Deming has acquired a reputation for delivering his message with venom." When another writer said, "He can be short-tempered and intolerant," Deming objected, saying it gave people entirely the wrong idea, and in a way it does. It is true that he is impatient and brusque to the point of rudeness with senior managers and reporters, but with workers and line supervisors he is friendly, gentle, and patient, and he will do anything to help someone who is struggling to learn. In the few social situations he allows himself, Deming is all but courtly. On the job, however, consulting or lecturing, his sole concern is making his point.

Deming tells people that what is required is "transformation," which Brian Joiner, the consultant, describes as orderly change as opposed to the organized chaos of revolution. Whatever it's called, little that management does in the old system stays the same in the Deming method. Scholtes says one of the things that separates the quality gurus "is how much they demand of managers, and it seems to me that Dr. Deming, more than any of the other leaders in quality, demands a great deal. . . . Nothing less is needed than the transformation of the western style of management. To a greater or lesser extent, the other teachers of quality strike me as letting the managers get away without very much change on their part." Myron Tribus of Exergy, Inc., says, "Deming will get you to your best level because he is holistic. The others give you various things you can do."

That transformation, Deming says, will let the United States prosper in "the new economic age," which he believes the United States must join to survive. "Nobody's sitting here *predicting* that we'll survive," he tells an American seminar. "We may not. There's no regulation saying we must survive. Purely voluntary."

Phil Crosby left ITT in 1979, and, he says, "My original plan was that I was going to do it all myself, maybe with a part-time secretary. I was going to make speeches, write a book a year, and do a little board-level consulting." He had decided to leave ITT partly because of the success of *Quality Is Free,* which he wrote in 1979. In it he quotes Harold S. Geneen, the hard-driving chairman he worked for at ITT: "Quality is not only right, it is free. And it is not only free, it is the most profitable product line we have." The book is written in simple, direct language with examples that any adult, in or out of business, can understand. To business people trying to learn about quality and running into the profession's disagreements on definitions, mathematics, philosophical discussion, and the use of special words, Crosby's approach had to be a welcome change. The book was a best seller then and has now sold more than two million copies in several languages. That success led to the establishment of Philip Crosby Associates, Inc., with schools in London, Paris, Munich, Genoa, Toronto, Singapore, Sydney, and Tokyo through the Japan Management Association. In the United States, Crosby schools are in six states, including the headquarters in Winter Park, Florida.

Crosby is the only one of the American quality experts who does not have a doctorate, and he has said that he is not, and does not want to be, a quality guru. He considers himself a businessman who learned by doing, saying, "My career has not been in a college. . . . I am a pragmatic business philosopher who writes about things other than quality." It was Crosby who created the Zero Defect movement at Martin Marietta in the 1960s and popularized the concept "do it right the first time," which was first used in the mid-'30s at Western Electric. He says he got to those ideas because, as he moved up through the quality ranks, nothing else seemed to work.

"Quality control, quality assurance and all these things, diligently applied," Crosby says, "still produced material that did not meet the contract, did not meet the requirements, always had variations. . . . I went to Juran courses and Deming courses and everybody else courses, and what I learned was that the best thing you can do is contain it. All dams leak. . . . But that was not satisfactory to the management that I had. They didn't want to always play catch-up, they didn't want to always play defense. They wanted to know why couldn't we make what it was we said we were going to make. . . . It finally dawned on me about prevention . . . prevention was always sort of a far-out thing in industry, but my education was medical, and in medicine, prevention is the whole thing. It's okay to fix, but it's better to stay well. . . . I began to see that the problem was management, not the workers." Crosby says management accepted the statistical theory that a few things will always be bad and the business school theory that to try to get everything right would be too expensive. "I thought, 'It must be cheaper to do things right the first time.' "

Zero Defects was his way of making *management* believe that it didn't have to accept that some things would always be bad, that it could learn how to do it right, and that doing it right could be the standard. Crosby says his idea got twisted into a "motivational program" with slogans, banners, and parades by the Defense Department "based on their concept that the problem was the worker." The other experts are opposed to sloganeering or exhorting the workers or putting the blame for a lack of quality anywhere but on management. Crosby agrees with them, but because of the government's motivational campaign aimed at workers, he is criticized. "Dr. Deming, for instance, never makes a speech," he says, "without talking about how I try to exhort the workers, and I never exhorted a worker in my life. I wrote six books full of comments about 'Don't try to exhort the workers, it's a waste of time. It's management's fault, management's problem.' " Deming denies that he talks about Crosby.

The experts all agree that it's management's problem, and they solve it and get quality by studying the process, finding out what it will do and how to improve it so that defects are reduced (Deming, Juran, Feigenbaum) or eliminated (Crosby). All four also say, although they seem not to hear one another, that statistical quality control is a useful tool, but that's all. Deming, who is most closely associated with statistics, says of his teaching in Japan in 1950, "It is entirely wrong to say that Statistical Quality Control did it. Absolutely not. Nothing wrong with SQC, but if that's all you have, we're on the way down, down the tube." He says the value of statistical tools is to show "manufacturing as a system, a system, not just bits and pieces." Crosby says, "Now, what Deming has is a theory, based primarily on statistics . . . and he has these herds of supporters, but there's no *thing* to do. . . . these are not *management* tools, these are technical tools for process control, and they're wonderful, but they have nothing to do with running a company."

Crosby likes to talk about his college program: "We have it all around the world. Nobody else has anything like that. There actually is a system. It's based on reality, it's based on real life, it's based on solid concepts. Anybody can understand it." People come to study specifically what to do based on Crosby's fourteen-point program, which expands on four basics he says are essential. (Deming also uses fourteen points, but his are basically philosophical and Crosby's are basically practical.)

Crosby calls his four basics Absolutes of Quality Management. The first is that "the definition of quality is conformance to requirements," not specifications but requirements. He estimates that only about 10 percent of the requirements for an automobile are technical specifications, the exact details of the design. "The rest of them are what does the customer want from us, and how do you describe that, and how do you meet those." Since there is no accepted definition of quality, Crosby's "conformance to requirements" is not accepted by the other three men, and he, in turn, rejects their definitions.

His second absolute is "the system of causing quality is prevention." Here, all the experts generally agree; the idea is not to find mistakes later but not to make them in the first place. It's obvious that if you rely on mass inspection to catch mistakes, you are driving costs up. At a minimum, even if nothing is wrong, the inspectors have to be paid. If they do find a mistake (and they will), add the cost of having to do the same thing, whatever it is, over again. To drive costs down, you make the system itself produce quality without inspectors. The experts agree on that goal, but not on the method of achieving it.

The third absolute is "the performance standard for quality is Zero Defects." One of Crosby's continuing fights with statistically based quality methods is that they all accept as inevitable that some things will go wrong at some times, the theory of variation. He says, "The quality control profession, of which I've been a part for all these years, bears a very big burden of responsibility because they have perpetuated this myth . . . that there are these laws of probability that are inviolate, and God wants it to be bad." Crosby says companies can and should produce defect-free goods and services all the time. The other three experts say, imply, or suggest that Crosby doesn't know what he's talking about.

The final of the four absolutes is "the measurement of quality is the Price of Nonconformance." Crosby, having lived through the period when "professional" managers, the legal-financial types, were rising to the top, knew that the first question from any chief executive about any suggested improvement was likely to be,

"How much will it cost?" He adapted a method that Feigenbaum had introduced at GE to demonstrate with hard numbers that it costs more *not* to produce quality than to produce it. Juran also believes it's important that the cost of not producing quality be known since it helps to keep top management interested. On the other hand, Deming says the cost of not producing quality is "unknown and unknowable. No one knows the cost of a dissatisfied customer." All four men agree that quality does more to increase profits than anything else you can do. Quality, then, is no longer simply morally and ethically rewarding, it actually makes a lot of money.

Crosby has taught more than fifteen hundred companies, starting with IBM. Alone among the quality experts, he tells people that quality is relatively easy, that if they do what he teaches, they can run quality companies. "I have never determined," he writes, "why people insist on making quality so difficult by laying out technical roadblocks or structured techniques that have to be obeyed." He says Zero Defects and "do it right the first time" are concepts that are easily understood and easy to teach. "My experience with all the other ways of doing things is there's only two guys [in the company] who understand it, and the other people don't understand it, and the two guys can't explain it [to them]."

Deming makes no secret of his disdain for Crosby's method. He tells a class, "How about 'do it right the next time'? Makes just as much sense." He has none of the executive polish that twenty-seven years in industry have given Crosby. And where Crosby is a skilled public speaker, Deming once told a class, "I know I'm repeating myself; I don't mind."

Crosby looks like an executive. He is carefully dressed and always neat, his graying blond hair well cut and combed. He swims regularly and appears trim and fit. A good conversationalist, he is filled with obscure bits of information that he uses to make or illustrate points. He is, in short, the sort of man who would be perfectly at home in any boardroom in the country. Deming wears custom-made suits, then he stuffs the pockets with a calculator, file cards, a small notebook, scraps of paper on which he's written one or two words, clippings, a pocket diary, and a small magnifying glass with a built-in light. His shirt pocket usually holds at least a half dozen pens and markers. His white hair is cut by his daughter Linda, who trims it as he wants it — so close to his skull that, at a distance, he appears bald. He is nearly twenty-six years older than Crosby, and even though he tries to keep his weight in check, he is thick in the middle. If you imagined him anyplace, it would be in the classroom, not the boardroom.

Whereas Crosby has a staff of about 325, Deming's whole staff is Ceil Kilian, the "temporary" secretary he hired in 1954. They work out of a basement office at his house in Washington, D.C., where Deming moved in 1936, before he became committed to the quality movement.

Juran is closer to Deming in method than the others, but they move apart on how difficult it is for a company to achieve quality, how important statistical methods are, and whether competition is good or bad. Deming says quality requires transformation, but Juran says managing for quality is analogous to managing for finance and does not require a revolution. He says financial planning, financial control, and financial improvement by management become quality planning, quality control, and quality improvement, which he calls The Juran Trilogy (a registered trademark of Juran Institute, Inc.). "The conceptual approaches are identical with those used to manage for finance," he wrote. "However, the procedural steps are special, and the tools used are also special." Unlike Crosby, Juran does not say quality is easy, but he makes less of the difficulty than does Deming. Still, Juran thinks that most quality programs fail most often because the people at the top did not realize how difficult the programs would be. Difficult or not, however, he says both finance and quality can be managed.

Christopher Hart, once a Harvard Business School professor, now a quality consultant, says, "Joseph Juran, like W. Edwards Deming, is a national treasure. Never has there been a person in a discipline who has such a broad conceptualization of what the field is about and a flexible approach to let an organization answer the question, 'What's an appropriate approach to quality for us?' Dr. Juran does indeed have the Juran approach, but it's a flexible approach, it's not dogmatic."

Even though Juran worked with Shewhart at Hawthorne, the only one of the quality experts who did, he is less impressed with statistics than Deming is. Juran thinks the idea of quality management began well before Shewhart's control chart, and he is quoted as asking, "How in the world did the railroads run when Shewhart wasn't around?" Juran, like many of the other experts, thinks statistics is a useful tool, nothing more. "I got started in that [statistical methodology] soon after 1924," he says, "and I know the merits of it and the limitations, and it has both. But achieving quality involves a great deal more than what tools you use. It involves finding out what the customers need. And who are the customers? How can we design our goods and services to respond to those needs? How can we produce those goods and services using the proper technology? There's a great deal in it." All of the experts now agree that customers, suppliers, and technology play important parts in a quality program.

Juran says that the three most important items in a quality program are that the top people be in charge; that the people be trained in how to manage for quality; and that quality be improved at an unprecedented, revolutionary pace. He points out that quality is already improving in the United States and has in the past, but it has not improved nearly as fast as it has in Japan. So while Juran does not see the need of a management revolution, he does see the need for a revolutionary rate of quality improvement. While he says quality has to improve radically just to match Japan's rate of improvement, he also says all that is necessary to achieve that is for senior managers to give as much attention to quality as they give to finance. Joiner says, "The global marketplace demands a higher level of quality, and the new question is the rate of improvement. Old management provides a rate of improvement, but it isn't fast enough. It is possible with the old way to do things better, but the key is how fast you can improve. One of the drawbacks of the old way of managing was it continually solved the same problem over and over and over and over again."

Juran's definition of quality is "fitness for use," and he says the first thing you have to know is what that means to your customer. What does he need from you to make your product usable to him? He has since expanded his definition to include product features and freedom from failure.

Unlike Crosby, who has colleges for managers, or Deming, who teaches four-day seminars, Juran relies mainly on the Juran Institute in Wilton, Connecticut, to spread his message. Classes are taught there and in other locations, but the institute was created in 1979 primarily to produce and market his videotape series, "Juran on Quality Improvement." Juran had resisted setting up any organization for fear that it would eventually control him rather than the other way around, and of course it did. In 1987, Juran transferred leadership of the institute to Blanton Godfrey, formerly of AT&T. "I hesitate to use the term 'good riddance,' " Juran wrote, "but the passing of that torch was for me a joyful occasion." He still consults and advises at the institute, but he now takes a less active direct role because "years ago, I promised my nine grandchildren that I would write my autobiography for them."

The three different methods that the three experts use to teach led Joseph Oberle of *Training* magazine to write, "You can send your top managers to Crosby's college, order Juran's videotapes and materials from his institute, or join a waiting list to pay for Deming to tell you, in person, what a fool you've been." Feigenbaum does not teach, and apparently that is why Oberle listed Deming, Juran, and Crosby as the "quality gurus" and put Feigenbaum in a list of four less well known men (at least, less well known in the United States). *The Quality Review* magazine rates Feigenbaum as a major player and credits him with developing the concepts of the cost of quality (the cost of nonconformance to Crosby) and of total quality control while he was at GE. In 1944, when he was twenty-four, Feigenbaum became GE's top quality expert at the headquarters in Schenectady.

Even with his success during the war, it was no easier for Feigenbaum than for Juran or Deming after the war. Feigenbaum had realized that "what I did to make quality better made everything in my organization better." He tried various techniques — statistics, motivation, training, all of which he says are important — but when better ideas were found, he still had to fight with the finance people, or the design engineers, or the manufacturing engineers. "So I began to realize, basically," he says, "that quality was not a group of individual techniques or tools. . . . it was, instead, a total field. . . . and I called it Total Quality Control. I did that in the latter part of the 1940s, and nobody would listen." He published his book on total quality control in 1951; "that book received some attention in this country [the United States], but very great attention abroad [Europe and Japan]." He then began to publish articles in the *Harvard Business Review,* "making the point to a disbelieving market that quality and costs are partners, not adversaries — a sum, not a difference — because the industrial mythology of the time was that better quality has to cost more, create greater production difficulties, stretch things out farther.

"Quality isn't merely a generalized concept. Quality is measurable," he says, and what companies have to do is "quantify quality, as we quantify production costs, as we quantify finance, as we quantify any other part of it. The essence of quality is that it's a way of managing, and it's a way of measuring the way you exercise your stewardship. When you make quality right, then you'll make your shareowners happy." It was Feigenbaum who used the cost-of-quality approach to persuade managers that "the return on investment from these quality installations greatly exceeded the return from other forms of business investment." That, he says, ultimately led to a recognition that total quality was something to think about, to work on. Now, he says, "total quality has ultimately evolved into the basic international quality standard [and] I became an overnight success after fifty years of getting ready for it. Well, it's good to have preparation."

Feigenbaum defines quality as "what the buyer says it is. . . . When you run a business, and you're driven by sales, and you recognize that it's the buyer who makes the sales, the very fact that he's your arbiter of quality, I think, is perhaps the most simple but profound factor that you have to recognize." Deming disagrees in one way. He says the customer can't define quality because the customer doesn't know what you can do; that is, are you offering everything you have, or can you develop something better or even totally new? To illustrate what he means, he says, "Did any customer ask for electric lights?" Still, it is now generally recognized that the customer defines quality, but you have to stay ahead of the definition, meeting as-yet-undefined customer needs if you want to stay in business. Think buggy whip makers.

Whoever defines quality, Feigenbaum says, the importance of quality to the customer is growing: "Our General Systems survey of buyer preferences in both consumer and in industrial markets [in the United States] at the end of 1988 showed that eight out of ten buyers put quality ahead of price or equal to price in their buy preference. In 1979, it was three out of ten. That's the biggest marketplace change in our memory." It is also the period during which Japanese imports, particularly automobiles, were capturing big chunks of the American market.

*

Of the four experts, Deming, who can be the harshest as a teacher, seems the most humanistic, insisting that it is every person's right to have "joy in work." He used to say "pride" until David Kerridge, a professor at the University of Aberdeen, pointed out that the Book of Ecclesiastes says "joy" in two different verses. Deming, whose one known hobby is writing liturgical masses, switched to *joy*. He estimates that no more than two in a hundred managers and ten in a hundred workers now have joy in their work. Deming wants to drive fear among workers out of the workplace, but Juran says a little fear is not necessarily bad. All agree that the worker is not to blame; Feigenbaum says, "It's my good fortune to spend a great deal of my time offshore in the Far East, in Latin America, in Europe, and in Africa, and in my experience . . . the American man and woman in the factory or the office, when given full and necessary support and leadership from management and from the company, has no equal in the world."

He is optimistic because "the concept that quality is, in its essence, a way of managing to achieve customer satisfaction, better price, better human satisfaction simultaneously is going through the management of the world today like wildfire." He is also aware of the danger that may cause. A friend of his at one of the companies where he consults recently showed Feigenbaum eight notches carved in his desk with a pocketknife. "Each of those," Feigenbaum says, "represented a quality improvement crusade in his company that had failed, and had died, and had been buried without autopsy."

There were any number of so-called quality programs in the 1980s that were highly touted and often written about, then disappeared. Deming says all of them were wrong. He is especially critical of management by objective and management by results, which he compares to "driving your car by looking in the rearview mirror." At his seminars he names a list of things that people say or have said will help with quality. The list is labeled "Wrong!" It includes automation, new machinery, and computers — "Money will buy gadgets; it will not buy knowledge" — hard work and best efforts — "We might be better off if some people did not put forth their best efforts" — accountability, slogans and posters, merit systems, incentive plans, motivational plans, work standards, just-in-time, and zero defects.

Wrong, all wrong, Deming says. None of them alone nor all of them together can lead to quality without an understanding of profound knowledge. However, while just-in-time, for example, cannot lead to quality, quality can lead to just-in-time. Once you can predict what your system will do, then just-in-time becomes the smart thing to do. Best efforts, which Deming says are ruining us now, are effective once people know what they are supposed to do. Deming rarely tells people with whom he consults what to do, preferring to let them teach themselves. He asks over and over again, "By what method?" Or, to put it another way, "You know where you want to go, so how do you propose to get there?" (That method of forcing students to find their own answers by continued questioning is attributed to the Greek philosopher Socrates. Those who know ancient Greek history are also likely to mention Zeno when they talk about Deming. Zeno was the father of stoicism.)

Robert C. Christopher in *The Japanese Mind,* perhaps the best single-volume explanation of Japan in English, quotes a Japanese union official as saying, "Productivity and quality control are both games we learned from the Americans." But the Americans aren't named in that book, and only Deming is mentioned in David Halberstam's *The Reckoning.* Paul Kennedy in *The Rise and Fall of the Great Powers* says, "The effort to explain exactly how the country [Japan] transformed itself, and how others can imitate its success, has turned into a miniature growth industry itself. One major reason was its quite fanatical belief in achieving the highest levels of quality control, borrowing (and improving upon) sophisticated management techniques and production methods in the West." But his reference sends readers to Ezra Vogel's popular *Japan as Number One,* which doesn't mention the postwar American teachers and generally credits intrinsic Japanese character for Japan's success. Still, Vogel is more understandable than the writer who traced Japan's twentieth-century success to the nineteenth-century Meiji restoration.

The Japanese quality experts are more recent than that.

Kaoru Ishikawa, who died in 1989, is the best known of the Japanese quality experts. Unlike Deming and Juran, who were poor, or Crosby and Feigenbaum, who were middle class, Ishikawa was as close to an aristocrat as any Japanese outside the imperial household could be. He graduated in 1938 from Tokyo University, which is its own guarantee of a bright future in Japan, but he had a much better guarantee. The Japanese social style puts the family name before the given name, because in Japan the family is more important than the individual, and the Ishikawa family had power.

His father, Ichiro Ishikawa, who died in 1970, was president of both the Federation of Economic Organizations, the powerful Keidanren, and the Union of Japanese Science and Engineering (JUSE), organized in 1946 to help reconstruct Japan's bombed and burned-out industry. As head of both the industrial and engineering groups after World War II, Ichiro Ishikawa was a man of enormous influence. Deming, in a speech in Tokyo in 1960, said the elder Ishikawa "came to understand the problems that confronted Japanese industry, and [with Kenichi Koyanagi] perceived what statistical methods could do for Japan." It was Ichiro Ishikawa who arranged for Deming to make a presentation to the senior officers of Japan's twenty-one leading companies at a dinner in July 1950 and the next month with forty-seven senior executives at a conference center at Mount Hakone, a hot spring resort west of Tokyo. Other meetings with the industrial elite were arranged in later years. Homer Sarasohn had to order Japanese senior managers to attend his seminars; Ichiro Ishikawa had only to invite them. The results were the same.

Ichiro Ishikawa's son did not have to struggle to make Japanese industrialists and scientists and engineers listen to him. The family name opened doors and guaranteed respectful attention. Kaoru Ishikawa was urging statistical methods of quality control at JUSE in 1949. His English translator, David J. Lu, wrote, "His life and the history of QC [quality control] in Japan are inseparable." Some American managers may owe him more than they know.

When Americans began going to Japan in the early 1970s to learn how its industries produced better quality at lower cost, many of them came back with a vision of quality control circles, small groups of Japanese workers who met voluntarily to discuss ways to improve their own work and to make suggestions for improving the system. The circles met in the plant, they were easy to observe, and they were unlike anything in the United States. The Americans somehow believed those quality circles were the answer and imported the idea. They should have thanked Ishikawa, who developed quality control circles in 1962 and persuaded Japanese management, not only to support, but to listen to the QC circle suggestions as part of the total quality effort. That was the key difference. American workers made suggestions every bit as good as their Japanese counterparts, but American managers usually weren't listening. In the United States, quality circles — the word *control* was dropped — were popular in the 1970s (the first was established in 1974) and early '80s, but often died for lack of the total quality program that existed in Japan. Since total quality is largely an attitude and mental process, American visitors to Japanese plants could not see it and therefore did not import it.

Crosby remembers Americans going to Japan and coming back with quality circles. He says, "Quality circles are a wonderful thing," but not by themselves because "pretty soon the people find out that management has not changed its wicked ways." He says that American managers jumped on quality circles because the concept put the burden of quality on the workers, not on the managers. If management is not committed to quality, then groups of workers, however dedicated, making suggestions, however worthy, won't matter.

Ishikawa may have gotten the seed of the quality circle idea from earlier experiments. Kenneth Hopper, the British industrial consultant, says something roughly akin to quality control circles started in 1948 at Procter & Gamble and in the late 1950s at Sumitomo Electric. P&G began to have foremen meet in what were called Group Method Working meetings to discuss work simplification, trying to find a better, easier way to get a job done. Hopper, who was with P&G at the time, remembers how enthusiastically the working groups were accepted and how the meetings eventually began to talk about any problem or suggestion, not just work simplification. The working groups eventually led to the creation in the 1960s of an advanced type of quality circle that still exists at P&G and has been adopted in other firms.

In Japan, Hopper says, Sumitomo Electric started an employee participation program, not as structured as quality control circles, but more extensive than anything then being done in that country. The idea was to involve the lowest level workers, those the company could not afford to educate formally. The results were good, as they almost always are for genuine worker participation programs, and under the sponsorship of JUSE, Sumitomo shared its experience with other Japanese companies. While it's impossible to say with certainty that Sumitomo influenced Ishikawa's thinking about quality circles, Sumitomo's experiment and Ishikawa's concept occurred in that order.

A good deal of what happened in the quality movement in Japan and why it happened is still being argued. Sarasohn, who now lives in Arizona, says the history of that period is being reshaped. "Perhaps I share some of the blame," he wrote in a letter. "When I returned from Japan late in 1950, I left Japan behind me. . . . I was naive enough, I suppose, not to think about documenting the facts of the Civil Communications Section's (CCS) accomplishments at that time. . . . I did not attach sufficient significance to the matter. It was a job undertaken, and a job accomplished. . . . Perhaps my ego would be happier now if I had capitalized on what we had done to rebuild Japan's electronics and communications industries."

Perhaps he should have. Ishikawa mentions only three Americans as contributing to Japanese quality, Shewhart, Deming, and Juran. He does not recognize Sarasohn and Protzman or the CCS and the days immediately after World War II. This reference *may* be to the CCS or to the larger Economic and Scientific Section: "Many so-called management techniques were imported to Japan after the Second World War. Of these, only quality control was fully naturalized to become Japan's very own, experienced great success, and was transformed into a 'new product' to be widely exported to nations overseas."

Ishikawa was influenced by the Americans' introduction of statistical control in Japan's telecommunications industry in May 1946. Joji Arai, the secretary-general of the International Productivity Service in Washington, D.C., says experts from Bell Labs studied the Japanese telephone system. "What they came up with was a finding that essentially the Japanese engineering system was not so bad, and the system itself, the hardware, was not so bad, but it was the management system that was wrong." To improve the system, the teachers used the American War Standards, the Z series, written for the War Department. Deming was one of the five Americans who wrote them, starting in 1940. Ishikawa says, "Dr. Deming, a recognized scholar in the field of sampling, is the one who introduced quality control to Japan." Ishikawa thinks that at first too much emphasis was placed on statistical quality control, but he says that ended with a visit by Juran.

In July 1954, Juran lectured in Tokyo and Osaka, giving a

two-day course for top management and a ten-day course for department managers and section chiefs. Masao Kogure, professor emeritus of Tokyo Institute of Technology, wrote that "the courses presented definitive answers to detailed questions posed by Japanese companies. . . . These lectures led the audience, who, having fared almost completely in the dark, to feel that a boulevard to prosperity had suddenly opened in front of them, and fired them with ambition to try new approaches to developing effective means of Japanese TQC [total quality control]." In time for the lectures, the first edition of Juran's *Handbook on Quality Control* was translated into Japanese and was widely distributed because there were "precious few such books available in Japan," Kogure wrote.

"The Juran visit," Ishikawa said, "created an atmosphere in which QC was to be regarded as a tool of management, thus creating an opening for the establishment of total quality control as we know it today." Deming wrote of Juran's 1954 visit, "His masterful teaching gave to Japanese management new insight into management's responsibility for improvement of quality and productivity." Conversely, Andrea Gabor, a senior editor for *U.S. News and World Report* who often writes about quality, feels that Juran has been given too much credit for his role in Japan. "In fact," she writes in *The Man Who Discovered Quality*, one of the books about Deming, "the Hakone conference and the content of Deming's lectures indicate that Deming well appreciated the importance of management's role." Nonetheless, Japanese authorities usually refer to both Deming and Juran in any history of quality in Japan.

Shoji Shiba, a professor of economics at Tokyo University, says part of the two men's success can be attributed to good timing, not because of the destruction caused by the war but because of the growing Japanese demand for consumer goods. "Deming and Juran," he says, "came on the eve of Japan's consumption revolution. Their ideas were enthusiastically adopted by Japanese executives and engineers looking to introduce mass-production techniques for consumer goods."

In *What Is Total Quality Control?*, Ishikawa wrote of the early history of the quality movement in Japan. Like the Americans, he got into it unintentionally. As a professor of engineering at Tokyo University just after the war, he went to JUSE to borrow the copies of American wartime statistical standards that had been made available by the occupation forces. Koyanagi, the secretary-general, refused to loan the Z series to him unless the younger Ishikawa agreed to teach some statistical courses in return. When he protested that he didn't know anything about the subject, Koyanagi argued that no one else did either. Ishikawa gave in and remained actively involved with JUSE until his death.

Later in Ishikawa's book, Feigenbaum is given credit for originating the concept of total quality control, but Ishikawa and Feigenbaum differ on who should run the program. Ishikawa says Feigenbaum's "Western-type professionalism led him to advocate TQC [total quality control] conducted essentially by QC specialists." The Japanese approach is different: "Since 1949 we have insisted on having all divisions and all employees become involved in studying and promoting QC." Ishikawa says because of the similarity in terms, "people may think we are imitating Dr. Feigenbaum's approach, which we are not."

Ishikawa does not mention Crosby, who was just getting started in Florida when Ishikawa was writing his book, published in Japan in 1981.

Robert E. Cole, a professor of sociology and business administration at the University of California, Berkeley, compared Ishikawa and his method with Crosby "because he represents the clearest contrast with Ishikawa." Cole says Ishikawa and Crosby agree on several things: "the importance of top management's providing continuous support and leadership and serving as a role model for all employees in their commitment to quality, the belief in setting quality standards and measuring performance along these dimensions, management's primary responsibility for poor quality (not workers'), a commitment to continuous learning, and the view that quality improvement will lead to cost reduction." Just as Ishikawa wants all the workers, not just the professionals, to work on quality, he wants them to know why quality is important. Crosby stresses the importance of showing management the cost of not producing quality (nonconformance). Ishikawa wants those figures shown to everyone.

Cole says the "single vision that is central" to Ishikawa's Total Quality Control is that he "places primary importance on the role of the customer; it dominates almost every facet of his discussion." But the definition of customer has changed. Ishikawa says that while he was working with a Japanese steel mill in 1950, he came up with the idea that the customer is not necessarily the person who buys the product or pays for the service. The customer is whoever gets your work, whoever depends on you to have done your part correctly — the next person on the assembly line, the clerk who makes out the invoice, the salesman — anybody who relies on you. That occurred to Ishikawa when he asked the workmen in one section of the steel mill why they didn't go to the next section and ask the workers there what was wrong. The workmen said they couldn't do that; the second group would think the first group was spying and run them off. The insanity of workers' thinking other workers were spies gave Ishikawa the idea of the new customer. "Company-wide quality control cannot be complete without total acceptance of this kind of approach by all workers," he wrote. "Sectionalism has to be broken down, and the company has to be ventilated so that everyone can enjoy a breath of fresh air. . . . That is the spirit of TQC." That identification of co-workers and colleagues as customers is now widely, although not universally, accepted among the quality experts.

Ishikawa won the Deming Prize in 1952. Eight years later it went to Genichi Taguchi, another of the Japanese experts.

The Deming Prize was created by JUSE and first awarded in

1951. It is credited by at least one American with helping to force statistically based quality control through Japan's industry since it can only be won by companies following the prescribed Japanese quality method or by individuals who have made a significant contribution to the understanding of statistically based quality through education or research. Deming donated the royalties from *Elementary Principles of the Statistical Control of Quality,* based on his lecture series, to JUSE to promote quality programs. JUSE named the prize in his honor.

Crosby says Genichi Taguchi is "a fine guy" but impossible to understand unless you have a Ph.D. in mathematics or economics, a comment that is unintentionally amusing since Taguchi himself does not have a college degree. He does have a 1989 award from Emperor Akihito for his work in industrial standards. Taguchi's work is theoretical, and Crosby says he doesn't see how Taguchi's theories would help an American manager run a quality company. Crosby says most American quality control professionals seem to believe that "if it's incomprehensible in Japanese, it must be good for you."

Like Crosby and Feigenbaum, Taguchi tries to put a value on what the lack of quality costs, but he does it in each step of the process, from a product's design to its sale and use. He maintains that quality is primarily a function of design; he wrote, "The strength of a product's signal (its quality) . . . is primarily the responsibility of the product designers. Good factories are faithful to the intention of the design. But mediocre designs will always result in mediocre products." Gipsie Ranney, a consultant in statistics and quality from the University of Tennessee, says Taguchi's theory applies just as well to society. "Every individual's time is valuable," she says, "and yet so much of that gets wasted with errors and mistakes and having to have things done over. That time could be spent in some pursuit that delivered value. . . . Any kind of activity that goes on in daily life that happens with non-quality is a waste. I think one of the things that the Japanese may see very clearly is the loss to society that comes from nonquality." That, she says, is implicit in the Taguchi Loss Function, which Scherkenbach, in his book on Deming's fourteen points, says "has its roots in some of Dr. Deming's earlier teachings." Where they appear to differ now is on the cost of a lack of quality. Deming and Taguchi agree on the loss function itself; they disagree on whether it shows what the loss actually is. Deming says it can't be calculated; Taguchi says, "These things can and should be calculated. There isn't any reason to be fanatical about quality if you *cannot* justify your fanaticism." While the mathematical theory may be complex (and somewhat shaky, according to one critic), the loss function is fairly easy to understand, at least in concept. The easiest way to explain it is an example that Deming uses at his seminars.

Imagine that there are twenty of us working in an office. We have determined by statistical analysis that as a group we will be most productive if the temperature is 68°F (20°C). Individually, we may prefer it warmer or cooler, but as a group 68° is ideal. If it is 67° or 69°, however, the difference is so minor that it is imperceptible, so our work doesn't suffer. But make it 58° (15°C) or 78° (25°C), and the loss in our efficiency is staggering. To put it in terms of loss function, the farther away the temperature (or anything else) gets from what is best, the greater the loss will be. Scherkenbach says that Taguchi "recognizes that there is an incremental economic loss for any deviation. . . . This view is quite different from the traditional view that there is no loss so long as the parts are within the engineering tolerances," normally called specifications.

Traditionally in industry, parts are made to certain specifications; that is, the widget ideally should be 500 millimeters wide, but the design engineer says if it's 495 to 505, that's good enough — an engineering tolerance (specification) of plus or minus 5 millimeters. A quality control inspector would approve any widget that was within these limits because, as far as the inspector is concerned, all measurements that fall between 495 and 505 are exactly the same. Logically, that can't be; 496 is not the same as 501 since 496 is four times farther away from 500 and, therefore, it would seem to be four times more likely to cause trouble. Actually, it's much worse, since the loss is a geometric progression, not an arithmetic one. Specifications still control most American industries and are so much a part of the industrial jargon that Cole, comparing Ishikawa and Crosby, referred to Crosby's "conformance to specifications," which is not what Crosby teaches. One of his absolutes is "conformance to requirements," which include but are not limited to specifications.

The practical application of the Taguchi Loss Function can save an enormous amount of money. Ford Motor Company was having trouble with a particular transmission. Those built in the United States were breaking down and driving warranty costs through the roof, but the same transmission built in Japan to the same specifications was not causing any problem. Engineers took twelve transmissions from Japan and twelve from the United States and pulled them apart. Every piece of every American transmission was tested and measured; every single piece was within specifications. Not one bad part had slipped past the inspectors. In short, there was nothing wrong with the American transmissions. They were what they should have been, except for their unfortunate tendency to break down. But Taguchi says that when parts that were near the outer limits of the specifications, essentially trivial errors, were assembled in one transmission, all those trivial deviations began to multiply, each one making all the others worse. What would have been an insignificant loss in one part became a transmission that couldn't work. Think of it as a kind of straw-that-broke-the-camel's-back theory.

When the Japanese transmissions were tested, the engineers

reported that the measuring device had broken. It had not. There was so little variation from part to part that for any practical purpose, every part was the same. Going back to our widget, 495 millimeters is not the same as 500, but 499.9 could be so close that it wouldn't matter; there is no loss from an imperceptible difference. By realizing from the Taguchi Loss Function that the closer they got to the ideal, the better the transmissions would be, the Japanese had ignored the outer limits of the specifications and had worked to continually reduce variation toward the perfect or near perfect. That is the point of statistically based quality programs — the less variation, the greater the quality. Deming tells his class that you do not have to achieve that ideal figure, that you probably wouldn't know it if you did, and the goal in any case is not the achievement of perfection but the reduction of variation, just as it was with Shewhart in 1924.

Deming's role in Japan has already been officially recognized by the Japanese. Deming was awarded the Second Order Medal of the Sacred Treasure, the highest award Japan can bestow on a foreigner. It was authorized by Emperor Hirohito and announced on May 31, 1960, by Crown Prince Akihito at the opening assembly of the International Statistical Institute conference in Tokyo. Prime Minister Nobusuke Kishi pinned a small emblem on Deming's lapel, which he has worn every day since, and presented the three-inch medal itself in a box. Deming describes the medal and his reaction in his 1960 travel diary: "The design of my medal is mirror, jewels, and swords. The mirror is about the size of a dime, platinum or paladium (sic), then oriental jewels in a circle, and radial swords, all set in solid gold, in a beautiful lacquered box, a delightful work of art. I can say that nothing ever pleased me so much as this recognition. The citation stated that the Japanese people attribute the rebirth of Japanese industry, and their success in marketing their radios and parts, transistors, cameras, binoculars, and sewing machines all over the world to my work there."* (Juran also was awarded the Second Order Medal by Japan, but not until 1981.) Five years earlier, Deming had noticed another honor he was being given, not by the Japanese government but by the Japanese people. In the beginning of his 1955 travel diary, he wrote, "I can not refrain from mentioning constantly to myself during this trip something unusual. This is my 3d invitation to Japan at the expense of Japanese companies. So far as I know, this is the only instance where a man from an occupying power was actually invited back and paid by the people that were occupied, to continue the same work that he was doing under the occupation (1947–1950)."

Since then, the Japanese have worked on quality methods with the dedicated passion that is usually reserved to religious zealots. Shiba, the Tokyo University professor of economics, says that in 1987 alone, JUSE and the Japan Standards Association ran 520 courses for 48,560 students. "TQC [total quality control] based on statistical methods is the core of all the courses," he reported. From 1960 to 1985, JUSE published 660 books on quality control, and it publishes three magazines a month on quality, including *QC Circles,* with a circulation of 170,000! Shiba says, "It would not be an exaggeration to say that Japan has more information on QC than any other country." Compare that to the situation in the United States.

---

* Deming's travel diaries can be great fun to read but are occasionally maddening. He will list in detail everything that was served at a dinner, who attended, where each person sat, how many geisha girls there were, how many waitresses, how attractive they were, who sang songs, what songs they sang — then throw in a sentence like this: "I forgot to mention that we waited with Prime Minister Kishi about half an hour in a small room before the announcement came for dinner. He is very humble and personable, not showing worry about the demonstrations against him." In thirty-eight single-spaced typewritten pages, there is not another word about "the demonstrations" — what they were about, who was demonstrating, or what happened to Kishi.

4

What's Taught

"I'm starting to realize, talking to some economists," Daniel Yankelovich says, "that the word quality is not part of an economist's vocabulary. There is no concept of quality in traditional economic thinking; there's price, but not quality." Quality is rarely mentioned in traditional courses on economics, and it is rarely taught in American graduate business schools, even though it is possible to argue on the evidence that quality is more important for would-be senior executives than what *is* being taught. According to the columnist Robert J. Samuelson, "Between 1962 and 1987 the annual number of MBA graduates [in the United States] rose from 5,787 to 67,496. There are now more than a million MBAs. If they were improving the quality of U.S. management, the results ought to be obvious by now."

The results *are* obvious, but improvement isn't one of them. The United States is thoroughly indebted at every level and unable to meet its social, educational, and economic needs because many American executives do not know how to compete successfully in either the world market or their own. One reason is that they have not been taught how to compete. "I think that the business schools," Yankelovich says, "were responsible for some of the worst things that happened in American business, some of the short-term financial orientation, and, therefore, they ought to take responsibility for reversing it."

"The issue," Armand Feigenbaum says, "is that there is not recognition in the educational system yet that quality is fundamentally a body of knowledge, an important body of knowledge, a teachable body of knowledge. . . . The essence of our ability to make the conversion from 'make it quicker and cheaper' in this country [the United States] to 'make it better' is largely going to be dominated by the ability of our universities . . . to teach quality as a body of knowledge rather than a series of hip-shooting exercises."

Feigenbaum does not blame the business leaders who decided to make quantity after the war because, he says, the CEO's job was to respond to the customers, the market, and "very clearly, what the market wanted was conspicuous consumption goods, wanted innovative goods. . . . And businessmen delivered that." He *does* blame them for what happened in the 1960s and '70s, when industry "was dominated by the conventional intelligence taught by management leaders, made clear in our great universities, that the way you succeeded in a company was make product quicker and cheaper; sell it hard; finance it cleverly. That was the answer to success." Like Yankelovich, Feigenbaum thinks the business schools have a responsibility to help solve the problem that they helped create.

He has suggested naming a full professor of quality at the major business schools. "When I say that [at a business school], I can see the eyes of these professors of finance, of operations research, of market research, begin to glaze over. And I can see them giving each other little looks, as if they thought that Feigenbaum was a reasonably honest fellow up until this, but obviously, he's lost his marbles." Kees van Ham, of the European Foundation for Quality Management, has the same problem in Europe. "We don't want them [schools]," he says, "to give only teaching in finance, marketing, operations, personnel, but also in this new discipline of total quality management. . . . but there's not one single school, neither in the United States nor in Europe, as far as I know, that is already doing this."

Rosabeth Moss Kanter, a professor at the Harvard Business School and the editor of the *Harvard Business Review*, disagrees, at least in part. "I think the business schools are certainly addressing quality issues," she says. "I'm not sure they're doing as much as they could. I think that that theme ought to pervade everything that's taught; I think that quality puts a premium on managerial competence, leadership competence, people issues, how we direct people, and I still feel that our business schools spend too much time on financial analysis and not enough on people issues, but they're certainly trying. That's clearly a major emphasis at the Harvard Business School."

The consultant Christopher Hart says, "It [quality] is an emerging new management discipline that will, in the future, have the same credibility as finance, as marketing, and we're seeing it emerge right now." Earlier, in prepared testimony to a House committee, Hart, then at the Harvard Business School, wrote that quality is not being taught in business schools because, first, it overlaps all fields, so no one has figured out who should teach it; second, no one has figured out exactly what to teach; and, third, no one would want to teach whatever was taught anyway because quality is not a recognized field, so a professor could not get tenure (the academic version of job security) by teaching it.

To Deming, the problems that business schools may face in teaching quality don't matter because he believes they are not competent to teach it at all. At a meeting with students and faculty at the Columbia University School of Business, Deming was at his confrontational best. "What exactly is the contribution of this school to production, to alleviating our deficits in trade?" he said. "How much of the students' time is spent here learning skills that could be learned better — and with good pay — on the job?" Then, speaking to a faculty member about the MBA candidates, Deming demanded, "But do they understand it all as a system? Do they even know what a predictable system is? Do they? Do they? They do not!"

At a speech in Ohio, Deming talked about business schools and what they teach, saying, "What should a business school teach? Profound knowledge, that's what they ought to be teaching, but it's absolutely impossible because there is nobody in the faculty that knows anything about it. . . . What they do is teach students how business is carried on. That's how to perpetuate it, exactly what we do not need. Nothing could be worse. . . . Can they improve? No, they cannot. The only possibility in a school of business is to forget it, and for the university to establish an institute empowered to grant degrees and empowered to draw the teaching from any part of the university." Would-be MBAs could be taught by mathematicians, statisticians, philosophers, poets, psychologists, and sociologists, not to mention economists, historians, and, one could assume, ethicists.

What seems to infuriate Deming and frustrate Phil Crosby is the insistence of most business schools on continuing to teach, in the face of mountains of evidence to the contrary, that *improving quality increases costs*. Crosby describes his visits to business schools. "The kids love me," he says. "They understand exactly what I'm talking about. Professors always ask some dumb question like, 'Well, how about the economic constraints on quality, Mr. Crosby? I mean, if we're going to get everything right, wouldn't that bankrupt the company?' And I always say, 'Well, can you tell me something where it's cheaper to do it right the *second* time?' " Japan does not have business schools, but the quality-raises-cost idea does exist. Kaoru Ishikawa once said that some Japanese executives "often make the mistake of thinking that improving quality means to raise the cost. This comes from the faulty notion that QC equals inspection." Quality equals less inspection, but persuading business schools of that is only a small part of the problem.

There is an inherent difficulty in teaching a subject as amorphous as quality. Academics talk of "a discipline." What they mean is an area of specialization, and a graduate student who tries to dabble in more than one area of specialization will run into trouble from academics whose view of life is a good deal more narrow than life is. "The worst thing we could do," van Ham says, "is to introduce a new discipline at universities which is called Total Quality Management. What we must do is integrate total quality management as a stream across the existing disciplines. . . . You know as well as I do that in the educational system and also in companies, the whole status system, the power system, the hierarchical system, is based on the department dimension and is not based on the process I mentioned." There have been successful interdisciplinary study programs recently in some U.S. universities, but they aren't the norm.

Quality has not been considered a hot topic, a subject that will make a professor's reputation and attract students to a university. Feigenbaum remembers that while he was getting his Ph.D. at MIT in 1951, the attitude of his professors toward his study of quality management was, "Here's a likely fellow; why is he fooling around with that third-string activity?" Quality cuts across all disciplines and involves a little bit of a lot of things. Peter Drucker in *The New Realities* talks about what a manager needs to know in the modern world: technology, humanities, liberal arts, psychology, philosophy, economics, history, the physical sciences, and ethics. If that's what a manager needs, it is not what a student gets at business schools. But it may be. Eventually.

Myron Tribus says, "As a former dean [of the Thayer School of Engineering at MIT], I can say it's easier to move a graveyard than to change a curriculum." Still, a graveyard can be moved, and a curriculum can be changed, and Tribus thinks that will happen in the United States. "I forecast that within ten years, the business schools will be solidly behind this [quality] movement, understanding it, probably claiming they invented it." (He could be right. The University of Chicago Graduate Business School started a quality program in 1991.)

The first attempt to teach industrial quality was a Western

Electric handbook, basically Walter Shewhart's statistical method, that was popular until after World War II, when it seems to have disappeared or perhaps been trampled in the American rush to produce quantity. From the ideas that were later developed from that handbook, a new definition of quality was born.

Quality used to mean an absence of defects. Curt Reimann, associate director for Quality Programs at the National Institute of Standards and Technology, says, "Consumers now have choices from around the world. Choices may be made on the basis of price; on the basis of features, variety, and service; on the basis of responsiveness; on the basis of quality. All of these factors in purchase decisions — price, features, variety, service, responsiveness, and quality, not just quality alone — are addressed in an integrated way in total quality management." That would be the definition of quality, in all probability, that would be taught in a business school quality program.

But how will that course be taught? Will Feigenbaum get his full professor, or will van Ham have quality taught throughout all the other courses? Either way, who gets to decide which quality program will be taught? Would Feigenbaum, Crosby, and Juran agree that Deming's profound knowledge is the essential course? Would Juran want to include The Juran Trilogy, and would Crosby think "do it right the first time" was worth teaching? Feigenbaum's cost of quality concept is rejected by Deming but remains popular, even with Crosby and Juran, and his total quality control has been widely accepted or adapted. Should they be included? How about the management techniques, the basics of day-to-day operations, taught to the Japanese by Homer Sarasohn and Charles Protzman? Should the work of Kaoru Ishikawa and Genichi Taguchi be included? (Americans and British, particularly, often suffer from "not invented here" syndrome and are reluctant to admit that experts from other nations can teach them anything.) What is the emphasis — pragmatic or philosophical? Should the quality course start with Japan, as the quality movement did?

"I exported to Japan," Deming says, "what had never been done before. I did not export American practice. . . . I took to them a new theory, a theory of a system. They learned it. Any company should be viewed as a system; a school should be viewed as a system. I taught them. It starts with somebody's idea of what the customer might wish to buy — in the future, of course. Prediction. That's the way it starts." Deming kept on the blackboard a standard flow chart that shows how all parts of the system come together and flow across the company from suppliers to customers in a cooperative effort. "That flow diagram," he says, "tells people what their jobs are, how they fit in. It's an organization chart." He also used the diagram as a way to explain the importance of quality in his meetings with Japan's top industrial leaders. "I convinced them they could export," Deming remembers. "I showed them my German camera, my British suit and shoes. I taught them about world trade and told them they could do it." Of his talks at those meetings and their result, he wrote years later, "It will not suffice to achieve brilliant successes here and there. Disjointed efforts will have no national impact. Quality in terms of present and future needs of the consumer became at once companywide and nationwide in every activity."

Each person involved in the quality movement tends to see his contribution as critical, but since Shewhart drew his statistical graph in 1924, what seems to have happened is that a quality philosophy has evolved that uses ideas from Deming, Juran, Feigenbaum, Crosby, Ishikawa, Taguchi, and others. They all seem to borrow liberally from one another and from their clients, but except for Tribus, who cheerfully says, "I steal from everybody," it is doubtful the experts would appreciate this comment. Nonetheless, even as each claims to be more or less independent, they all seem to be cooperating and collaborating, even if it is at arm's length. However it is happening, the evolving quality philosophy may have implications that go well beyond the customer's present and future needs.

Peter Scholtes sees a greater advantage for people than just better goods and services at better prices. "I think that Dr. Deming and all the other leaders of the quality movement," he says, "have gotten us to stop looking at ourselves and start looking out there, at the employees, at the customers, at what's going on out there in the world and serving that. . . . For me that element of the quality movement makes it more than a new economic era, a new industrial revolution. For me that element, the caring and the carefulness and paying attention to others, elevates what Dr. Deming is teaching into the equivalent of a new renaissance."

Aside from that cultural change and the economic benefit, Scholtes sees a far more personal benefit for the world's peoples. "Part of my background is in psychology," he says, "and it's my own belief that more therapy, more good, solid healing of people will take place in a good, sound workplace environment than on all of the psychologists' and psychiatrists' couches and in all the counseling rooms in the world. Because people can go to a place, and if they can find joy and pride in what they do day in and day out, and if they have good relationships with the people with whom they work, that's healthy. That's health giving."

But that is not what you say to a CEO to get him to adopt a quality program, nor is it likely to convince the dean of a graduate business school to alter the curriculum. You could better use the arguments made by Donella Meadows, a professor of Environmental Studies at Dartmouth College, in a paper on quality of life presented at the National Geographic Society's centennial symposium in Washington, D.C., in January 1988. "Those who have seriously investigated the implications of Business as Usual continued into the long-term future," Meadows said, "have concluded that such a future is physically impossible and socially undesirable." Natural resources will be used up, and the environment will become more polluted and poisoned. "No cosmetic corrections, conflict-of-interest rules, or charitable contributions," she continued, "make a quantity-oriented system moral or sustainable. . . . One likely future is total or near-total destruction. The other is the achievement of something close to Quality on a global scale."

As if to underline that thought, a 1991 Worldwatch Institute report says, "If growth proceeds along the lines of recent decades, it is only a matter of time before global systems collapse under the pressure. . . . For humanity to avoid the wholesale breakdown of natural systems requires not just a slowing in the expansion of our numbers [global population] but a shift from the pursuit of growth to that of sustainable progress — human betterment that does not come at the expense of future generations." A quality program would help since it eliminates waste and rework, thus saving resources.

Meadows argues that it can be done because "within the bounds of physical possibility, real system goals are usually realized. . . . It follows that if a society aims for Quality, if it rewards Quality, discusses Quality, devises ways of measuring and monitoring Quality, takes determined and effective actions to restore any absence of Quality, identifies itself openly and constantly with Quality, it will almost certainly get Quality."

She might have included in her list that if American business schools stop teaching quantity and start teaching quality, it would make a difference. The curriculum of that quality course, which Tribus thinks is no more than ten years away, is likely to reflect what happens in American business and industry where quality programs are in place; different companies use different programs or combinations of them. Business schools are likely to follow the same pattern, and each school will do what the dean or faculty thinks best, as each company does now. Some companies start with one expert and never consider any other approach. Others use the Chinese menu approach: take one from column A, two from column B, and create their own systems. Still others start with one expert, then switch to another.

Milliken & Company, the textile firm, first contacted Crosby in

1981 and studied his method. It didn't begin to study Deming's idea of statistical process control until 1990, then recently sent twenty of its people to a Deming seminar. The company is now promoting process improvement, not as a way to look at each process individually, but as a way to look at the entire business, start to finish, with the supplier at one end, the customer at the other.

While the other experts generally scorn Crosby — one of them says, "He doesn't bring much to the party" — the fact is, Crosby has a benefit that the others do not: he can talk to business leaders in their own language, and he has been incredibly successful at getting companies interested in quality. Hart says, "Phil Crosby is owed a tremendous debt for the enormous attention he has drawn to the field of quality." Deming, Feigenbaum, and Juran are all considered academics, and even if that's not true, they are often viewed with suspicion in the business world as outsiders who "don't understand." Business people will go to Crosby because he is one of them, and he has been successful in their world, and they may find it easier to hear from him that if their company has a problem, they probably caused it — a truth that students at business schools might find hard to swallow.

On that point, however, all four men are adamant. Where there is a quality problem, the odds are overwhelming that the problem is in the system, and since only management can change the system, management is to blame for the problem. The obvious question for all managers to ask, assuming they accept that responsibility, is how to fix the system. That is also the first question for a business school planning a quality curriculum.

Asking the four experts what to do gets four different answers, but not *completely* different. They agree that management is responsible, and they agree that unless there is a corporate commitment to quality through the organization, nothing will happen. Juran believes that commitment can start at the top or in middle management, but Deming and Crosby think it must start at the top. "It's easy to say it starts at the top," Crosby says, "but you've got to say *what* starts at the top. Just having the president go to school or class or show up at the meetings, that isn't enough." John Stepp, the former Labor Department official, says the chief executive has to "walk the talk." He can't just say he's in favor of quality, he has to show it. The work force has to *see* the commitment; they've already *heard* it too many times to care. At Milliken & Company after Crosby, at Ford Motor Company after Deming, and at Motorola after Six Sigma (see Chapter 6), when the top officers meet, the first item on the agenda is quality. It used to be finance. That's the sort of walk that gives the talk meaning.

Another agreement among the four is that you have to be specific and systematic. You can't take a sawed-off shotgun and blow all the problems away at once, so management has to identify the most critical problems and solve them first. Juran talks about "the vital few versus the trivial many" and working on the most important problem first. It sounds so obvious as to be self-evident, but as Brian Joiner says, "Most answers are obvious afterward." Another point of agreement with the experts is that quality takes time, and anything that promises a quick fix may be quick, but it won't be a fix. Americans tend to be impatient, to want everything solved by Friday, and that impatience can destroy a quality program before it gets started.

All four experts say that while management has to lead, the total work force must be involved in the quality effort, and all four agree that the work force must be given a bigger say in how work gets done — worker participation. Juran in particular stresses team efforts, and Deming says management must make it possible for all people in a company to cooperate, to work together. Feigenbaum remembers that "when I was growing up in industry, the conventional intelligence was that good management meant getting the ideas out of the heads of the bosses into the hands of the workers. Today, we know that is wrong, that good management, instead, means leadership to mobilize the knowledge, the skills, the attitudes, of every man and woman in the organization." Business schools would have to teach how to lead and listen rather than how to give orders and require obedience.

Even if every business school in the United States began to teach accepted principles of quality management, the quality problem would not go away. If what is needed to produce quality is continual improvement, then what is needed for management is the continual opportunity to learn. Robert Chapman Wood, a business consultant, says, "Clearly, the U.S. quality movement needs opportunities for followers of different schools to talk and to explore what they can learn from each other." The teachers themselves have obviously learned from one another, and there is a core of quality principles that they all accept to some degree — that the worker is not the problem, management is; that to solve the problem takes a corporate commitment from the top down; that what you do has to be systematic, specific, and continual; that you must study the system to learn what needs to be done; that you must include your suppliers and your customers; that employees must be educated and trained; and that quality must be a part of the system, not an inspection. America's business leaders also have to learn and keep up with what has happened or is happening in other countries.

Tribus says the Japanese contribution to the quality movement was that "they brought a focus. Deming persuaded the Japanese that they should use these quality methods. . . . Juran went over and taught them ideas about management, particularly project management. . . . and although the pieces of the system were known to all of us, no one had ever seen the power of it when they were all put together." The Japanese have worked on the system since 1950, Tribus says; "until now they have a tremendous educational package, a tremendous number of examples, and a large number of people who for forty years have grown up through this thing and are now at the top and applying it systematically. We [Americans] don't have that. . . . What the Japanese did was create a top management culture that understands quality in a very deep sense. Mr. Toyoda [of Toyota] wrote the chapter on automotive quality that appears in Juran's handbook. . . . Where do you find that person [who understands the quality movement] as the CEO of a company in the United States? They come out of accounting and finance, and they come with the terrible things that business schools have done to them, and now they run the business, and they think that's the way to run a business. . . . That [Japanese] culture began when Sarasohn, essentially at gunpoint, stuck them in a room and said, 'This is the way you're going to manage, or else!' "

Tribus credits Deming for making quality the driving force. "Sarasohn and Protzman taught them many things," he says. "Their book is full of detail on organization and all kinds of things that the Japanese needed to know [and] there was an undercurrent that said 'quality is the most important feature'. . . but when Deming came, he sort of twisted it around a little bit and said, in effect, 'If you go for quality in everything you do, these other problems will take care of themselves.' "

Joiner says of Japanese companies, "The way they've taken those lessons [about quality] and refined them, improved on them, and polished them, and really taken them down deep into the soul of the management of companies is vastly superior. They're able to work with people, to help people work together, to understand the system, to take data on a system, and use the brainpower of everybody in the company." Joiner says Deming "taught them statistics, and that's a key ingredient. Without statistics, you can't do this. . . . He taught them to view the organization of the system, too, I think, and view the customer as being part of that system. . . . He taught them to work with their suppliers to help them get better and better." All of that could be taught in a school.

(Perhaps this is the moment to stop just long enough to urge that you not get hung up about statistics. What is required is not an advanced degree, but a working knowledge. As used by most people in most quality programs, statistics is a tool, a method of measurement. To say that you cannot learn a quality program because you have no background in statistics is the same as saying that you cannot learn to write because you can't make a pencil. Don't confuse the means with the end.)

Joiner also says the Japanese were smarter than Americans about Frederick W. Taylor's scientific management. "Taylor had two negative things," he explains. "He said you don't need to be concerned about what the next person does with what you send them — let management worry about that — and he built up the bureaucracy in manufacturing. He was also the first to bring in white-collar people to figure out how to do the work and then tell the blue-collar what to do. The Japanese threw out the bureaucracy and the 'white-collar think' and the 'blue-collar do,' and we kept those two pieces and threw out the part about the scientific analysis of work. They kept the good part and threw out the chaff, and we did the reverse, which was a major factor in getting us to where we are today in quality and management."

That alone would not account for Japan's business success. Scholtes says, "The thing that Dr. Deming taught the Japanese that I think was revolutionary was quality as a business strategy, that the way to become competitive is not by selling things at a cheaper price, or all the other strategies that are being used in the business place, but to give reliable goods and services to people and constantly improve them. . . . You can't give people a reliable product without having a reliable process to manufacture them, so the method of doing the work and the outcome of the work are so intertwined, so inseparable, that you have to work on both ends of it. What he taught the Japanese was to start with the customers."

Michael Maccoby sees a broader concept. "Deming is a prophet," he says, "not the kind who predicts the future, but one who speaks deep truths. . . . Deming's vision is not merely that of new management systems, but of a different spirit for American industry. He recently said, 'People are entitled to have fun, to have joy in learning and work.' Even when work is drudgery, as it sometimes must be, people need to see the importance of it and to have a sense of a positive future. People need to feel needed."

Crosby says Deming did teach the Japanese, but he didn't teach them what people think he did. Because of Deming, Crosby says, Japanese companies "sent all these people to statistics school and so forth, and what they got out of that was not how to do statistics, they got out of that that management is serious about all this stuff, that they're really serious." It is that knowledge throughout the company of management's commitment that Crosby and others believe is essential to all successful quality programs. "What made them [the Japanese] successful and what Deming taught them," Crosby says, "is you can lay out the process, and then if you meet all these things in the process, it will all come out right at this end. You stick it in this end, and it all comes out right at that end, which sounds kind of simple, but they didn't know that, and most companies don't know that. Now what people [Americans] think he taught them was that if you measure this process, it'll come out good at the other end, so American companies bust their tails measuring the process, and out the other end comes junk, because while they're measuring the process, it goes out of control."

What Deming teaches in seminars and consultations are his fourteen points. That is not what he taught the Japanese in 1950; the fourteen points were not written until almost thirty years later. The French expert Jean-Marie Gogue remembers, "In Tokyo in 1978, during an international conference on quality control, I was listening to Dr. Deming, and his paper was a first approach of the fourteen points." Robert E. Cole, the Berkeley professor, says, "Much of what is now called the Deming method . . . are not ideas that Deming taught the Japanese but principles that he learned while watching the Japanese develop." Tribus puts it this way: "I think that Deming's fourteen points grew out of the contrasts between what he saw working in Japan, and what he saw in the

United States. These are really fourteen points for American or Western managers to observe, because there was no need for him to teach them to the Japanese by that time." Ishikawa wrote in the Japanese edition of a book on Deming, Andrea Gabor reports, "that Deming had borrowed many of the ideas for his Fourteen Points from Japanese TQC and Joseph Juran." The statement is not in the English translation, and Gabor thinks it indicates that the Japanese are now beginning to resent the fact that their highly successful quality movement started with an American.

Not everyone agrees on Deming's influence in Japan. Cole wrote in a review of a book about Deming, "If there had been no Dr. Deming, the Japanese would have successfully developed their quality-improvement strategy all the same. It may have taken longer, but it would have happened. . . . Great Man theories of history, however entertaining to the reader and appealing to the journalist and television producer, leave much to be desired as causal explanations.

"The Japanese learned much from American experts such as Deming, J. M. Juran, and Edward (sic) Feigenbaum. But they also evolved a system of quality improvement that is distinctively Japanese. No American in the early '50s was talking about quality improvement as a participative system of management that involved all employees and all departments. This was a Japanese innovation." Ishikawa might have agreed. In his book he said, "The fundamental principle of successful management is to allow subordinates to make full use of their abilities." He credited the Swedes with having named that idea "industrial democracy."

Cole and Ishikawa ignore Sarasohn and Protzman, but part of the CCS management course that senior Japanese industrialists were ordered to attend was a section on industrial relations, including how employees should be treated. Sarasohn remembers that "we were feeding the Japanese very difficult concepts when we talked about quality, when we talked about company philosophy, for example, they could not understand because some of these words did not exist in the Japanese language. We talked about democracy, for example. At that time there was no Japanese word that meant democracy as we in America meant it. . . . so I learned Japanese because I had to speak to them from the point of view of a mentality that they could identify with." Just as MacArthur saw part of his job as reforming the feudal political system, Sarasohn and Protzman saw part of theirs as reforming the treatment of workers in industry. So, apparently, did Deming a year or so later.

Tribus says, "Deming also hit very hard at the human side of it, and that was important in Japan, because the Japanese treatment of their workers was left over from the shogun warrior days. The Japanese had to adapt to a different idea." As will a good many American employers, who will have to be taught that employees can think, plan, and solve problems only if management will teach them how and encourage them to use what they have learned.

5

The Workers Aren't the Problem

"No organization can survive," says Deming, "with just good people. They need people that are improving." Without people who are improving, no country can prosper for long in the global economy. Robert Reich writes, "The skills and insights of a nation's work force, and the quality of its transportation and communications links to the world (its infrastructure), are what make it unique, and uniquely attractive, in the new world economy. Increasingly, educated brainpower — along with roads, airports, computers, and fiber-optic cables connecting it up — determines a nation's standard of living. . . . A work force possessing a good basic education, which can efficiently bring the fruits of its labors to the global economy, can attract global capital for its performance of moderately complex tasks. . . . But without adequate skills and infrastructure, the relationship can be the opposite — a vicious cycle in which global money and technology are lured only by low wages and low taxes."

The need for a better-educated work force — industries now routinely want high school as a minimum, preferably two years of college — is a relatively new phenomenon in the United States. "Back in the 1960s," Daniel Yankelovich recalls, "[President] John Kennedy said, 'A rising tide raises all boats.' And it was true of the America of the '60s and '70s in this sense, that if you had a college education, you could make a good living. But if you didn't have a

105

college education, you could also make a good living. . . . Today, if you have a college education, you can make a good living, but if you don't, you can't." In 1973 there was a 15 percent gap in pay between a thirty-year-old male high school graduate and a thirty-year-old male college graduate. By 1989 the gap was 50 percent, not because the college graduate's pay had gone up — it had not — but because the high school graduate's pay had gone down. Unless high school graduates can get advanced training and continuing education, they must scramble for whatever dead-end jobs are out there, and that is new in the United States.

A man we know, who was born early in the twentieth century, supported a wife and two daughters well, owned his own home, and put both children through college while working as a welder, a job for which he was trained by his employer because he was "willing to work" — at that time about the only requirement for a strong young man who wanted a job. His education, he says, was "three years in high school, two in the same grade." Today, it is doubtful that he would even be considered for any job with a future. Without a high school education, which essentially is nothing more than proof that you have the capacity to learn, there are limited job openings. A University of Georgia survey released in April 1991 says that job openings during the '90s will require better-than-average education and training.

Worker training and retraining is critical in the United States. Pat Choate, the political economist, says, "Our major problem in education in the 1990s is, how do we improve the skills of people over the age of twenty-one?" Because of the post–World War II baby boom, "roughly 92 or 93 percent of the people who'll be working [in the United States] in the year 2001 are already adults and most are already at work. We're going to make it or break it with the people that are already here, and the people that are here don't have the types of education and the skills that they require."

Herb Striner, the professor emeritus and consultant, says, "We

[Americans] are going to have to understand that the investment in human resources in this country is far below the level of investment in human resources in other countries. . . . We have one of the poorest-trained labor forces in the industrial world." Choate says, "When one takes a look at the top third of our workers, we find people that are as good or better than any in the rest of the world. . . . When we take a look at the middle third of our work force, we find increasing slippage and an inability to read, write, count. . . . When we go to the bottom third of our work force, we find Third World standards, and we just absolutely don't measure up. . . . You cannot compete with that level of workers."

In fact, the workers themselves cannot compete. "If you're relatively unskilled in the United States," Reich says, "you are competing with unskilled workers around the world who are pouring into the world market — twelve thousand people are entering the world market every hour, most of whom are willing to labor for a fraction of the wages of unskilled workers in the United States. It's supply and demand." When John Stepp was associate deputy undersecretary of labor, he told an audience, "In the American apparel industry, for instance, the average wage today is $6.52 an hour. In South Korea, apparel workers make approximately $1 an hour, in Taiwan, $1.43, and — get this — in China, 26 cents an hour. We cannot, and morally should not, try to compete with these countries on the basis of labor costs." Apparently, however, American workers are being forced to do just that. According to the Council on Competitiveness, "Since 1969, real average weekly earnings (for Americans) have fallen by 12 percent." Comparative wage rates are as much a political as an economic issue, and the political objective should be to raise the lower rate, not lower the higher one.

In its report *America's Choice: High Skills or Low Wages!*, the Commission on the Skills of the American Workforce reported, "What we are facing is an economic cliff of sorts. And the front-line working people of America are about to fall off it." The report said that 70 percent of the American work force is in danger unless they get better education in school and better training on the job. The commission is neither the first, nor will it be the last, group or individual to say that. Richard Rosecrance, a professor at UCLA, wrote, "We should ponder why a Japanese eighth grader typically knows more mathematics than an American with an MBA." Generally, America's major industrial competitors in Europe, Scandinavia, and Asia have better educational systems, a national standard to certify a school graduate's skills, and superior training programs. Still, despite the number of warnings, reports, and comments, the American Society for Training and Development (ASTD) says, "Very few [American] companies seem aware of the fact that learning on the job contributed more to productivity increases over the past sixty years than technology or capital, and more than formal education."

ASTD says American business and industry already spend about $30 billion a year on employee education and training, but the American Workforce Commission says only about $10 billion of that goes to train workers who don't have a college education, that is, generally speaking, the people doing the work — production workers, clerks, secretaries. Most of the money is spent to train skilled technicians, salespeople, and managers. John Hoerr, writing in *Business Week,* said, "Frontline workers in factories, stores, and offices receive little or none of it [employee training]." He quoted Sue Berryman of the National Center on Education and Employment as saying, "The whole work force must be trained, and it must be continuous training, not a little splat here and there like an injection." In most U.S. companies, however, there is not even that "little splat." The commission says that 1 percent of America's companies provide 90 percent of the training, perhaps because the majority of American firms cling to mass production standards, for which workers in low-paying, dead-end jobs need only minimal skills. As quality manufacturers prosper and take over more global markets, those dead-end jobs will go to the lowest-wage country, which, for the moment, the United States is not.

Some American companies say they are reluctant to train because workers, once trained and more highly skilled than when they were hired, quit and go to a competitor for higher pay. In Germany, workers can just as easily quit and join a competitor, but it doesn't matter. All major German companies provide training, so, in effect, each company contributes to the national pool of skilled workers, and each takes from that pool the skills it needs. An official of an American car company in Germany says he could save money by not training his workers and apprentices, but the company would lose its reputation as a "good employer" and in the future might not be able to attract the skilled workers it needed.

At major corporations in Japan, the question never comes up. All companies do extensive training; few workers change jobs. Daisaku Harada, the head of the Japan Productivity Center near Washington, D.C., says, "You have to remember that in order to produce a quality product, you have to have not only understanding management, but also you have to have well-educated, skilled labor. . . . to have well-educated, quality employees, you have to spend the money to train and to educate them." Even when they locate in the United States, foreign firms are more inclined to provide training and avoid layoffs than are American firms.

Layoffs are a second reason that American companies tend not to train. Just as newly trained workers may quit and go to the competitor, newly trained workers may be laid off if quarterly profits are down. In either case, the money spent on training has been wasted, particularly since under American tax law companies get some benefit for capital investments in equipment, but not for investments in people. The issue, therefore, is not training but job security. In its short form, job security means that if a company wants to get loyalty, it has to give loyalty; and if it wants a skilled work force, it has to train its employees, all of them. Labor officials believe that management is less interested than workers in job security, probably because if you can temporarily save a company's short-term profits by laying off workers, you don't have to know how to manage a company. Ernest D. Lieberman, who studies American management, wrote, "In manufacturing, direct labor averages only 10 percent of the costs, but draws 75 percent of cost-cutting efforts. This means 90 percent of true costs . . . are barely touched." Workers in the United States have always been the first to feel anything that goes wrong, either in their own companies or in the economy. "We tend to treat workers as expendable or replaceable parts," Stepp says. "This is hardly a way to treat people if our goal is a high degree of commitment."

That is the goal. All the quality experts agree that active worker participation is a key to any program's success. Kees van Ham, of the European Foundation for Quality Management, says, "Full participation or involvement of all employees is one of the major aspects of any successful total quality management action. Without full participation, you cannot succeed." In some U.S. companies, worker participation programs by themselves have helped keep the companies in business and even prosperous. At Northern Telecom's repair plant at Morrisville, North Carolina, 420 employees work in teams, are their own bosses, and make their own decisions. In earlier years, under a traditional management system, the plant lost money. Since 1988, under the employee-controlled system, revenue is up 86 percent and the plant is profitable. Its operation is being studied by other Northern Telecom managers as well as officials from other companies.

Romac Industries in Seattle, which produces repair clamps for water mains, started with three people more than twenty years ago. It now has three hundred people, two plants in the United States, and international connections in Holland, Australia, and Japan. Almost from the beginning, workers have voted on one another's pay raises. Management has nothing to do with it. Any employee can put a notice on the bulletin board saying he wants a raise and why he deserves it, and his fellow employees vote yes or no. The immediate reaction of most American managers is that those workers would vote themselves enormous raises and bankrupt the company. In fact, at the end of the first year the plan was in effect, the company had to declare an across-the-board pay raise to keep salaries competitive in the market. The workers had asked for little and approved less, demonstrating for the umpteenth time that given responsibility, workers act responsibly. Manford McNeil, the founder and chief executive of Romac, remembers that not everyone agreed with him when he suggested the plan. "When we first started our voting program," he says, "we had a director. I had a terrible time selling the program to the director, and he said, 'Well, maybe it will work for twenty people, but it sure won't work for twenty-one.' We've got pretty close to three hundred people now, so I know it works for three hundred. I don't know if it will work for three hundred and one or not."

There are no time clocks in Romac plants and few supervisors. The time clocks went when McNeil realized that blue-collar workers punched them and white-collar workers did not, showing that white-collar people were trustworthy, blue-collar people were not. The time clocks were collected, taken to the foundry, and melted. McNeil says, "In the last analysis, people can only and will only manage themselves, and we have to foster that." He encourages his employees to make their own decisions. "There is a much higher quality of decision made at that level," he says, "than there is at this level. . . . There is no inherent wisdom in the corner office on the third floor." Jim Mullen, the founder and president of the Mullen advertising agency in Massachusetts, wrote that a key to executive success is "to make good decisions," but only a very few. "When you come to terms with the fact that your employees know more than you do," he wrote, "it's one short step to accepting that, in their areas of expertise, they're quite likely to make better decisions than you will." William Potter, the president

111

of Preston Corporation in Easton, Maryland, agrees. "First of all," he says, "the person doing the job knows more about it than anyone else. Secondly, the more that individual understands what the business is and what he can do to contribute to the business and make it a success, the better off you're going to be." When a Teamsters newspaper printed part of a Preston management memo on issues that needed to be discussed in future contract talks, Potter sent the union the rest of the memo so it could print the whole thing. That way his union and nonunion employees at all the trucking terminals would know what problems faced the company.

Both Potter and McNeil share financial information with their employees. McNeil says he does it because "I think it's important that people who you're expecting to make decisions have information to make decisions, and if you withhold that information, then don't be surprised if they make a bad decision." Over the years, Romac has lost only two employees to Boeing, Seattle's biggest employer by far. Both went for higher pay, but one came back and told McNeil, "There's more than money to the job site." McNeil says Boeing is certainly not a bad place to work, but it doesn't have Romac's culture.

Yankelovich says, "People have a need to feel pride in their work. Nothing satisfies that need more than being associated with a quality product. . . . it isn't just a matter of mechanical incentive systems or money." Rick Madrid works at New United Motors Manufacturing, Inc. (NUMMI), the auto company in Fremont, California, owned jointly by GM and Toyota. Under GM until 1982, he would have been a foreman; under NUMMI since 1986, he is something of a teacher–group leader–worker. He describes himself as being a motivator, saying, "My job is to motivate the team, to teach the team their jobs, to help them build confidence in themselves, to try to build pride and loyalty." Under GM, the plant at Fremont was among the company's worst, but as a joint venture plant with Toyota, using Japanese management techniques, it is highly productive, one of the company's best. Madrid was at the GM plant and is now with NUMMI. Asked to explain the difference, he says, "Under the old system, eight hours was an interruption of my leisure time. I was here to earn some money, and that was it." Under the new system, when he came out of a restaurant in Monterey one evening and saw a car he knew had been assembled at NUMMI, he slipped his business card under the windshield wiper with a penciled message: "I helped to build your car." In GM days, that would have been a ludicrous if not a suicidal gesture.

Maryann Keller, the auto industry analyst who wrote *Rude Awakening*, the study of what went wrong at GM, says the company initially was not prepared to accept what it learned from NUMMI. "What General Motors, when it became involved with Toyota, really expected," she comments, "was that some sort of Rube Goldberg machine was going to be placed in NUMMI, and that they were suddenly going to have this great technological revelation put out before them. Then they can go and buy the same machines, and lo and behold, they would have the same productivity. As it turned out, NUMMI is by today's standards nonmechanized; it is really quite old-fashioned in terms of what one might find in a typical General Motors assembly plant today. And it turned out, of course, that the secret of NUMMI was in its selection and training of its workers, and in the manner in which the work was organized and it was managed." Eighty-five percent of the work force at NUMMI in 1986 was the same as it was at GM in 1982, but under GM the absentee rate had run as high as 25 percent; under NUMMI it was 2 percent. After an initial period of resistance, Keller says, GM is getting the message; "they don't seem to be afraid any more to learn that the message of NUMMI is one of management change and workplace involvement by the hourly work force." GM's top managers now accept that NUMMI works, but that acceptance causes its own problem. NUMMI now limits the number of GM officials who can visit the plant on the same day. Platoons of visitors studying the quality system were interfering with that system.

Companies around the world send managers to study plants that work, which helps to boost the morale of the people doing the work at those plants. Roger Milliken, the chief executive of Milliken & Company, says, "Our people get excited about the fact that leading companies from all over the world are visiting with us. It makes them feel a sense of pride about the company, and you can see it. The letters of thanks I get always say they can't believe the enthusiasm of our people, their commitment, their understanding, and their excitement about what they're doing. That's very gratifying."

It is more than gratifying, it is profitable. "We've gone through some tough times here," McNeil says of Romac; "the industry has, because of competition and that sort of thing, and the people in that plant kept us competitive. They were the ones that allowed us to stay in business." Louis Schultz of Process Management International talks about an electronics corporation that pulled its manufacturing back from overseas after a seven-year quality effort "because they do it better and cheaper in Minnesota, so the United States worker is still an excellent worker. If we create the right environment for them to be able to make their own contributions to improvement and use their minds, the United States can compete."

Frederick W. Smith, the founder and chief executive of Federal Express, says the company "from its inception, has put its people first because it is right to do so and because it is good business as well. . . . We refer to our employees as our most strategic asset because, quite simply, they are." In 1990, Federal Express became the first service company to win the Malcolm Baldrige National Quality Award (see Chapter 8). Federal Express doesn't put anyone to work without extensive training in a total quality program, teaching each person how to work both as a member of a team and independently. Smith told the Baldrige Award ceremony audience, "In trying to understand the service side of quality, one must necessarily grasp the significance of the human side of quality." Rosabeth Moss Kanter of the *Harvard Business Review* explains it this way: "Now we're putting much more responsibility in the hands of workers to correct problems themselves because that saves time, that's a better guarantee of quality, so they need much more knowledge and much more information, so the role of everybody from the shop floor or the service center on up becomes much more important. After all, business policy, business strategy, can be articulated at the top of the firm, but what it really means in practice is what the ordinary worker does, because that's often what the customer sees."

Federal Express has 40,000 couriers and customer service agents handling 300 million shipments each year. Smith says every personal meeting every day by every employee is an opportunity to make or lose a customer for the company. Each employee is told that the object is 100 percent customer satisfaction, and every employee has the obligation and right to do whatever is necessary to satisfy a customer. No management approval is needed. Every employee is, in effect, the boss.

Michael Maccoby describes quality in that situation, which is becoming more common, as the difference between a symphony orchestra and a jazz quartet. Deming often uses the orchestra (see Chapter 3) as an example of how a well-run company operates efficiently, with everyone working together to achieve the company's goal. Maccoby says in that case the company's chief executive is like a conductor, and "the conductor's job is to translate his vision [of how the music should sound] through words and gestures in rehearsal and performance. The musicians follow the leader." Companies like Federal Express, however, are more like a jazz quartet. The leader selects the music and the beat, but "the instrumental parts are not written down. . . . the responsibility of interpretation shifts from the leader to all the players. Each has the freedom to improvise within the musical structure, to initiate or to react to what the other players of the ensemble are playing. The concept — the vision of how the music should sound — is a shared vision."

The Commission on the Skills of the American Workforce says the most productive organizations worldwide are doing away with the accepted hierarchies and bureaucracies and letting workers become their own managers. American companies like Boeing, Cummins, Ford, IBM, Kodak, Motorola, Procter & Gamble and others operate at least some teamwork plants. Stepp says that P&G has reported that "productivity is at least 40 percent greater in those plants where they have introduced teams than in their more traditionally organized and managed plants." Corning's new automotive filters plant at Blacksburg, Virginia, used highly trained, self-managed production teams to make a $2 million profit in its first eight months of production. Corning had expected a *loss* of more than $2 million in that period, so the training had a $4 million payoff. To do that, the company had carefully picked 150 workers from 8,000 applications, then spent $750,000 to train them, not only in how to make filters with the newest and best equipment, but also in how to solve problems and work in teams without supervision. "The competitive advantage can never be in hardware," Keller says; "the competitive advantage is in the people, the systems, how the work is laid out."

As work becomes less a matter of rigid control and more a matter of cooperation, the need for management declines, which causes its own resistance. Milliken says, "It's hard for management to understand that they're not indispensable." Kanter says, "The role of managers is changing dramatically . . . the classic middle managers — supervisors and managers of managers — and people who were sort of built up in an infinite hierarchical progression, they're an endangered species. We're not going to have very many of them anymore." It is worthwhile to remember that middle managers are also workers, who, like those below them, have been doing exactly what they've been told to do by their bosses.

And they were hired by their bosses — in incredible numbers.

"More than half of the modern American corporation," Rosecrance wrote, "consists of workers uninvolved in operations or production work, an astounding fact. . . . The ratio in typical corporations in Japan is about one-sixth of the American figure." He says that applies as well in the military and in public schools. William Brock, a former secretary of labor, says, "In the city of New York there are more school administrators than there are in all of France. In the state of New York there are more administrators than there are in all of the European Community, and the EC has twelve countries and 320 million people." Rosecrance's solution is for workers to take over more management duties to reduce the ratio of managers to operators (or teachers to administrators). He says that needs to happen right away. "In the more distant future," he adds, "the distinction between white and blue collars may disappear."

There is not the slightest hint that it is disappearing in America now. In December 1989, *Fortune* magazine published a cover story called "The Trust Gap," which said that as the disparity grew between what the top people were paid and what the workers made, the workers felt less connected to their companies and less respectful of their managers. The workers didn't trust top management, didn't think management cared about them or their opinions, and generally believed that no matter what went wrong, the workers would take the heat and top management would get a bonus. American workers have good reason to believe that. It's true. Senior managers often do everything they can to distance themselves from those they consider the unruly riffraff who make their products. Entrepreneurs and small business owners usually started in the shop and worked beside anyone they hired; at Romac, McNeil was simultaneously president and welder. Financial, legal, and marketing executives — today's standard American chief executives — have not worked on a shop floor and, in most cases, have no desire to. One CEO mentioned in the *Fortune* article could not bring himself to talk face-to-face with his plant's employees.

The magazine gave examples of how the gap between who gets what could be closed so that, as it quoted one consultant, "employees *do* feel they're living in a society of equals." Apparently, any U.S. corporate chief executive who read the article decided to ignore it. The *New York Times* reported in March 1991 that despite the recession, the nation's top executives got bigger pay raises in 1990 than any other group of American workers. The article said that chief executives of large companies now make seventy to eighty times what the average worker makes — other sources say it can go as high as a hundred times more — and that is double what it was fifteen years ago. Canada, which is second in pay disparity, is only half the U.S. rate.

Bill Totten is an American who has lived in Japan since 1968; in 1972 he founded Ashisuto to sell American computer software to Japanese firms. It's a successful business. As the founder, majority stockholder, and president, his total income, he says, is eight times his average employee's pay, and after taxes it is only six times the average. "That is typical of Japan," he says. "What's typical in the United States? A ratio of about 93 to 1. And the people with that 93 to 1 ratio are not the company founders. They are the hired guns." He complains that those "hired guns" think nothing of firing the employees. "In Japan employees get a very fair share," he says. "That is why they are more productive. And productive employees don't get shoved out the door as soon as profits take a downturn." Totten insists that what he does in Japan now is no different from what he remembers happening when he was growing up in the United States in the 1940s and '50s. At some point after that, as Kenichi Ohmae suggests, greed took over (see Chapter 9).

Stepp says, "When you look at our [American] compensation systems and our reward systems, it is hard to find anything in those systems which would engender motivation, or provide incentives, or enable the employee to feel a linkage with the organization." Choate says, "In Japan, 93 percent of the Japanese think that if they work harder and smarter, they'll get something out of it, that the benefits will flow to them. The firm will reward them for their efforts. It's just the reverse in America. Less than 10 percent of American workers think that if they make any extra effort, they're going to get anything out of it. They think it will go to their boss, the stockholders, to somebody, but not to them."

Ohmae says workers could believe they would be left out only in the United States "because in Europe, and more so in Japan, corporations are defined as a social entity. It's not really a money-making machine. . . . Profit is not the objective. Profit is the result of doing the right thing. The objective should be to serve customers . . . and to serve its own employees. Then, if any money is left, maybe someone who is called 'stockholder' ought to have a distribution. But it's in that order as far as I am concerned." Stepp would agree: "In fact, I think it is no exaggeration to say that rank-and-file workers have more stake in the success of their organization than anyone else — more so even than stockholders and company managers. . . . Businesses are learning that if they're going to be in the business of providing satisfied customers, they must first be in the business of providing satisfied employees." Kanter says, "I used to say that the Golden Rule of customer service was 'Do unto others as your boss just did unto you.' "

Joji Arai says that the current American view of ownership started in 1930, when Harvard and Columbia Law School "had a fierce argument about for whom the corporation exists." Arai said the idea that workers had a claim to ownership lost "to the argument that the corporation's sole fiduciary responsibility was to the investors." The Japanese never accepted that, so Japanese workers expect to share in the company's success; American workers do not. Reich says that because of that difference in worker expectation, "there is less alienation [in Japan]. The Japanese managers or the American managers working for Japanese companies are not getting nearly the salaries, perquisites, and benefits relative to other American managers. Therefore, the gap between the blue-collar worker and the white-collar is much less." Reich says that treating workers with respect, giving them responsibility, job security, training, a sense of pride, and perhaps a bonus based on productivity "gives a worker a sense that he or she is not easily replaceable, that the company is a product of its workers. Too many American companies are really collections of financial assets; they're not companies at all."

Nucor Corporation of Charlotte, North Carolina, is a company, the seventh-largest steel company in the United States, with twenty-two plants, twelve more than it operated in 1980. The twenty-third will open in 1993. Nucor has not had a losing quarter in twenty-five years, and in 1990 its net income went up 30 percent. It operates on an incentive production system, which is a fancy way of saying that everyone at the company is paid for productivity. A worker's base pay, including an executive's pay, is typically lower than the steel industry standard, but everyone gets a second paycheck based on productivity. The more steel that is turned out, the fatter the second paycheck, and it is not at all unusual for workers to double their weekly pay. The employees work in teams and must meet agreed production standards for their base pay. Any more steel they produce is money in their pockets. But that is only part of it.

Ken Iverson has run the company either as president or chairman since 1965. By any industry standard, he is a successful executive, and by any industry standard, he deserves some perks. He doesn't see it that way. Iverson still drives his own car, carries his own bags on business trips, and flies coach on commercial airlines. There is no company plane. There is also no executive dining room or a reserved parking place for anyone, and any executive who considers himself too good to answer his own phone isn't good enough to work at Nucor. Out of fifty-five hundred employees, only twenty are at headquarters. Iverson tells his

employees everywhere that if they cannot get satisfaction anywhere else in the company to call him. He means it. His aim is to
"reduce any difference between management and anyone else at
the company — destroy corporate hierarchy." He attacks differences wherever he finds them. At most steel mills, safety helmet
colors vary with rank, and the chief executive's is often gold. At
Nucor everyone, including Iverson, has a green helmet, except
for maintenance workers, who wear yellow. Yellow helmet or
green, no employee at Nucor has been laid off for lack of work in
more than twenty years, and when the company hits a bad patch,
the first people to suffer are Nucor's eighteen officers. When the
return to shareholders is less than 8 percent, they get no bonus.
In one year, Iverson and his officers took in effect a 60 percent pay
cut, but no employee was laid off. In return, the employees are
just as loyal to the company as it is to them. Employee turnover is
all but nonexistent.

Nucor is a nonunion company, but it has never tried to keep
the United Steelworkers of America out. The union hasn't tried to
organize a Nucor plant in twelve years. That time, company supervisors were sent out to protect a union organizer handing out
leaflets after company workers threatened him.

At Romac, McNeil says, "we are nonunion, but I like to think
we're not antiunion." He sees a "tremendous future" for unions if
they will give up confrontation for constructive cooperation. "C.
E. Wilson, who was president of General Motors and then became
secretary of defense under [President Dwight] Eisenhower," Mc-
Neil remembers, "made a statement that the adversary relationship between management and labor in this country is a necessary
ingredient in the American way. I don't think that is true at all."
Fred Smith at Federal Express says his company has unions, but
none in the United States. "The unions in the United States," he
says, "have accomplished many of the traditional goals they
fought so hard for. Anybody who says that the average working
person hasn't benefited enormously because of the efforts of

labor leaders over the years is not being objective." But, he says, most of the traditional labor goals are now law, and even if they weren't, "most people that run organizations the size of Federal Express find these things to be both the right thing to do and good business as well." He says some unions have become involved in quality, productivity, and management, as he feels they should, "but many still insist on adversarial, political posturing."

Unions in the United States have steadily lost membership since 1955 when 36 percent of workers in the private sector were organized. By 1990, only about 12 percent were union members. (If public sector jobs are included, union membership is 16 percent.) Some scholars are suggesting that if nothing changes, union membership among American workers in the year 2000 will be 5 percent. While union membership was going down in the United States, in the seventeen industrial nations that are competitors, average union membership *increased* to 53 percent. In other countries, the pay difference between union and nonunion workers is about 10 percent; in the United States, the difference can be as much as 25 percent more for union workers. Stepp says, "What has happened in Europe is, there's a greater sense of what we call a social contract between labor, management, and government, each looking at the national interest, each coming to the bargaining table . . . with some shared understandings about what's good for business, and good for workers, and good for the country." In the United States, because workers had no job security, unions have always tried to get as much money as they could as a kind of cushion against unemployment. There was no shared understanding of mutual advantage. That constant drive for money may have built a public resistance to unions; their strikes for higher wages may have hurt the companies, but they usually hurt the customers more.

In each country in Europe, unions are different and labor laws are different, but in no country is there a resistance to unions; they are seen as natural political and social representatives of the labor force. "By law in Germany," Striner says, "all publicly held companies with over two thousand employees must have 50 percent of the board of directors elected from the [union] workers. That's radical, but it works." Japanese unions are not across an industry, as in the United States and Europe, but at each company. "Japanese unions, being so closely linked with a given employer," Stepp says, "always see the union's success and the success of its members as being linked to the success of the enterprise." He says it is sometimes difficult inside a Japanese company "to distinguish who is a union leader and who is a management leader." Actually, it is not unusual for a rising Japanese executive to spend time as both.

The AFL-CIO, the principal American labor organization, sees hope for future union growth in self-managed teams and worker participation programs, where the union can help to communicate quickly between management and labor. Unions can also be crucial in training and education programs. Ford Motor Company and the United Auto Workers (UAW) jointly sponsored a four-day Deming seminar and routinely administer the Education, Development and Training Program, an auto industry first that started in 1982, at Ford plants and UAW halls. It is an education, training, and social package that includes programs not ordinarily associated with industry, such as helping employees and their spouses learn financial planning and budgeting, planning for retirement, and a referral service for social service agencies. Employees can brush up basic language and math skills or take college-level courses for credit. The program is run by an eight-member board, four from Ford, four from the UAW; since neither side can outvote the other, cooperation keeps the program working.

The Teamsters union is actively involved in worker participation at Preston Trucking, as is the Communications Workers at U.S. West, the baby Bell in Denver, and the UAW at NUMMI. The UAW sees a bigger role in the future at NUMMI, helping to make decisions about what kind of cars to build and how to build them. The idea is to help management build quality because, a union official says, "our livelihoods depend on what they do. I think that we're going to have to be part of that decision-making process, where we never were before." Yankelovich says, "I think there's a great deal that the union can do about quality. I think that they can kill it or cooperate and enhance it, and if they see their mission in those terms, it will make a huge difference. . . . So there is an opportunity for the unions to redefine their role, to redefine it in terms of putting the national interests first, and if they do, I think that they will begin to reverse the trend [of declining membership]. If they don't, I think they'll just continue to go downhill."

Stepp says, "Unions are becoming less and less the voice of working people, and working people in a democratic society, it seems to me, must have both a political voice and an economic voice." If that voice disappears, what replaces it? If there is no more collective bargaining, what replaces it? "These are momentous issues," says Stepp, "yet, they're not being discussed. It ought to be a rich part of the public debate, yet when you hold your ear to the outside, all you hear is silence. . . . And I'm bothered by that."

Whatever American unions may do, the consultant Lou Schultz says, "the worker's role has changed. You know, at one time we hired them for their arms and legs, and now we need their minds as well. . . . It's not sufficient for management to study and learn new things and to lead the company in certain directions, but the entire organization must learn." Not only has the worker's role changed in the United States, the worker has changed and will change even more in the next few years. Until now, the typical American worker has been a white male. Increasingly, American workers will be women or minorities, often immigrants with an imperfect command of English. Increasingly, companies will have to be even more deeply involved in unfamiliar social issues: flexible work schedules, child and elder care, job sharing. Except for dying, dead-end companies, training will be increasingly essential, and the need to keep trained workers will be an absolute necessity of success. "Forty years ago," Reich says, "when we talked about labor, we talked about a cost. Labor was a cost on the balance sheet. These days, if a company is doing it right, labor is an asset, particularly your labor that is able to solve problems and identify problems and see the connection between the solutions and the new problems that are being identified. . . . That's your key asset. . . . If you lose your key problem solvers and problem identifiers, you've lost everything."

Reich believes that the 20 percent of Americans who work with their brains are doing best in today's economy; the other 80 percent, those who basically still work under the old system of quantity production, are watching their income decline or their jobs disappear. Yankelovich says that's unacceptable in the heterogeneous, pluralistic American society. "The economic decline in income," he says, "is not the worst of it. The worst of it is that the decline in income will not be across the board; it will not occur in a society in which people are cohesive and feel a sense of community. It will result in a deeper alienation, in resentment, and in demagoguery. Whenever you get a circumstance like that, the demagogues are never far behind."

Yankelovich says the American standard of living has already begun to erode, but relatively few people have noticed: "One of the reasons that the public isn't more agitated is because the lack of competitiveness and the decline in income has been masked." American women going back to work in record numbers masked the decline by creating two-earner households. Two incomes improved the household standard of living or, at worst, kept it from declining. Also, in the last ten years, increasing numbers of American teenagers have taken jobs for longer hours, often to the detriment of their schoolwork. "And again," Yankelovich says, "they started out like the women, first for the luxuries, but before you know it, the family is dependent on the money that they bring in."

To make American workers more productive, the Commission on the Skills of the American Workforce made several recommendations, including that the government require all companies to spend 1 percent of their payrolls on employee training. The commission also supports a national educational standard and the creation of centers around the country to help those already out of school reach that standard. While its report has been generally praised, it has not been put into practice in any of the states, where education and, to some degree, job training are controlled.

Not long after this report was made public, a legislative subcommittee in North Carolina proposed cuts in the public school budget that would eliminate four hundred to five hundred teaching jobs, reduce money for supplies and textbooks, shorten summer school by a third, cut teacher training money by 10 percent, and inevitably put more children in each classroom. The legislators saw their choices as cutting costs or raising taxes. Improving the public school system with a quality program was not considered. North Carolina ranked forty-ninth of the fifty states in SAT (college placement) scores in 1990, and thirty-seventh in percentage of high school students graduating.

Striner says, "Education, training, is absolutely key to quality, key to productivity gain, and key to our remaining competitive and holding U.S. companies in the United States. . . . Unless we take this seriously, unless we really begin to invest in training and retraining, we're going to have an increasing flight of American companies to other countries." They used to go for cheap labor, and a few still do, but the major companies go for a different reason now, Striner says; "what is proving to be the carrot are well-educated, well-trained employees." American workers are losing their jobs, but they are themselves all but powerless to keep those jobs by fixing the system. That takes leadership and change.

6

The Company That Saved Itself

Motorola, a $10.8 billion global company, is one of the leading providers of electronic equipment, systems, components, and services for the world market. The American company makes semiconductors and communications equipment and is especially dominant in wireless communication — two-way car radios, pagers, and cellular telephones. The company has 100,000 employees, more than half of them in the United States. It was founded in 1928 to make car radios, hence its name: *motor* from motor car and *ola* from Victrola, the most popular phonograph of its day. As new and better consumer electronics were invented, Motorola moved step by step from primitive car radios to advanced color televisions. It has long been one of America's better-known consumer electronics manufacturers.

Motorola was one of the companies mentioned in the 1980 television documentary on productivity, *If Japan Can, Why Can't We?*, but not in a way its management liked. In the early 1970s, Motorola had decided to get out of consumer electronics and into high technology industrial electronics. In 1974, Motorola sold its television plant in a Chicago suburb to Matsushita. By 1979, using the same American labor force, modestly improved equipment, and Japanese quality management techniques, every hundred Matsushita television sets built at the plant averaged 4 defects. In the closing days under Motorola, every hundred sets had 150 defects.

In 1988, Motorola was one of three American companies to win the first Malcolm Baldrige National Quality Award, created by the U.S. Congress and administered by the Department of Commerce to recognize quality achievements in manufacturing and service (see Chapter 8). In ten years, Motorola had moved to the top of the quality mountain by developing a thoughtful, companywide approach to quality. Using the employee participation programs started in the 1960s, Motorola got the best ideas of its own people, those who do the work day by day. Research and development continued to get funding no matter what, and money was poured into education and training. The program was worldwide, so that foreign subsidiaries with local managers and workers knew the same quality program that headquarters knew. And Motorola made good use of the U.S. government (of which, more later).

What it didn't do is equally important. Motorola did not dash off willy-nilly, desperate to get something done. It didn't decide that quality circles or statistical process control or any of the other tools was *the* answer. In short, they didn't confuse technique with philosophy. Perhaps without knowing it, Motorola used the Shewhart Cycle, one of the techniques W. Edwards Deming taught the Japanese in 1950; in fact, he taught them so well that in Japan to this day, it is known as the Deming Cycle. Essentially it says that when you start a project, there are four steps. First, you plan what you are going to do; second, you do it, preferably in a small, controlled test; third, you study the results of the test; finally, you act on the study, which gets you back to planning for the next step.

That does not explain why Motorola developed a quality program. The reason started with one man at a senior management meeting in 1979. "Well, the specific incident that triggered our interest," Robert Galvin, the former chief executive, now chairman of the Executive Committee, says, "was a statement by a very successful sales manager of his day . . . who told our officers, who were then in assembly, that our quality was very poor." According to the popular story around Motorola, what Arthur Sundry, the senior sales executive for the Communications Sector, told seventy-five members of senior management was, "Our quality levels really stink." That would have been the end of his career in any number of companies around the world, but he went on to become president of the sector and executive vice-president of Motorola before his retirement late in 1990. Galvin says Motorola has always encouraged its people to speak up, to say what they mean, not what is expected. His father, Paul, who started the company with the first car radio, was known for his ability to make an instant decision, then change it without rancor or resentment if anyone could show that he was wrong, and that attitude continues today. Still, it is unusual for a successful manager, a man obviously moving up, to be so openly critical of his own company's goods.

"And we took cognizance of the fact," Galvin says, "that if he felt our quality was bad, maybe we all ought to examine our standards. . . . Maybe it was also a demonstration of the fact that back within our inner feelings, many of us were beginning to question [Motorola quality]. . . . So we had a very personal, a very emotional buy-in, almost on an instantaneous basis, which got us started."

It was not a smooth start or an easy one. "We muddled and stumbled for a good period of time," Galvin says. "First off, like the good farmer, we really knew how to farm better than we were doing at the time, so we set ourselves to just plain getting back to some basics. From there on, we began to reach out and to listen to anyone and everyone who had some thoughts."

From David Kearns, the chairman of Xerox Corporation, Motorola learned how to "benchmark," which essentially means you search the world to find the corporations that are best at doing one or more of the things you do, then study how they do it. It's the same concept that built the state-of-the-art, high technology, computer-integrated pager assembly line called the Bandit Line, in Boynton Beach — take every good idea you can get. While studying what other companies were doing, Motorola officials learned that some of their Japanese competitors had levels of quality *a thousand times higher* than Motorola's, and those companies intended to improve. Motorola had already left consumer electronics to the Japanese, and it became obvious that without a dramatic increase in quality, Motorola could lose parts of its new business in industrial electronics as well. But how do you persuade everyone in the company to believe that, and, equally important, how do you get them to act on that belief?

"Basically," says George Fisher, the chief executive since January 1988, "you had better demonstrate the need or the fear or something that's emotional up front. . . . we put on something we called 'Rise to the Challenge.' The intention of 'Rise to the Challenge' was to make it evident to everybody that there was a need; in fact, this scared the heck out of everybody. If we didn't accelerate the pace of change, especially with respect to areas like quality and cycle time, we were going to fall woefully behind all of our competitors. . . . I think that because of that initial fear that was created out of the 'Rise to the Challenge' program, we had an easier sell, a sell that made creating change necessary not just because we said it or somebody in the organization said it, but because all the people identified with it." From the beginning, the program has had a single, easily understood although unattainable goal — total customer satisfaction.

Initially, however, even though people knew something had to be done, no one quite knew what to do or how to do it.

"We went to the intellectual experts, the people in academia," Galvin says, "learned a great deal from them. We brought in consultants, talked to our customers. . . . we began a process of reaching out to learn from every source we could. Finally, we engaged in very formal training to teach ourselves all manner of the new ways and means."

American business and industry, starting in the 1980s, was spending about $25 billion to $30 billion a year on employee training and education. Even at that, Robert Reich, the Harvard political economist, says that when Japanese take over an American plant, they typically spend about $1,000 more on training for each employee each year than their American counterparts. That helps give them a more productive work force. "Japanese managers are able to manage American workers better," Reich says, "because they're investing more in the training and education of American workers . . . they're willing to give their workers a greater degree of job security . . . they're willing to give the workers more responsibility [and] they're willing to listen to workers in terms of suggestions." Bill Smith, an engineer active in Motorola's program, tells people from other companies studying at Motorola that job security is part of "a quality culture" and allows employees to suggest ways to eliminate their own jobs, knowing they'll be trained for another job. "Motorola is more of a lifetime employer than most Japanese companies," Smith says. "If you have been with the company for ten or more years, you're a member of the Motorola Service Club, and as such, it requires the written concurrence of the chairman of the board to terminate you." Job security is important, as are responsibility and communications, but training is first among equals; without training, no quality program can succeed.

Of Deming's fourteen points, one deals with training and another with education. Training, Deming believes, should continue until employees have learned all they can; then, unless conditions change, additional training isn't worthwhile. Education, however, should go on forever, his only suggestion being that what is being studied should *not* be directly related to the business. At Ford Motor Company sites, there are joint company-union programs in which employees can take high school English or math, college courses, or pretty much anything else, Deming says, "except basketball." He thinks that's a mistake because basketball "teaches teamwork. Pretty important." The theory is that as you learn to think about anything, you will be better able to think about what you do and about how your job can be done better.

Interestingly, two of Crosby's fourteen points also deal with training and education, but his concern is, as always, more practical. Education, he says, should make certain that every employee is personally concerned with the need for quality and the importance of a quality reputation to the company. Like all the other experts, he insists that every employee be extensively trained and, when necessary, retrained.

Many if not most companies suddenly faced with international competition in the global market try to graft a so-called quality improvement program onto the existing internal communications or training program. Our experience is that the add-on approach is doomed; it sounds reasonable, but it does not work. What does work is what Motorola did. Top management found a philosophy of quality improvement on which they could agree and to which they could commit. They then developed a new quality communications and training program for everyone in the company.

Motorola has its own university, with training facilities at each of its locations worldwide. At the 325-acre headquarters in Schaumburg, Illinois, about 30 miles west of Chicago, the school is in the Galvin Center, named for both father and son, a $10 million, 88,000-square-foot building that opened in 1986. The company needed the expanded facility because of the amount of training involved. Every Motorola employee must take a minimum forty hours of training each year. That's a full work week of training for every employee, every year, starting at the top. "We learned the hard way," Fisher says, "in one of the mistakes we made early on that unless you start at the top with your training programs, you have a phenomenon where people are going back to their jobs after taking a course, they want to implement some new process or procedure, and they're all enthusiastic to do it, and, lo and behold, they go in and talk to their boss, and he doesn't know what they're talking about [and that] made it clear that we have to start educating from the top of the organization down. . . . Otherwise, how can you make reasonable demands on the people if you don't understand it yourself? That doesn't mean we all have to be experts in statistics or some of the other tools, but we have to know what's available at all levels."

William Wiggenhorn, the president of Motorola University and corporate vice-president of Training and Education, explained what happened in the early days. "Workers began to wonder why they'd take the training," he wrote. "They'd learned how to keep a Pareto chart and make an Ishikawa diagram [statistical tools], but no one ever appeared on the floor and asked to see one. On the contrary, some of their immediate managers wanted product shipped even if it wasn't perfect. Top managers, on the other hand, began to wonder why it was that people took the courses so carefully designed for them and then went back to their jobs and did nothing different."

That need for intensive training from the top down often leads to resistance among managers at companies that are starting quality programs, and it may have contributed to what Galvin remembers as "a rather ordinary organizational resistance, but not an intense one." He says there was no widespread disagreement or objection at Motorola; "they just were I'm-too-busy kinds of objections." Those objections were simply overruled; training was essential, and that was that. Training is part of Galvin's answer when he is asked what advice he would give other chief executives who are thinking of starting quality programs.

"I don't know that I would advise," Galvin says. "I would observe that there is a basis for an act of faith. The act of faith is that it will never cost money to have a quality program, that you will always have lower costs and better products when you have a quality program, and you must believe in that. As a supporter to that, you're going to have to have extensive training, and you must have an act of faith that training is never going to cost you any money. You will indeed rotate some dollars to a line item called 'training' in your budget, but you'll get benefits back far greater than the cost that you put in. And with these kinds of acts of faith, then one can more readily justify the energies and the resources that go to quality."

When Galvin says "training is never going to cost you any money," he says it with the same quiet confidence with which he answers all questions. It's impressive if you know that Motorola originally intended to spend about $7 million a year on training; it now spends $60 million a year on training and education and another $60 million in wages paid to the employee-students. But when Galvin says the dollars spent on education and training are an investment, Wiggenhorn has the figures to back it up. In the early 1980s, independent research showed that in those Motorola plants where the workers had learned quality skills *and* where managers understood and supported the program, every $1 spent on training returned $33. As Armand Feigenbaum has said, "The return on investment from these quality installations greatly exceeded the return from other forms of business investment."

Neil Dial, the manufacturing operations manager for the Paging Division at Boynton Beach, says training and education are necessary because requirements have changed. "It used to be manual dexterity you looked at," he says, "and today you're definitely looking at people that can be able to read and communicate. . . . It used to be that a lot of decision-making was held at the managerial level, and then the people in the factory were left to execute sometimes an unguided plan that they did not necessarily have inputs into. Now, in the total participative management culture, the people down at the factory-floor level are definitely an integrated part of the decision-making process." Wiggenhorn wrote about the differences. "In the old days," he explained, "our selection criteria had been simply, 'Are you willing to work? Do you have a good record of showing up for work? Are you motivated to work?' We didn't ask people if they could read. We didn't ask them to do arithmetic. We didn't ask them to demonstrate an ability to solve problems or work on a team or do anything except show up and be productive for so many hours a week." The work force was, therefore, motivated, reliable, and largely unable to read or do simple arithmetic. "To meet our business needs," Wiggenhorn continued, "we found we had to add remedial elementary education" to Motorola's training program. The costs went up.

As Galvin says, spending that kind of money takes an act of faith. However, more than that act of faith is required from the chief executive. "I think the single most important thing," Galvin says, "is that the chief executive officer has to decide that it is his uncompromising objective to accomplish the highest-quality standards for that business, and that his personal involvement will be ever evident, and he will be the role model. Without that, you cannot have a program of this nature. . . . If the rest of the organization does not discern that the leader is all for a quality program, then there will be some degree of compromise." When he was chief executive, to be certain that his most senior managers understood his commitment, Galvin would go to quarterly corporate meetings, insist that quality reports be given first, then walk out before quarterly profit-and-loss was discussed.

Fisher believes that leadership from the top has to be real and consistent. "Perhaps the most sensitive area," he says, "where you could lose a lot of gain [in a quality program], is where you lose credibility with your people. You can't just talk about quality one day a month, or one day a week, or have it your 'hot button' this year. It's got to be a way of life, and you had better walk the talk, as they say, or your people will see right through it."

The American Society for Quality Control (ASQC) sponsored a survey on quality of 1,237 full-time American workers in 1990. More than half the workers said their companies claimed it was extremely important that the customer know the company was committed to quality, but only 36 percent said their companies *were* committed. There were similar disparities between talk and action on making quality the top priority in the company and on competing by producing top-quality goods and services. According to the workers surveyed, American managers talked a good deal more than they acted. Reich agrees with the workers. "American managers right now," he says, "are very good at quoting all of the bromides of the new management theories — quality circles, pushing responsibility downward, flattening the pyramid. It's extraordinary the extent to which these buzzwords have dominated all American management. It's also extraordinary how little has changed." Daniel Yankelovich of the Public Agenda Foundation adds, "When it comes to quality, management gives their people mixed messages. On the one hand, they say quality is very important, they give a lot of lip service to it. But if you look at the reward systems, if you look at the incentives, if you look at what people are paid to do and are rewarded to do, it's not for quality."

Another finding of the ASQC survey was mentioned by the Council on Competitiveness. Where quality programs were being used, only 29 percent of the workers were satisfied with the rate of improvement; 25 percent were actively dissatisfied and didn't think the program was going fast enough. Motorola did its own survey to find out if it was pushing its 100,000 employees too hard and too fast and putting on too much pressure. "It's interesting to me," Fisher says, "that a preliminary conclusion would be that our people, generally, would rather see us change faster in many respects, because many of our people, most of our people I suspect, understand that competition is really keen, the world's moving really fast, and unless we move faster than the best in the industry, we won't be the leader ten years from now that we are today." Fisher says he was a little surprised, because he had more or less expected that demands for perfection and sweeping changes were putting too much pressure on the organization. "In fact," he says, "what the organization is telling us is, 'You better change even faster.' " Smith says that when Motorola employees were first asked if they could make no more than three mistakes the next million times they did something, "they sort of scratched their heads, and they said, 'God, that's a tough goal, but it's possible.' And I don't know what the magic of it is," Smith adds, "but people tend to accept a finite number, however small it might be."

Of the courses at the Motorola training center, about 40 percent are about quality, and what is being taught is the Chinese menu approach. Motorola has studied or consulted with the four American quality experts, as it has with many of the lesser-known consultants. It took what it found useful from each of the experts and added the suggestions of its own people to create its own approach with its own standards and its own goals. Some of it, as in all the quality programs, is so logically simple that it seems obvious, but as Richard Buetow, the senior vice-president and director of quality, says, "All this stuff is intuitively obvious — after you figure it out." What began at a management meeting in Chicago in 1979 led to a companywide program in 1987 to reach Six Sigma quality during 1992.

Six sigma is a statistical term just as *pi* is a mathematical term. (Unless you're a statistician, just accept that six sigma is a method of defect measurement and let it go at that. The explanation isn't as important as what six sigma means.) At Motorola it means that there will be no more than 3.4 defects per million parts or, to put it another way, that you will get it right no less than 99.99966 percent of the time. As a comparison, the average American company operates between three and four sigma, or about 67,000 to 6,200 defects per million. At the three or four sigma level, almost any honest effort to improve quality will have some results, however limited. Once you move toward five sigma, you must have a planned improvement system, including statistics; honest effort won't work at that level. Because improvement does become more difficult at higher levels, six sigma is a way to force innovative, breakthrough thinking and revolutionary rates of improvement. You cannot get to six sigma by improving 10 percent at a time. None of the quality experts has a Six Sigma program; it was suggested by Bill Smith, the Motorola engineer, and Galvin liked the name. Incidentally, we are using Motorola's sigma figures; statisticians say that what sigma means mathematically depends on the situation.

Whatever the program is called, if you listen to what's being said at Motorola, you can hear which expert opinions have been rejected and which accepted. Kaoru Ishikawa, the Japanese expert, developed the concept of the next person in the company who depends on you being a customer. Motorola rejects it. "For a while," Fisher says, "people at Motorola thought they had 'internal customers.' They don't. There is only one customer — the person who pays the bills. That's the person we're serving." Fisher talks of the costs of not producing quality, then adds that the cost of a dissatisfied customer who'll never buy a Motorola product again can't even be measured. In one sentence he paraphrases Crosby's fourth absolute — "the measurement of quality is the price of nonconformance" — and Deming's teaching that what a lack of quality costs is "unknown and unknowable." As far as Fisher and Motorola are concerned, both statements are demonstrably true, and they are part of what everyone at Motorola has been and is being taught.

"I am very, very much a believer," Fisher says, "that our training program is perhaps the most important single element of the drive that we've made in quality over the years and, in fact, the most important element of a cultural transition in the company." Training not only teaches the tools of Motorola's quality program and how to use them, but it gives everyone in the company a common language, which Fisher calls the company's "cohesive glue. . . . We talk the Six Sigma language around the world. If you go to Singapore, they will talk the same language with respect to cycle time and quality that the people here in Chicago, or the people in Texas or Phoenix, will talk. As a result, we're able to build on a common linguistic foundation in addition to a common set of tools, in addition to a commonly communicated message across the whole organization — all done through the training program."

The Motorola program equates time and quality. Galvin says the only way you can perform perfectly is to improve your quality. As quality goes up, the amount of time needed for any job goes down. "One can focus on time and accomplish quality," he says. "One can focus on quality and accomplish time." He says when people begin to believe that what must be done will be done correctly and exactly on time, "you have the perfect combination for operational perfection."

There is a solid business reason for a concern with time as well as quality. Whoever gets a new quality product to the global market first usually makes the most money. Says Fisher, "If, in fact, you are out there early enough, then you will make enough money to refuel your ability to finance future product developments." He paraphrases a study by McKinsey and Company, which essentially says that getting a project to market *on time* is more important than that project's budget. "If you spent 50 percent more than your budget on a project like some of the products we develop," he says, "your profit over the life cycle of that product might diminish by 4 percent. If, on the other hand, you miss the market, you're late by six months, your profit is diminished by 33 percent — *a third.*" He says that in the high tech electronics business, companies that are always followers are also financially weak. Being first to the market with quality products that customers want is what gives Motorola the largest market share in about 60 percent of what it sells. "You don't do that without being consistently a product and technology leader," he says.

That is not something Wall Street appears to understand. When Motorola's stock fell in the third quarter of 1990 because of a lower-than-expected gain in profits — not a loss, a gain; but not as big a gain as Wall Street wanted — Fisher was asked if it wouldn't be wiser *not* to increase research spending, as he planned to do. "For us not to make the wise investments in probably the highest-growth area in the electronics industry — wireless communications — would be insane," he answered. "We are the world leader in all aspects of that, whether it's paging or land mobile or cellular." Fisher says that he wants stockholders to "get a decent return over the long term," and the best way to do that, he believes, is for Motorola to stay on top.

The question and his answer illustrate another problem facing American management as it changes to a quality program: the company has to stay in business, not only persuading its employees to change, but persuading investors as well. Deming tells a seminar, "You must hang a sign on the door, 'Open for business during renovations.' " Ben Carlson, the executive vice-president at Vernay Laboratories, said that when the company was going from standard American business management to the Deming quality method, every day he tried to spend one minute more introducing the quality program in the company and one minute less running around the plant "stamping out fires." When a company adopts a quality program, old problems do not magically solve themselves and everyone does not instantly join the new program. "I presume that various of us," Galvin says of Motorola, "bought into a quality objective at a slightly different pace. . . . What happened in the company was that the successful people, at the early stages, became role models for those of us that maybe came along a little slower. We discovered that others were doing it well, we could join with them, and we didn't want to get left behind." Still, it is an added pressure on the chief executive to keep the company operating profitably, satisfying shareholders, while fundamentally changing the company's complete culture. Ishikawa called total quality control "a thought revolution for management."

It is not just a thought revolution; it is a completely new kind of competition that can be almost weird. Rosabeth Moss Kanter of the *Harvard Business Review* says, "I often tell people that it's like the croquet game in *Alice in Wonderland.* That's a game in which nothing remains stable for very long; everything is in constant motion around the players. So Alice tries to hit the ball, but the mallet she's using is a flamingo, and just as she's about to hit the ball, the flamingo lifts its head and looks in another direction, which I think is a perfect image for technology, for the tools we use. Just as one set has been mastered, there's another set facing in still another direction that requires adaptation, learning, change, a flexible attitude, the ability to incorporate new knowledge, work differently with suppliers, and so forth.

"And then the ball that Alice is trying to hit, that's also alive and moving and changing. It's a hedgehog, and it's a living creature with a mind of its own. So rather than just lying there, waiting for Alice to whack it with whatever she's got, the hedgehog, when it feels like it, gets up, unrolls, moves to some other part of the court, and sits down again, which I think is a wonderful image for our employees and customers, the human factor in business. They're no longer lying there, waiting for us to whack them with whatever we've got. They're fickle, they're demanding, they're less loyal, they have more choices. . . . So because of that motion on the part of employees and customers, companies, too, have to be more flexible, able to incorporate change, able to respond before the hedgehog moves, and that means an innovative, flexible organization.

"Then the last part of that croquet game," Kanter continues, "is that the wickets through which Alice is trying to hit this ball are card soldiers ordered around by the Queen of Hearts, and every once in a while, seemingly at random, the Queen of Hearts barks out an order, and suddenly the wickets reposition themselves on the court. The whole structure of the game is changing around any individual company. The Red Queen might be a government agency that barks out an order — 'regulate here,' 'open the regulations here,' 'raise tariffs,' 'lower tariffs,' 'GATT agreements' — but the structure is in constant motion, constantly being renegotiated. Or the Queen of Hearts might be a corporate raider — nowadays a corporate raider really means a corporation — barking out an order, 'buy that stock,' and suddenly there's the structure changing. Or a technological breakthrough that causes industry structure to change, or voluntary mergers and acquisitions.

"So managers are trying to do their job while the tools are changing, their customers are changing and are more demanding, and the very structure of the industry and regulation environments in which they operate are changing. It seems a little out of control, a little chaotic," Kanter says, "but it puts a premium on companies that are more flexible, faster-moving, more adaptive, and much more willing to embrace change as a way of life."

The quality demands, George Fisher says, create for senior management "an increasing pressure, increasing every day with the awareness that unless you are a world-class performer with respect to quality, your corporation is likely not to grow very rapidly, certainly not to gain market share, and, as a result, not to be as profitable as it should be." Another part of the pressure on everyone in the company is the understanding that the job is never finished. "You can achieve perfect quality," Fisher says, "zero defects per unit, world-class cycle time, and do everything perfectly, and still not have *total* customer satisfaction. We really have set an objective for the corporation that is never-ending. You never get there. Our people understand that you never get there. You have to continue to work." Not only does a quality program never end, it gets progressively more difficult. "Going from three to four sigma was relatively easy," Fisher says. "Going from four to five, we had to be much more creative in those areas. Where we're moving from five to six right now, it is much more difficult. . . . the solutions to get there cannot be conventional, evolutionary solutions. People really have to think quite differently." T. Scott Shamlin, then the director of manufacturing operations for the Paging Division, told a news conference, "Raising levels of expectation must be done quantitatively — you can't just tack on 10 percent or 100 percent to existing levels of performance and call it a goal." You can't just set goals; you must develop methods to improve performance. Starting a quality program puts you in a race where no matter how hard or fast you run, you never reach the finish line, because there isn't one. Despite the difficulties and the problems of adopting a quality program, Fisher says, "I think enlightened companies are recognizing that quality is not a necessary evil, but a necessary prerequisite to really being successful."

Being a quality company means going beyond your factory floor, for example, to both your suppliers and your customers. Fisher says you have to go to your customers to find out what they want, then show them the new technology that is available: "We marry our technology development with a deep understanding of our customers' business needs." Fisher says that by understanding their business needs, not just their communications needs, Motorola can design products the customers can't even imagine. "That design process," Fisher says, "increasingly has to integrate what the customer feels [and] what our suppliers can provide, so there are two major external forces in addition to getting the parts of the company working together. No longer do you have a situation where the designer can design a product and throw it over a wall and expect a manufacturing organization to simply make it. Today, in order to get the quality and the cost you need, you really have to have an integrated team effort starting with the customers and suppliers and [going] across all the divisions within Motorola or within any company like ours." Design and manufacturing people work together from the first day, and the idea is to design a product that is easy to make without error. The analogy is a garage with a door so narrow that only the most skilled driver can get through. You can either pray for skilled drivers, or you can make the door wider.

Tim Leuliette of Siemens, the German global giant, says, "There really today is no such thing as product engineers and manufacturing engineers who live in separate wings in the building and talk over lunch. Rather, there are engineers, and the way a product is designed is to have the product and the process designed at the same time." He talks about the change in a high-speed precision part. "The old product had thirteen minutes of direct labor; the new product has a minute and forty-seven seconds of direct labor. The old part had thirteen grinding operations; the new part has two." Leuliette says Siemens, which supplies auto makers all over the world, works with its customers and suppliers constantly to build better, less expensive parts for their cars.

Galvin says one of the earliest mistakes Motorola made while it "muddled and stumbled" toward an answer was that "we didn't talk to our suppliers enough at that time. We could have learned so much more from them, as we are now learning from them. . . . suppliers know an awful lot to teach their customers." Galvin takes as an example a plastic part. A Motorola designer will know what the part must do, but the plastics manufacturer will have ideas on how to make it more efficient, more reliable, and less expensive because that's his business. "Now we're listening to our suppliers much more on those things that they are the experienced experts on," Galvin says, "and our designs are better, our designs are less expensive, and, frankly, we get our designs quicker because we're doing them the ways our suppliers suggest are the best."

Motorola wants to help its suppliers improve; indeed, the company insists that they improve. Charles Gonsior of St. Paul Metalcraft is quoted as saying, "If we can supply Motorola, we can supply God." The Motorola communications division used to buy from about five thousand suppliers. It is now down to fewer than two thousand and wants to get to only four hundred. The company notified all its suppliers in every division that it would continue to do business only with those that would agree to apply for the Baldrige Award within five years. The agreement did not have to be a formal contract — a one-sentence letter would do fine — but if there was no commitment from the supplier, there would be no future business from Motorola, period. Galvin is aware, however, that improving Motorola's suppliers may help his competitors, who often buy from the same sources. It doesn't bother him. "If we cause that our suppliers, who supply our competitors, get better, we would be helping our competitors to compete. But I believe that this is in the general best interest of our country and, therefore, our company. . . . We depend on our competitors. We'd like to get more orders than they get, but it's more than just the fact that they're there to compete with us. They are often our suppliers and often our customers. So we learn from each other, and we gain from the energies of the [free] enterprise system."

Fisher has a similar opinion. "When you're playing in the major leagues," he says, "your competitors are major league players. In our case, the Japanese are superb. People have often said that if the Japanese didn't exist, we should have invented them just because they make us better, and I think there's truth in that. . . . We beat them more often than we lose to them, actually, in head-to-head competition, but I think we're better because we have to compete with them." Fisher believes the global competition is going to get worse with more major league players, saying, "There are emerging countries in the world that have pockets of excellence that are amazing. You look at Korea, Singapore, Malaysia, Hong Kong, Taiwan, there are pockets of excellence in companies in those countries in the electronics industry that are outstanding." He believes the economic union of the European Community in 1992 is going to contribute to the competition. "Europe," he says, "which has always been very strong from a fundamental technology side, will become increasingly strong in its application of technology. I see very stiff competition and good competition coming out of Europe. It's already there in Japan, and then you have it emerging in many parts of the world, but don't discount the United States. . . . The fact of the matter is that some of the best companies in the world today in some of the most competitive areas, the areas that I know in electronics, are American companies."

Leuliette of Siemens would probably agree with the "pockets of excellence" analysis, and he emphasizes the companies, not the countries. Motorola and Siemens are both successful global companies — multinationals, if you will — so nationality, Leuliette feels, doesn't make that much difference. "There's no question that the pressure of the Japanese in many industries in the '70s made certain companies, not countries, but certain companies aware outside of Japan that the quality role had changed," he says. "Today, when you look at quality, you say, 'The Japanese are here, and the Americans are here, and the Frenchmen are here, and the Germans are here.' Well, wait a minute. Our company has operations all over the world run by Koreans, run by Frenchmen, run by Japanese, run by Americans. Who are they? Are they Germans because they work for a German company, or are they Americans because the entity is in America? No single country in my mind today controls quality."

Leuliette is an American who is part of Siemens's management board, the top executives who run the company. As a general rule, large European companies tend to have teams rather than individuals at the top. That concept is spreading in the United States. "I think in fact to run a company successfully today," Fisher says, "you need a team of people. There is more of a collegial requirement in governing large corporations. In a technical company, the technical content is increasing." Fisher, whose master's degree is in engineering and whose doctorate is in applied mathematics, says that in negotiating agreements with other technical companies, it is easier for him to learn the necessary law or financial matters than it would be for a lawyer or an accountant to learn the technical matters. Even at that, he believes one man cannot do it alone. "The world's way too complex," he says, "and none of us is all that good. That's expecting a lot of a single individual, to be all-knowing and all-wise." Galvin seems to agree, saying, "We can't expect that any one of us is going to be smart enough entirely on our own." He says that while cooperation is essential, each individual is responsible to "reach out" for training and education so that he or she can contribute to the group. That, Fisher seems to feel, could be the key. "I think," he says, "that to the extent that we're able to leverage the intelligence and the thinking ability of other people with diverse backgrounds, [that] will be the extent to which we are successful at running these corporations."

The corporation that the chief executive will run with the help of others is changing; it has to change. "You've got to understand," Fisher explains, "what the process of serving a customer is. Most organizations are formed on a vertical, hierarchical structure, militaristic structure, but if you think about how you serve a customer. . . . you serve him *across* the functional organization within the company." Starting with the supplier and moving across the company's divisions, not up and down the way the organizational chart is drawn, requires cooperation from all levels of all divisions, what Deming calls "optimization." It is, according to Myron Tribus, the consultant, corporate president, and former dean, the first major overhaul of the organizational system since the hierarchical system was laid out in biblical times in the book of Exodus. He compared it to the change required when man discovered that the earth was not flat, but round.

However great the upset, Fisher thinks the traditional organization has to change. "Parochial organizational boundaries," he says, "more often than not, get in the way of serving a customer effectively. So, we are trying to create a culture which increasingly reinforces the fact that we have to be cooperative with each other, less competitive with each other, less attentive to organizational boundaries, and certainly more participative to get everybody involved in the process, always with the focus on the customer. . . . I don't mean to pretend that we know all the answers, nor have all the things I'm talking about been implemented perfectly in the organization. We have a long way to go."

The across-the-company cooperation was used to plan, design, and build the Bandit Line in Boynton Beach. People from every part of the company were included. Len DeBarras, the manager of manufacturing operations, remembers, "All of the product developers, the equipment people, the people from marketing, the process people, were put together in a room, and they were given eighteen months to do the project." A project of that complexity normally takes a minimum of thirty-six months. The first thing that went was the start-from-scratch approach typically used in America and Europe; the idea here was to use as much off-the-shelf technology as possible and take the best ideas wherever they were found. The not-invented-here syndrome was out. Shamlin, the director of manufacturing operations, says team researchers visited the best factories they could find in the United States, Europe, and Asia, factories that did everything from assembling cars to grinding optical fiber lenses. They talked with suppliers and with universities. They talked with customers and learned that what bothered them was not so much product quality but delivery and billing mistakes, the so-called soft side of the business. Bandit takes the order, makes it, packs it, ships it, and bills it — automatically. Every pager is different — what manufacturers call a lot size of one — and instead of taking thirty days, as it used to, it takes twenty-eight minutes.

Just a few days from its deadline, Bandit went to work. Motorola news releases described it as a "factory of the future." It is an automated manufacturing line with twenty-seven programmable robots (made in Japan) controlled by an integrated computer network. Shamlin calls it "a new robotic factory, a new product, a new computer control system, a new material system, a new ordering system, a new management system." All of it was designed, built, and put into operation in eighteen months, and there is nothing like it anywhere else in the world. The question, of course, is whether all that effort is worth it.

Buetow, the quality director, told a reporter that the Six Sigma program saved the company $500 million in 1990. Fisher says tremendous progress has been made at Motorola, but it's progress, not perfection: "A corporation like ours that's doing a pretty good job in quality, and maybe a world-class job, still wastes probably something on the order of 7, or 8, 9 percent of their sales revenue on defects. . . . just in the quantifiable costs associated with doing things imperfectly. . . . That's throwing away about $900 million a year for us." Imagine what would be thrown away if Motorola were still at four sigma, making about 6,200 defects per million, instead of being between five and six, heading toward 3.4 defects. Siemens, by the way, is at 20 defects per million with a goal of reaching 10 per million. "I hope," Leuliette says, "when they reach that, they set their target for five." Which would be within rock-throwing distance of six sigma.

What has happened at Motorola has attracted attention from major North American manufacturers. Digital Equipment Company has already adopted its own Six Sigma program, as have IBM, Corning, Northern Telecom, Boeing, Caterpillar, Xerox, and Raytheon. All of them share information with Motorola, which may be one of the more profound changes in U.S. corporate culture. For the first time that we can find, major American industries are cooperating — to everyone's advantage. The Baldrige Award requires winners to share quality ideas with other American businesses and industries, and Galvin says, "We will share all of our fundamental ideas with any of our competitors." That cooperation seems to be replacing the competitive attitude that has always existed, even between companies that were not in the same field. Cooperation among federal, state, and county governments and private business in the mid-nineteenth century is what eventually made American farms the world's most productive (see Chapter 10).

Six Sigma started when one man made a critical comment that a chief executive, Robert Galvin, heard and believed and decided to act on. His decision led to Six Sigma, his unswerving commitment launched the program, and if he wanted to brag a bit, no one could blame him. He does not — except for one thing. Galvin is trim and fit, partly because he climbs the fourteen flights of steps to his office each day and partly because he wind-surfs on the pond near his home. That's where the bragging comes in. He can, Galvin says with obvious pride and supreme confidence, teach anyone to wind-surf in fifteen minutes. He taught Akio Morita, Sony's chairman, in 1986. Morita now refers to him as "my teacher," an enormous compliment in Japan.

7

A Coach, Not a Dictator

W. Edwards Deming believes that the basic problem for the United States is that most of its leaders, political and business, have not yet figured out that the country is in an economic crisis, which means there's no concerted national effort to overcome that crisis. In that regard, the Japanese after World War II were in a better position: they knew they were in a crisis, and if they needed a reminder, they had only to look out the window — if it wasn't boarded up for lack of glass. The American crisis has been the rather boring, slow erosion of the nation's earlier success, about as riveting as watching rust form. Both Deming and C. Jackson Grayson, Jr., of the American Productivity and Quality Center, use the "boiled frog" story to illustrate the difference.

If you take a frog and put it in a shallow pan of scalding water, it will jump out. If the same frog is put in tepid water over a low flame, it will sit calmly and gradually boil to death. The United States is gradually boiling to death because, as Grayson explains, "Americans don't really respond to things until they see it as a crisis." Herb Striner, the professor emeritus at American University, agrees. "I've been looking at the process of change," he says, "and what triggers change, because this is what we're really talking about. . . . And what's fascinating is that all across the board, it doesn't matter which discipline or what problem you're looking at, there is a tremendous resistance to change. . . . I found that the real problem with people who were trying to compete with the Japanese was that it was not an economic problem, it was a behavior problem — the resistance to change. Most instances of change result when there's a crisis; we're driven to it." The current U.S. economic situation, he says, has reached crisis proportions, but too few people seem to have noticed, or if they have, they don't know what to do. Leading American companies have changed or are changing, but they are a fractional minority of the private companies, and a fractional minority isn't enough.

John Stepp says that as business people became aware of the slipping American economy during the 1980s, management had three basic reactions: "We had widespread experimentation ranging from 'Let's keep the old system intact' — tighten the screws — to 'Let's play along with a few new things, but let's not go too far because who knows what may happen in terms of our own power and perks and rewards,' to those who have finally said, 'Look, we live in a new world with new requirements, and the old ways are no longer working, and we've got to fundamentally rethink what we're doing and why we're doing it.' "

It is that fundamental rethinking that some experts favor. "What we need," Deming says, "is a transformation to a new style of management. It's not just improvement. You've got to move into a totally new state. Metamorphosis; total change." Robert Reich believes part of that fundamental change will have to be in how managers think about their own companies. "Too often, too long," he says, "American managers have viewed their companies as simply collections of assets to be traded, to be cashed in, to be manipulated, to be rearranged. They don't view them as collections of people to be nurtured and developed."

Fundamental change can only be made at the highest level because it deals with corporate organization and philosophy, but once that fundamental change is made, it can also be made to spread. Major corporations are already pushing quality out from their plants into the general economy. When Motorola won the

Malcolm Baldrige National Quality Award, it told all its suppliers that they must prepare and apply for that prize within five years, as we noted in the last chapter. After Ford Motor Company began to work with Deming, its suppliers were told to adopt quality methods or lose Ford's business. General Motors divisions that are now consulting with Deming work not only with their suppliers to achieve quality, but with their suppliers' suppliers as well. IBM, Rochester, Minnesota, a 1990 Baldrige Award winner, used a three-step approach with its suppliers.

"First off," Laurence L. Osterwise, the general manager, explains, "we spent some time asking our suppliers to either apply for the Baldrige Award or to understand the categories and examination items and ensure to their own satisfaction, and eventually to ours, that they had a total quality management system. . . . The second step was sharing what we learned about ourselves from the self-assessment and the Baldrige examination and how that learning would benefit us and our customers. Now, we have gotten to the stage of saying, 'We are actually going to work with you in your self-assessment of your company to the Baldrige guidelines.' And so we have teams trained to be able to work with a supplier as they write an application [and] they say, 'You know, certification and a reasonable self-assessment are not an inquisition. . . . As long as you're willing to work with us and help us get better, that's better for you, it's better for us, and we're more willing to participate.' "

Adopting quality programs may have been marginally easier at IBM, Procter & Gamble, and Federal Express because those companies were founded on the idea of quality. Osterwise says that for IBM, it's simply a return to the company's basic beliefs. "I sort of sit there," he says, "and marvel at the wisdom of Tom Watson, Sr. [IBM's founder], when he said, 'These are the three things that we believe in: respect for the individual, striving for excellence, and service to the customer.' " Fred Smith of Federal Express told a Baldrige Award audience: "Federal Express was designed from day one to meet customers' expectations, and every day since then, we've been working very hard indeed to exceed those expectations." At P&G, Edwin L. Artzt, the chief executive, says, "The founders of the company passed along this principle of quality and customer satisfaction. . . . that was the niche they wanted this company to fill, and so it was built into the roots and culture of the company. They were uncompromising about it. They were not expedient; they were principled, and they were very committed to passing it on down through the generations of management."

However, even when the basic company ideal is quality and customer satisfaction, without a total quality program, a company isn't going to do as well as it could. "We have always had systems," Artzt says, "to continuously improve and upgrade the quality of our products and our operations. . . . But as we learned when we got into the more sophisticated form of total quality system, our approach was incomplete. . . . What total quality systems, or the continuous improvement program, have brought to us is a more sophisticated and more effective way of achieving what we've always tried to achieve."

In 1987, John Akers, IBM's chief executive, invited customers to attend the company's strategic planning conference for the first time. Over two days, the customers told IBM that the company had to do a better job of sharing its plans, that it had to do everything faster, and that it had to be more consistent. Osterwise says, "That woke us up."

Joji Arai, the Japanese productivity expert, says American businessmen have been waking up over the last few years because "they have seen the erosion of their marketplace, they have seen the erosion of their technological superiority in some fields, they have seen the decline or slowdown in the level of compensation to their own people, [and] they have seen the possibility of future Americans not being able to pursue the good old 'American dream.' They know that they're responsible for their society. After all, the economy is made up of business activities." Because of that "waking up," Arai is optimistic about America's future. He says some Japanese who visit the United States take too narrow a view and focus on technology. "I'm afraid," he says, "that many Japanese get the wrong impression as to the dynamism of American society; they don't see the excellent part of the United States, the big potential that this country has."

But that big potential remains essentially that — potential. "I did a study for Motorola back in 1980," Daniel Yankelovich says, "where the business leadership regarded the problem of the threat to competitiveness as the most serious, most urgent problem they had seen in the past twenty years. That was more than a decade ago, and its urgency has grown, and its seriousness has grown." Yankelovich believes the problem is leadership. "The public," he says, "already knows there's a problem. What is missing is an explanation of why there's a problem and what to do about it." Osterwise seems to agree. "I think that, clearly, most Americans believe that there is a crisis," he says, "[but] they haven't personalized it because they don't understand what they can do to change it. . . . I think we've come a long way, and I think there's a fairly good — understanding is probably not the right word, but awareness that it's a crisis. It's a matter of survival."

Stephen Schwartz, who carries the unwieldy title of IBM senior vice-president of market-driven quality assessment, says that IBM adopted quality with "the clear understanding that this was an issue of survival, that this had to be number one on the hit parade; it was just not one of a number of things, or it wasn't a 'Gee, of course, we're interested in customer satisfaction and quality, but where is this week's profit coming from' kind of thing. It had to be numero uno in what they did." Tim Leuliette of the Siemens management board says the Newport News plant that makes fuel injectors was all but closed when a team that wanted to keep it open started from scratch and designed a globally competitive product and a quality process to produce it. It worked, Leuliette says, "but that was driven by the survival instinct."

Survival, therefore, is a matter of leadership, and it is developing in private industry. Roger Milliken, chairman of Milliken & Company, told a Baldrige Award audience, "I think the worst words in the industrial lexicon are managers and managing. The words should be leading, leaders, and coaching." Tom Mallone, Milliken's president, told a company group, "Our job as leader is to create the environment that gives our people the opportunity to contribute to the maximum extent they're capable of, and for us to thank them, make them heroes for doing so, and let them have a lot of fun in the process." The consultant Louis Schultz says, "Leadership today, which is probably a better word than managing — leadership means pulling the whole organization together. It does not mean abdication of responsibility to lead. We cannot have anarchy. Leaders must lead, but by leading, they get all the inputs of all the people. They get them focused and moving in the same direction of their own accord. People want to do what's right; people want to do a good job; they want to be proud of themselves, their organizations, and their work. But they have to be in the right environment created by leadership that will enable them to do that."

Joseph Juran says that a person doing a dull job on an assembly line will do what is required, but no more. The same worker in, say, a softball game will use much more energy. "It's more taxing, and he may get exhausted," Juran says. "But he does it because now he's with people that he himself has chosen to work with, he's not having to take orders from a boss he had no voice in choosing, and there's an element of volunteerism and freedom that is not present in the working place, but that doesn't have to stay that way. . . . One of the main things about getting workers enthusiastic is to give them interesting work that will stimulate them." Juran's observation of the industrial worker applies equally well to others. "Studies have shown," says Carolyn Burstein, a government official, "that up to 40 to 50 percent of white-collar professional work is at the discretion of the individual." The worker can do more or less; only he or she can decide which it will be. A worker can be led to do more, but cannot be bullied into it.

Osterwise at IBM says that the idea is to excite creativity, sharing with employees the concepts, techniques, and tools they need. "I think, if anything," he says, "one of our competitive advantages [in the United States] is our people's ingenuity and innovative spirit, and we've got to find out how to most effectively foster that." That can be done better by leaders than by managers. "It's fairly clear," he says, "and should have been obvious to everyone, that people would rather be led than managed and empowered as opposed to controlled." Osterwise says empowerment "starts with the authority, the responsibility, then the accountability. It causes people to be more thoughtful when they really get that authority and responsibility and more dedicated and committed." But that requires extensive training, since to give people power without the skills to use it, Osterwise says, "will, in my opinion anyway, lead to anarchy and disaster." Osterwise says IBM has suffered some "false starts" from employee empowerment, "but the experience is that those are probably not as serious as not having the empowerment and, thereby, having a reticence to act."

If employees cannot act, or are afraid to act to satisfy the customer, nothing management does later to try to make up for it is likely to satisfy. "All of the communications and human resource programs in our company," Smith says, "in fact, all of the training and the reward systems, the technology and the measurement systems . . . have everything to do with empowering our employees. There's no simple answer to how do you empower people. No one-stop-shopping or one-size-fits-all program I can suggest to you. And yet this question is central, we believe, to the quality issue in any organization. And it is absolutely critical in the service industry." Having power will be a new role for lower-level employees, but as they do more of what used to be management, managers at all levels will also have new roles.

Rosabeth Moss Kanter of Harvard says, "The CEO and senior

management have to do two things. . . . First of all, they have to be strategists, not just in the old-fashioned sense of analyzing the business and analyzing the industry, they have to be very visionary imaginers of a new corporate future. . . . they have to anticipate tomorrow's competition, and more than that, they have to create markets or imagine a better future. . . . So the quality of the thought process and the imagining of top managers is much more important than it ever was. . . . The second essential task of top managers . . . is to be like middle managers, the coaches and facilitators of the actions other people take. The new CEO . . . spends more and more of his time directly thinking about people matters and the corporate culture, and that's a change, that's a new role. They have to be the cheerleaders and the champions of all the action that's going on lower in the organization. After they've imagined the vision, they have to be the communicators and the marketers of the vision."

The traditional American management system includes none of that. It is authoritarian, and Marvin Cetron, who wrote *American Renaissance,* says, "The authoritarian management — do this, do this, do this — that's for the birds. It doesn't work, and everybody knows it doesn't work." The system Kanter suggests above he calls "consultive management." His firm, Forecasting International, did a study in 1983 of what types of firms were failing and found that "the largest number of firms going out of business were the authoritarian, the second were participative — everybody's called together and everybody discusses what they want to do; the workers and the managers, everybody — then they do it, then they go out of business. . . . But the most important one that works is called consultive . . . bringing people in, getting their views, making sure we modify things to get people involved. . . . but you, the boss, make up your own mind. That's consultive management, that's the best." It may be the best management, but it is not, in the United States, the accepted management. It is not what is taught.

Michael Maccoby, the psychiatrist and business consultant, says, "One of the difficulties of learning what Dr. Deming is talking about is the fact that people have to unlearn so much that they've been taught that really isn't true." William Scherkenbach, the statistician at GM, agrees: "We've been carefully taught a lot of things that just aren't so." Which means that the way most of today's corporate leaders made it to the top, what they were taught, has to change. Reich, the political economist, says the necessary change can be threatening to all levels. "If you're at the top of the old pyramid," he says, "you got to where you were because you were very good at doing the old kind of work — you were good at controlling, you were good at being the font of all wisdom and daring, you were good at strategizing in terms of high volume, you were good at thinking of change as a more or less linear process in which you could predict the course of change. If you were in the middle, you were good at controlling people below you and making sure that everybody did their job. And if you were at the bottom, you were good, basically, at doing the same thing over and over and over."

There is a fourth group that may face potentially threatening change — the stockholders. A question that was first debated more than sixty years ago is coming up again: Who owns the company; who should benefit first from its success?

Milliken says, "Business has an obligation to its customers, and to its suppliers, to its community. As somebody who visited us from somewhere in the world said, 'CEO stands for customers first, the employees second, and if that's done well, the owners will come out all right.' " IBM has a similar idea; Osterwise talks about the "five ups" that concern Akers at corporate headquarters, five things he specifically wants to go up: customer satisfaction, quality, people (employee morale and participation), market share and revenue, and, finally, profit. "By the way," Osterwise says, "if you get the first three, the fourth and fifth naturally follow. . . . If you dramatically reduce your cycle times, if you eliminate your defects, if you focus on customer satisfaction, volume will, in and of itself, take over. That's not to say that . . . one of your major measures is still not revenue, profit, and market share. Indeed, they are. They're just not *the* measure."

Kenichi Ohmae, the Japanese consultant, understands the need for a corporation to make a profit, but he is also concerned with society's need to share in that profit. "American corporations today have lost their own raison d'être, and the reason I say this is that a corporation is the only unit in society creating wealth. Bureaucrats and other institutions consume wealth, but they do not create wealth. Corporations create wealth. They create services and products. They create employment. As such, corporations should not belong only to the capitalists, those who have equity and capital. Corporations should be social entities serving the critical role of producing wealth, jobs, and security in society, and protecting vendors, distributors, people who are dependent on that corporation. They should worry about the entire group of people who are making the corporation successful.

"Now," Ohmae continues, "the American theory is not that. The American theory is that this [company] belongs to the stockholders, and, therefore, if the stockholders decided to throw this part of the business to that other company and share the profits, it's okay. What about the employees? What about the subcontractors? What about all those poor people? What about the municipalities that are expecting this company to continue? You see, I think you have to go back to this definition of 'What do you mean by a corporation in America?' Unless you go back to the original definition of a corporation, not the capitalist's definition, you will continue to have a problem. Corporations have a social responsibility."

Yankelovich says he remembers a time when corporate chairmen talked about the need to balance the different interests of the various groups to whom the corporations were responsible — shareholders, employees, the community, suppliers, customers.

"In the 1980s," he says, "we moved away from that concept of corporate responsibility to the concept of corporate responsibility to the shareholder, and the shareholder suddenly became number one, and everybody else kind of fell to the bottom of the heap." The shareholder was not even an individual, not the widow that people imagined, totally dependent on her dividends to survive. "Seventy percent of the American stocks are held by financial institutions," Ohmae says, "and these financial institutions are basically fund managers and, as such, the owners of American corporations have become almost blind fund managers, and these corporations have become only numbers on the screen." Yankelovich says, "It is maybe Wall Street's biggest mistake to push this idea that the main and only responsibility of the corporation is to its technical owners, the shareholders. That just doesn't wash. It won't wash politically, much less in the 1990s than in the 1980s."

Arai says investors who are smart enough to take a longer view should be as interested in quality methods as workers and managers. "Even the investors have to look at their interests from both short-term and long-term perspectives," he says. "If all the companies you bet your money on keep going down the drain, you have to keep switching your investment decisions. Ultimately, you discover that the chance of your making money is fifty-fifty, while if you employ the long-term perspective in making investments, you can always bet on, say, 10 percent or 15 percent growth if management is pursuing the new [quality] principles of business. . . . Long-term investment may turn out to be more beneficial on the part of the investors." It's the same thing Osterwise means when he says, "I think there are at least three stakeholders that I can think of right off. The employee is one of them. The community is another one, and the stockholders deserve a *real* return on these investments."

If long-term investment is a better idea, so is long-term employment. In the United States, in companies where there are no

161

union contracts, the theory of employment at will has generally been the law; that is, the boss hires you when he wants, so he fires you when he wants. (That has been challenged successfully in court in several states since the 1970s, but those legal challenges are a separate issue.) In quality companies, employment at will is a thoroughly discredited theory, having given way to job security. If, as the experts generally agree, your employees' brainpower is the only asset you have that another company can't duplicate, then firing or laying off employees that you have trained and educated — throwing away your best assets — borders on criminal stupidity. As we've already said, Motorola does not guarantee lifetime employment, but after ten years, only the chairman of the board can fire you. IBM's Osterwise says as far as he is concerned, the proper attitude is, "Let me tell you, folks, if we figure out how to reduce the defects, shorten the cycle time, and have higher customer satisfaction, you don't really need to worry about your job." At Federal Express, workers are protected by a Guaranteed Fair Treatment program that, Smith says, "has been viewed by many legal scholars as among the best in American industry." Job security, however, comes at a price, and the price is quality. "I think there aren't many people in industry today," Osterwise says, "or in IBM as a subunit of industry, that believe that if you don't continue to improve, that you are going to survive. So they may think that we have a full employment practice and history at IBM, but they don't believe that that's any God-granted right."

The importance of job security, according to Osterwise, is that "it does provide people with a feeling that they can act without fear." That is critical to another part of corporate leadership — encouraging your employees to take risks. Kanter says that quality companies "have an attitude that permits experimentation, sometimes that's connected to a continuous improvement philosophy, but they encourage a multiplicity of experiments, constantly pushing the frontier throughout the company, and they're much more open to the idea of change, they have much more flexible structures in which they're not rigidly bound by what's my territory versus what's your territory."

George Fisher, who is leading Motorola to Six Sigma quality, says, "There is no doubt that you had better encourage a culture which allows people to make some pretty big mistakes, otherwise, you won't get very big gains." In trying to reduce defects to 3.4 per million while staying ahead in a high technology industry, Fisher says the company can't play it safe, it has to take chances, even if some turn out badly. "You can't take risks without expecting some failures," he says. "So it's your batting average that counts, not whether you ever strike out." He says mistakes cost money, but not allowing for mistakes would cost even more: "I think a bigger challenge for us is how we develop, first, a creative environment, where people really are encouraged to take risks and try some new ideas. But, perhaps as importantly, a receptive environment, where if you have a good idea, my natural instinct is to build on that as opposed to tear it down. . . . Somehow we have to create on top of this creative culture a knee-jerk response that says, in [George Bernard] Shaw's words, 'Why not?' Rather than why, why not?" (The Shaw quote is from *Back to Methuselah*: "You see things; and you say, 'Why?' But I dream things that never were; and I say, 'Why not?'")

At IBM, Schwartz says, "You want people to move from a mode of, let's say, risk avoidance to a mode of risk management, and you don't 'shoot' people for taking prudent risks. . . . so the first thing is creating an atmosphere where people are not afraid to fail. You also have to let them know that you don't want them to go off half-cocked without giving any thought to what the outcome of a failure would be. . . . but we're seeing people taking prudent risks, and we're getting a lot of pay-back from that. . . . That's the only way we're going to get the change that is required at the pace that is required."

At Federal Express, Smith says, "We've learned that you've got to let people take appropriate risks to serve customers even if that means a mistake or two once in a while. Well-intentioned efforts are just as important, I assure you, as successes. And if you hang your sales or customer support people who try to do something that doesn't quite work out, you'll just get people who won't do anything." Christopher Hart, the Harvard Business School professor turned consultant, says the idea of zero defects is powerful, but not always appropriate. "There are many situations," he says, "where that is absolutely not what you want your people to be thinking about because it will inhibit innovation. It leads to incremental improvement . . . instead of blowing it up, coming in with a totally radical way of doing things." In the United States and Europe, there is still resistance to the idea that totally radical change is needed in the way companies are organized, in the roles that employees at all levels have to play, and in the need for a new and better system of leadership. All of those things are new and therefore threatening. Reich says people find a great deal more comfort in the certainty of the past, explaining, "There is always, when times get tough, the argument, 'But it was so successful twenty years ago when we did it the old way. Why don't we go back to basics?' In the United States, every time there is deep difficulty and great stress, you hear people say, 'Let's go back to basics. It worked well before.' Great success in the past," he says, "is one of the major impediments to change in the future. . . . Remember, we are all the products of our accumulated experience. Most of our experience took place in an older economy that is irrelevant to the future. . . . These changes can be very frightening.

"I think a big portion of leadership," Reich continues, "whether you're talking about political leadership or leadership in the private sector, is helping people face the tasks in front of them and not escape from them, helping them with their fear. With regard to public leadership and the economy, it means not letting people escape into blaming the Japanese, or blaming the Europeans, or blaming welfare mothers, or blaming fat cats at the top. It means focusing on the real problems we have. . . . In the private sector, it means also helping people not escape by simply paying lip service to the aphorisms and bromides of modern management. . . . It means actually getting on with the job."

Deming talks more about leadership than any of the other experts, although they all agree that leadership is critical. Describing a leader, Deming says that "he understands how the work of this group fits into the aims of the company, its constancy of purpose. . . . He tries to create for everybody interest and challenge and joy in work. . . . He teaches them cooperation; he works by cooperation. He tries to optimize the education, skills, and abilities of everyone — helps everyone to improve. He's coach and counsel, not a judge. Judging people doesn't help them." Deming says there are three sources of power a leader can use: the formal power of his position, the power of his knowledge, and the power of his personality. A successful leader, he says, "develops knowledge and personality" so that people come to him for help and advice. He uses the formal power of position sparingly and only because "this source of power enables him to change the system, equipment, material, methods, to reduce variation in output." Formal power, therefore, is used only to order fundamental changes.

"One of the important questions for leadership," Maccoby says, "is how do you make it so people want to follow you. It's not enough to be right. A lot of people have been right, and nobody followed them. People have been right and gone to the Inquisition. . . . A leader has to create a relationship with the followers where they believe he's working for their common good, even though they don't like some of the things he does." Maccoby tells the story of George Washington dealing with rebellious American officers after the Revolutionary War. Angry that they hadn't been paid while civilians were making money in currency speculation, the officers wanted to take over the young American government. " 'The whole world is watching us,' " Maccoby quotes Washington. " 'The whole world believes we're going to end up another little military dictatorship. Nobody believes in the perfectibility of man, and this whole experiment, gentlemen, is in your hands right now.' They had such faith in him and respect for him, and he touched their deepest values. He made them see they could create something great, [but] only if they could put aside the immediate goals and work for the common good. That's a leader."

Maccoby says President Franklin Roosevelt did the same thing and gave the American people a positive vision, something they could believe in, when he said during the Great Depression, "The only thing we have to fear is fear itself." Maccoby says, "The leader has to be honest about the situation. . . . but he's got to give them a vision of what's possible if they work together." When a leader successfully does that in the private sector and one or more companies begin to work on quality improvement, those programs can have unplanned benefits in the public sector. In Michigan, a lot of UAW members and salaried auto company employees have learned Deming's quality method at Ford and GM, and they are beginning to ask why public schools cannot adopt the same method. They can. A quality program is under way at Mount Edgecumbe High School in Sitka, Alaska (see Chapter 10).

Jim Martin, who helped interest Mount Edgecumbe in the Deming quality method, was working with a Community Quality Coalition (CQC) in Phoenix, Arizona. Coalition councils are now at work in five states and about fifty communities. Founded by Myron Tribus, the CQC brings together large and small business executives, educators, and labor and local government officers to talk about quality. The idea is to improve community life by protecting or creating jobs, improving management skills, and training or retraining the work force. Typically, the CQC offers a training course in total quality and statistical methods through a community college. It has had a number of successes. In Meadville, Pennsylvania, it brought together five tool-and-die shops to revive a shaky industry, and in Erie, Pennsylvania, the council helped police cut the response time to emergency calls by 75 percent and also saved the county $300,000 in prison funds. But that's not what Tribus remembers about the city. "When you land at the airport," he says, "and you get into a taxi and tell the driver, 'I want to go to such-and-such hotel,' the driver will call his dispatcher, who will call the hotel and tell them you're on the way and verify your reservation. . . . The people in Erie want you to know that this is a friendly town. Now, that gets beyond just issues of business. . . . It creates a better life, and that's part of the quality movement, and it's spreading into these other areas." In Palm Beach County, Florida, Richard Miller, who helped start the local council, says, "I think it [quality] is the only hope for this country." The CQC councils are private, community-funded organizations, not government agencies.

In the United States, business leaders, and to a considerable degree the public as well, tend to neither trust nor respect parts of the federal government. Phil Crosby, one of the quality experts, tells a class of businessmen, "The difference between the public sector and the private sector is that someone is in charge of the private sector." He gets a big laugh. A study of the growth of the American government pointed out that "bureaucratic regulation places power in the hands of appointed rather than elected officials. Since the civil servant is not accountable to his charges, he is no more concerned for their welfare than a slaveowner, that is, to see that they are productive of revenue." The distrust is not just of bureaucrats but of elected officials as well. A consultant said, "The Congress is not required to be economically literate. It's an accident when some are." Certainly, Congress has not demonstrated any desire to lead the country toward solving the quality and productivity problem. John Chancellor, a television journalist and commentator, wrote, "The only clear message the Congress has sent to the voters is that its members place the highest priority on getting reelected. Nothing else seems to matter."

Even when attempts are made by some government agency to

improve quality for the American public, they often seem to make things worse. The easiest example, the one Deming uses often, is the Department of Transportation's well-publicized, well-intentioned attempt to improve the on-time performance of America's airlines. Each month the agency publishes the statistics for on-time arrivals in the preceding month. As Deming points out, that is the same as driving by looking in the rearview mirror: it tells you what happened last month, but not what's going to happen this month. Soon after the monthly list began to appear, air travelers noticed that more planes seemed to be arriving early. The airlines, as anyone could have predicted, had simply rewritten their schedules to include more time for each flight, thus reducing the number of late arrivals but guaranteeing that there would be even fewer *on-time* arrivals. Fewer flights would arrive late, but a great many more would arrive early. What should have been done, Deming says, would have been for the Department of Transportation to get airline executives and employees, government officials, and airport authority members together to analyze the problem. Of course, at that point the Department of Justice might have raided the meeting and accused the airline executives of anticompetitive collusion. The various federal agencies do not have a coordinated quality improvement policy.

There is, however, a U.S. Federal Quality Institute, a government agency with thirty people that grew out of an Executive Order in the mid-'80s to find ways to improve productivity. According to Burstein, an executive with the agency, the order "focused on efficiency and saving money, because we were looking for the first time at huge [federal] budget deficits." She says that after a year of dealing with private companies that were working on the same problem, "we found out that productivity is a by-product, a result of quality improvement. We gradually evolved by late '87, early '88, into a quality improvement effort." The institute was established in the summer of 1988. Burstein says there already have been some successes, especially at the Internal

Revenue Service (IRS). It sent representatives to the Juran Institute and eventually trained 10,000 of its 130,000 employees in Juran's methods. They trained or are training the others, and improvements are gradually being made. In one section that handles billions of dollars, errors were cut in half; the IRS is trying to eliminate errors totally.

The institute has learned from private industry that inspectors do not mean accuracy. "In a bureaucracy, in a white-collar environment," Burstein says, "we had all kinds of layers of supervisors and managers that really were, you might say, glorified inspectors." They cause the same problems in government that they do in industry. Schultz, the consultant, spent some years in the federal government, and he says that to send a letter outside your own agency typically takes the approval of three to eight managers. Each one, of course, wants at least one change — otherwise, how could each demonstrate his or her own worth — and those changes guarantee from 300 to 800 percent rework on every single letter. "I think the first thing to realize," Schultz says, "is that government people are no different than the rest of us [but] they are working within a system that makes it very difficult to achieve pride and satisfaction in their work. . . . there are tremendous systems problems in government that have to be changed."

The efforts being made to change those systems and improve quality in government are not obvious to the American public. One man, told that the Federal Quality Institute existed, said, "I didn't know the words *quality* and *federal government* even went together." In the past they often did not, and not all agencies of the government are working on quality programs yet. Burstein says, "Most of the [federal] agencies are just at the very beginning stages; some are not even at the awareness stage. . . . Those that have begun to implement [quality programs] are taking the very first steps. . . . Give us a couple of more years, certainly ten years, and we'll see whether or not this whole movement really took in the Federal Government, or whether it was just a fad." Burstein seems optimistic. She headed a task force of fifteen government officials who studied the major American corporations that had made themselves quality companies. "We learned how these companies were able to change huge bureaucracies," she says, "because every one of the companies. . . . is similar to the federal government in structure. Ford is a huge bureaucracy. IBM is a huge bureaucracy. . . . We were eager to find out how large, complex bureaucracies were able to change. We figured that if they can do it, so can we."

Burstein is lavish in her praise for the major American corporations that have helped the Federal Quality Institute. "We have gotten a lot of assistance, and they have been models. . . . From their standpoint, they are so thrilled that people in the federal government are interested in improving the quality of service to them, because they're taxpayers, too."

Companies and government agencies working together on quality may help to change the traditional relationship. There has been as much of an adversarial or, at best, a standoffish relationship between the U.S. government and American business as there has been between management and labor. Manford McNeil, the founder of Romac Industries in Seattle, asked if he ever had any help from the federal government in expanding overseas, says, "I'm not sure who Washington, D.C., is. I wouldn't know which door to knock on back there. We've pretty much done it on our own [but] I don't think they've harmed us."

On the other hand, Stewart Dahlberg, a vice-president of Bee Hat in St. Louis, credits his company's success in exporting to a Commerce Department seminar. Bee Hat now sells to sixteen countries, and exports account for 12 percent of its sales. (They used to be only 1 percent.) Dahlberg is quoted as saying, "It's simple really. Anyone who has a quality product can start exporting tomorrow from their basement." He found overseas customers on a Commerce Department list of foreign companies looking for American products. (Commerce sells the list for twenty-five cents per name.)

Pat Choate, the political economist whose knowledge of Washington is formidable, says, "A major problem that we have in this country is the disaffection and the disengagement between our business leaders and our government leaders." He says no more than a quarter of America's top business leaders spend any time in Washington trying to shape public policy, trying to get the federal government to help solve social and economic problems. "In Europe and in Japan," he says, "half to three quarters of the time of the top people in the corporations goes to work with government and shape the environment in which they operate."

Finally, the United States, except for a relatively brief period during the Persian Gulf crisis, seems almost to be adrift. It does not have an economic goal — except to borrow enough to stay afloat — but the country's major economic competitors do. The twelve nations of the European Community are moving purposefully toward economic unification, potentially increasing their competitive ability by early 1993. Japan is already moving toward economic leadership in the next century. "The Japanese really are concerned about national objectives," Striner says, "and doing what has to be done to achieve national objectives. It's a form, if you will, of real economic warfare. . . . Japan does indeed have a very strong sense of their destiny as a country. Their value system is one where there is a very high priority placed on the objective of Japan being Japan. The United States doesn't quite have that." If the United States is going to get that sense of purpose, it will take leadership, and leadership from the private sector may be more important than from the public sector. Juran says, "The amount of help the government can give is probably limited in any case. And up to now, we really haven't had that much."

Kees van Ham, of the European quality foundation, says, "I think, generally speaking, the government has a supporting role. It's not up to government to take the initiative. They can't, because they are not in a competitive environment, so they are most probably not learning as rapidly as industry is about the evolution of the quality concepts and what's happening in other parts of the world. . . . so my experience is that only initiatives which are led by industry, which are led by senior managers of industry, are about to be successful." Van Ham says governments do have an influence on and a responsibility for education and infrastructure, "so the role of government is more in facilitating . . . than in taking the initiative. The major reason being that companies are more under threat, are more forced by their competitors and customers to move, and they can explain to government why quality has to become the new value for society."

Yankelovich believes it is then government's role to explain that to the people, involving them to change national priorities just as employees are being involved at major companies to change corporate cultures. He believes that explanation should come directly from the president of the United States and that both the reasons for the decline and the steps necessary for a recovery must be credible. "I think the national interest of the United States in economic terms," he says, "is to make sure that the American standard of living is rising rather than falling. That's because, not only does our economic health depend on that, but our social stability and our political health. . . . I don't think that in the United States we have had a clear vision, and I *know* we haven't had a strategy for achieving it. . . . Every corporation in America that's successful has a vision, and a strategy, and objectives to achieve it. That's not [industrial] planning in the sense of picking winners and losers. It is having a sensible national policy [on economics] in the same way that a country has a policy with regard to its national security. We do not have a policy with regard to our economic security and well-being, and we have to have one."

Yankelovich believes the United States has knowledgeable leaders in industry who could become national leaders, but not quite yet. "I think you have a very good cadre of potential leaders in the business community," he says. "You have institutions like the Business Roundtable and the Business Higher Education Forum — business leadership groups who are very concerned with this issue [of quality]. The missing piece for them is that they don't have a clear understanding of how to build public consensus." Political leaders know how to build consensus but don't seem aware that quality is the answer to America's economic and social crisis. That creates a conundrum for the United States: the people with a national voice don't have the answer, and the people with the answer don't have a national voice.

Fortunately, that situation may be changing.

8

The Baldrige Award

Laurence Osterwise is a suit-and-tie man who looks like what he is, a rising IBM executive. He routinely puts in a long day at the office, then goes home for "a couple of hours with the kids, make sure everybody's homework is done." There's more office paperwork, then at eleven o'clock "the lights go out and whatnot." In the fall of 1989, "whatnot" for four straight nights was wandering out to the back porch, climbing into the hot tub, looking up at the stars, and asking himself, "Is there a greater meaning to all of this? I mean, what is the deal here?" It is not the sort of question you expect from a successful executive on his way up until you learn that he'd just been kicked right in his corporate beliefs, and it hurt. IBM is a proud, hard-driving corporation, jealous of its reputation and perceived as a well-run, high-quality company. Osterwise had been told, in effect, that all of those things might be true, but they weren't true enough.

The IBM computer division at Rochester, Minnesota, which Osterwise heads, had been a finalist for the 1989 Malcolm Baldrige National Quality Award. It lost. "When Curt Reimann [the Baldrige director] called me and told me we hadn't won," Osterwise remembers, "he said that it was a painful call for him. I said, 'Hah! You should be on this end of the call!' This was a tremendously painful, devastating occurrence. We thought we had a good organization. We didn't win, and when the Baldrige ex-

174

aminers told me point-blank that part of the reason was 'a lack of consistent focused leadership,' I said, 'Well, I mean, is this really important to me or isn't it?' I don't mean the winning, but being a high-quality organization focused on total customer satisfaction."

After four nights of talking to himself in the hot tub, he came up with his answer: "I don't know where the word came down from, but I said, 'The greater meaning in all of this is, we've got to learn.' We had learned a lot. So let's apply the learning, and if we get good enough to win, that's great. If not, we'll learn some more, and we'll continue to get better. So I said, 'Well, okay, that's what I'm going to go back and tell the team.' I came into my staff meeting a week later with a new set of priorities for the rest of my life. It started with total customer satisfaction and quality improvement." Also, he says, people had told him "point-blank that I wasn't as committed as I should be, and I wasn't walkin' like I was talkin'. And I said, 'Okay, I can take that. I'm a big boy.' "

The question was, having been hurt once, should IBM at Rochester set itself up to be hurt again. Osterwise didn't mind going through the self-assessment required by the Baldrige Award examiners, even though it's a lot of work. He had a different concern: "What impact would it have on our morale if we went after this Holy Grail again and didn't win? What would it tell us about ourselves? It was somewhat of a personal decision. I said, 'Well, that's not going to matter. We will only get our maximum learning out of doing it for real, so we're going to do it for real.' "

Which is exactly what the Baldrige Award was designed to do: encourage American companies to improve themselves and continue to improve themselves.

The award program was established by the Congress as "The Malcolm Baldrige National Quality Improvement Act of 1987 (public law 100–107)," and is run by the National Institute of Standards and Technology, an agency of the Commerce Department. A joint public-private program, it's administered by the government (through an outside contractor), financed by private business and industry, and run as a partnership. Stephen Schwartz of IBM likes that cooperation. "A partnership approach," he says, "between [the United States] government and companies is very important. Adversarial relationships are not very productive for anyone. They're not productive for the country, they're not productive for the government, and they're certainly not productive for the companies. So a partnership relationship between industry and government is terribly important."

The 230 examiners, senior examiners, and judges — collectively known as the Board of Examiners — who recommend the winners to Reimann and the commerce secretary, are from "industry, professional and trade associations, universities, health care organizations, and government agencies." The Baldrige is the highest quality prize in the United States, and it is normally presented to as many as six winners in the late fall by the president.

The award is named for Malcolm Baldrige, a popular secretary of commerce who died in a rodeo accident in 1987. The prize itself, made by Steuben Glass, is a fourteen-inch crystal stele with an 18-karat gold-plated medal embedded in the top central part. On one side of the medal is the presidential seal; on the other are the inscriptions "Malcolm Baldrige National Quality Award" and "The Quest for Excellence." It's a handsome piece, but no one would go through the difficulty and expense of the self-appraisal and examination just to win it; it isn't *that* handsome. The entry fee for a large company is $3,000, which would buy a nice decorative piece if that's all it wanted. The real prize, as Osterwise realized, is a process, a way of continually improving the company's ability to deliver quality goods and services. Even the companies that don't win the award get a thorough review from the examiners. Wayne Cassett, who works with Reimann, says, "In that sense, there are no losers because [each applicant] gets assessments from some of the most qualified people in the field."

The companies are judged in seven categories, but the categories are not equal. In recognition of the more or less accepted definition of quality as being whatever the customer says it is, Customer Satisfaction (Category 7) is worth five times as many points as Strategic Quality Planning (Category 3). Overall, there are a total of 1,000 points: Leadership (100), Information and Analysis (70), Strategic Quality Planning (60), Human Resource Utilization (150), Quality Assurance (140), Quality Results (180), and the big one, Customer Satisfaction (300). The seven categories have thirty-two subcategories, all of which are outlined in a forty-one-page guidebook for applicants in 1991. There is also some easily understandable advice, such as this opening sentence from the paragraph on employees: "Meeting the company's quality objectives requires a fully committed, well-trained work force that is encouraged to participate in the company's continuous improvement activities."

The Baldrige Award is not a how-to book, telling companies how to get quality in their businesses. Brian Joiner, the quality consultant and a Baldrige judge, says, "The award does not tell you what to do. It helps you to assess how well you're doing. . . . The Baldrige Award is more like a yardstick. It helps you to see where your deficiencies are."

More American companies are getting interested in the Baldrige Award, which Motorola's Robert Galvin predicted. "What is likely to happen," he says, "is that the Baldrige Award is going to become popular, meaning substantially supported. Tens and tens of thousands of companies are coming out of the woodwork now, demonstrating their interest. The leadership companies, role-model companies, are all beginning to take a very serious interest in it."

By April 1991, about 150,000 companies had written to the Baldrige office for an application form, and Reimann expects the number will reach 250,000 by the end of the application period. Additionally, companies may copy the application for its own divisions or for another company, so the number of companies that request applications is fewer than the number that actually have them. However, nowhere near that many companies will apply, nor does Reimann expect them to — yet. "Increasingly, we hear that companies plan to apply perhaps five years from now," he says. "They understand that this is something that is very, very difficult to do in a short period of time. We also see companies apply for the Baldrige Award in order to get feedback from our Board of Examiners. That's a very different kind of thing than the competition."

The requirements are deliberately complex; the self-examination that has to be filed as a first step is detailed and demanding, and the examiners are experts who do not believe their job is to make you feel better. Joiner says the application is an "extremely useful way for companies to do self-examination . . . a different lens than they've been historically using to examine how they're managing their businesses. . . . to find weaknesses in their approaches to management. . . . It helps top management ask itself the right quality questions: Are its leaders really focusing on quality? Are they really understanding quality? Are they really managing in a quality way? Are they really getting the best from their people? Are they really working with their people well? Are they really finding out what barriers there are to people being able to do a good job? It is very helpful in thinking about what is it that you want to look for in an organization that's trying to be effective in terms of quality."

The executives filling out the application do not necessarily see it that way, especially not at first. Osterwise remembers his group reading the application in 1988, realizing that there were some questions about things that IBM didn't even do and resenting the questions. "You don't know the right questions to ask," Osterwise remembers thinking of the Baldrige application. "And who are we? We're the gurus from the Midwest. At any rate, it took us a little while to get over that and say, 'These aren't bad questions.'" IBM, Rochester, filed in 1989 and did well. "We know we were in the final four," Osterwise says. "That's great, except there are only two winners." After the company decided to try again, it began to correct both the problems found through self-examination and the problems the examiners found, which Osterwise describes as "major weaknesses, but not from the score or the competitive viewpoint catastrophic."

IBM in Rochester was one of 97 applicants in 1990, the year that the number of application requests reached 180,000, which was a substantial improvement over 1989, when 65,000 applications were sent out but only 40 companies applied. In the first year, 66 applicants had come from only 12,000 requests. By the next year, the word must have spread that the examination could be rigorous, that the Malcolm Baldrige National Quality Award was not going to be handed out lightly. (Incidentally, it's no easier to get on the Board of Examiners, a volunteer group. This year, 1,332 people volunteered; 230 were selected.)

No matter how many applicants there are, only two awards are given in each of three categories — manufacturing, small business, and service — and if no company is judged worthy of quality standards, no award is given. Federal Express Corporation won the first service award, in 1990. In the three years so far, all six awards for manufacturing have been awarded — Motorola and the Commercial Nuclear Fuel Division of Westinghouse (1988); Milliken & Company and Xerox Business Products and Systems (1989); and Cadillac and IBM, Rochester (1990). There have been only two small business awards — Globe Metallurgical, Inc., of Cleveland (1988) and Wallace Company, Inc., of Houston (1990).

Officially the Baldrige has three aims: to promote quality awareness, to recognize the quality achievements of U.S. businesses, and to publicize successful quality strategies. That is being done among corporations, large and small, but public awareness is lagging. "In fact," C. Jackson Grayson, Jr., of the American Productivity and Quality Center says, "recent surveys by the American

Society for Quality Control show that most Americans still don't know the Baldrige Award exists." Nonetheless, he's an enthusiastic supporter because the award is "a good way to sort of amplify the effect because if you reward the [quality] companies and then say, 'Here are the standards they use,' people will start to say, 'Hey, maybe we can do it, too.' . . . So I'm optimistic because I see the role-modeling taking place at companies that have done it, and done it in the face of tough competition." Joiner sees the award's influence spreading. "The National Quality Award was an idea whose time had come," he says, "and I think it has really helped to develop the national attention on quality. Companies taking full-page ads in the *Wall Street Journal, USA Today,* the *New York Times,* and so on to advertise that they have achieved this level of excellence in quality. . . . Companies going to visit each other because of quality . . . and how they're going about achieving quality. I think it's a very major plus."

Reimann thinks the biggest winners may be the employees of quality companies: "All of the award winners are presenting . . . information about the changes in leadership, changes in the culture, changes in the investment in employees, evidence that employees are better off — improved safety, lowered absenteeism, lower turnover, all of the manifestations of employee interest in the work and feelings of contribution." He says companies that apply for the Baldrige "are realizing that in order to gain the respect and the contribution of employees, they have to invest in employees. They have to respect their human dignity, and they have to invest in the long-term, in training and education. They have to be sensitive to morale." There are also pluses for executives, Reimann says. "There is now a discourse taking place between senior executives based on the Baldrige Award . . . because senior executives [from different companies], it turns out, listen to each other more than they listen to quality professionals, and I think that's a very, very healthy development."

Almost everyone in the American quality movement approves of the Baldrige Award. Joseph Juran says, "Setting up the National Quality Award . . . has been a really useful thing [for the U.S. government] to do." Armand V. Feigenbaum testified before a House committee that the award "deserves enthusiastic support" as "the visible expression of America's national will to recognize quality leadership in the face of widespread skepticism about our commitment." Feigenbaum, who worked out a system to measure how much it costs *not* to produce quality, has said, "The widespread application of Baldrige standards could add 7 percent to the gross national product [in the United States]." Myron Tribus believes "the creation of the Baldrige prize has been extraordinarily important. I find people that a few years ago were not interested and were difficult to reach have changed their tune. . . . People like the executives at Motorola have made the case very compelling."

The exceptions are Philip B. Crosby and W. Edwards Deming. Crosby says the award has "the unintended result of leading us back to the days when executives felt no personal responsibility for quality and happily delegated it to the quality department." Deming says the Baldrige guidelines are, in fact, "misguided." His concern is that because the Baldrige Award has no quality theory of its own, there is no basis for improvement. One of his favorite comments is "Experience teaches nothing without theory." He is adamantly opposed to any sort of comparative or ranking, he doesn't like setting goals, he is against rewards and recognition to individuals or teams, and he worries that as companies study award-winning companies, they will try to copy without knowing what they are copying. Told that the Baldrige Award "has brought dialogues between people who never talked about quality before," Deming shoots back, "Dialogue is not going to do it. There is no substitute for knowledge, and dialogue is not going to produce knowledge."

Joiner, who teaches the Deming method, has some of the same fears, but he sees a middle ground. "I think they still need to understand a theory of how to achieve quality," he says. "I think that's what Dr. Deming brings to the party. There's a danger that companies will just go and copy one another without understanding; that, of course, won't work. But seeing what other people are doing and understanding it with the aid of theory is a very powerful force to help move the country forward." Reimann says, "I think the first stages of benchmarking or comparison may very well be looking for and at things that can be copied. But I believe that the successful companies take it back, and there is a great deal of theory and discussion. I don't believe that theory need precede benchmarking; I think that benchmarking can drive interest in theory." If so, that may satisfy Deming's main objection, but it hasn't yet. Deming says that sharing knowledge does not create knowledge. "These guidelines," he says, "are an attempt to substitute wishful thinking for knowledge." Crosby feels the guidelines try to substitute "techniques" for commitment. "Quality is a culture," he says, "a way of life deliberately selected and constructed, not a set of procedures."

One effect of the Baldrige Award has been increased benchmarking, getting competitors to talk to one another and share information about achieving quality — not the traditional approach in American business and industry. There is a new openness with customers, suppliers, and companies that aren't direct competitors. That pleases Reimann and concerns Deming. He remembers how American industry copied quality circles from Japan in the early 1980s, then watched them fail because management hadn't been trained and didn't understand that they actually had to respond to the suggestions from quality circle workers.

It is ironic that Deming is dubious about the Baldrige Award since it was prompted by the Deming Prize, Japan's highest industrial award and the focus of Japanese productivity improvement since 1951. Unlike the Baldrige Award, however, the Deming Prize requires each company to meet a set of precise requirements with the help of consultants from the Union of Japanese Scientists and Engineers. The prize committee recognizes only one road to quality. Reimann says the Baldrige guide-lines "do not require a company to implement a particular set of rules or systems, because the observations are that there are many paths to carry out the same aims."

As a sidelight and another bit of irony, Florida Power and Light won the Deming Prize in 1989, the first American winner in the award's history. The Florida utilities board refused to let the company pass on the cost of the Japanese quality consultants to the utility's consumers, the ultimate beneficiaries of the quality improvement program. The *Wall Street Journal* told the company's publicity department that winning the prize, which is televised nationally in Japan, was not a news story. Neither, apparently, is the Baldrige Award. The paper's coverage so far seems to con-centrate on the cost of applying.

Applying for the award forces companies to consider how best to get information about their customers' current and future needs, and, as Reimann says, "Quality systems are about customer satisfaction." We've said it before and may again, but it's critical: unless you know what the customer needs, you can't produce quality. Reimann hopes the award will create a national forum in which everyone will discuss what goes into a successful quality system. He is not married to the Baldrige Award's categories and subcategories. "This is, in part," he says, "an experimental pro-gram. We're trying to identify those factors in leadership and the factors in the management of human resources which most effec-tively produce customer satisfaction." Joiner would like to see one new criterion that would force companies to reveal what they do differently, if anything, on the last day of the month, or the quarter, or the year. That's when companies routinely do out-rageous, often destructive, things in order to meet company quotas or profit goals (see Chapter 2).

Reimann also sees a potential danger. "I personally believe," he says, "the criteria could be misused by seeing them as a shorthand check list, not realizing the tremendous thought that has to be put behind every element and the long investment that the leadership of the company has to make. . . . I think competing for the Baldrige Award should be undertaken with great care by a company. It should be a culmination of its commitment to quality, and it should seek to learn from the process and take very seriously the commitment it then makes if it does win the award to help and cooperate with other organizations around the United States."

Schwartz says there can be a trap in applying for the Baldrige: "If the primary reason you're going after it is to win the award rather than to change your business, that could be a danger because your eye is on the wrong ball. If the quest for the award is part of a process of changing your business for the better, then I don't think there really are that many dangers. I think it's a wonderful tool. But if the only thing you're focused on is the award and you don't make the fundamental changes in your business, then I don't think the time will be well spent. And, by the way, you'll never win the award because it is a tough taskmaster when it comes to inspecting how you're doing."

Galvin of Motorola is willing, even eager, to help companies that are serious about improving their quality. "In fact," he says, "it is our obligation, having won the Baldrige Award, to open ourselves to inquiry and to offer our thoughts. That, therefore, puts us face to face with leadership people all over America." George Fisher, Motorola's current chief executive and the chairman of the U.S. Council on Competitiveness, says Motorola's people "can be justifiably proud, and they find themselves sometimes used as the benchmark in the world," and that is flattering. "The down side of all that winning awards and the nice recognition that we get for it can create complacency. And I think it's very important for us to realize that we've only really just begun what is a continual process. . . . our fundamental objective, and we state it on little cards that we hand out to everybody, is total customer satisfaction. . . . Our people understand that you never get there. You have to continue to work."

There has been a developing corollary to the Baldrige Award: business schools are beginning to pay attention. "They understand that there is something there that they don't understand," Reimann says. "In the last year, I've had interactions with as many as thirty or forty of the business schools. In the first months of the program, none. . . . It is now routine to hear from business schools, [and] there have been regular forums." Xerox sponsored a forum for business schools in 1989 and '90, and it will continue under Procter & Gamble's sponsorship. "These forums," Reimann says, "are bringing people together from business schools to look at what quality is, what needs to be done to improve curricula, what research needs to flow from it, and so on. These are very, very important developments in quality in the United States."

Christopher Hart, when he taught at Harvard, told a House committee, "The Malcolm Baldrige methodology makes it clear that it [quality] is everybody's game, and it brings structure to an area in which there has so far been a lot of confusion." Hart also suggested another, more important benefit from the Baldrige Award. "I believe that Japan's Deming Prize may have been the major driving force behind the current 'quality dominance' of Japanese products. The prize is not only prestigious — it is also a practical tool. . . . With its excellent design, the Baldrige Award could well have the same galvanizing effect in the United States that the Deming Prize has had in Japan." Josh Hammond, the president of the American Quality Foundation, says, "It's amazing that a simple little gimmick like the Malcolm Baldrige Award, in its simplicity, has managed to get people to do what they should have done."

Reimann says U.S. companies got complacent with their enormous success after World War II and didn't get out of it until the Japanese started moving in with higher quality and lower costs. He says that was what he calls the American "wake-up call," a phrase Deming likes. "In effect," Reimann says, "companies wake up to wholly new ways of doing things." He thinks "the exposure to Japanese companies has given many American companies a wholly new view of how companies can be organized and people motivated. That's been very, very interesting and exciting. . . . to a certain extent, we're seeing those concepts now become more widely known by way of the Baldrige Award. What we're trying to find out from the companies is what they did and how they did it so that strategies can be shared with others."

IBM has taken it one step further. It has rewritten the Baldrige Award application to use IBM's terms and phrases, modified the contents only slightly, and uses it "as an internal international assessment tool." Schwartz says, "We have found it is a wonderful total physical, because it tells you what your problems are, where you have shortcomings, and it is a wonderful way to point out what you need to work on, and then to take a constant review of how you're doing. . . . it's a wonderful tool for just understanding the health of an organization."

Osterwise sums up IBM's effort at Rochester: "What we're doing is enabling, empowering, and exciting creativity . . . giving people the tools and the ideas on which to build and grow. . . . I think you reward [and] recognize individuals or their accomplishments, their innovations, their inventions, their education levels as they seek improvements. And you also recognize teams at all levels. You recognize teams that do superior inventions or focused efforts to improve customer satisfaction in monetary ways . . . or you do it in small ways, in bulletin board pictures of teams, and team luncheons, and things like that appropriate to the contribution and the effort."

Deming says that when individuals are forced to compete, you make it impossible for them to cooperate. Osterwise disagrees: "We recognized a team of seventy people. . . . But we sat down and said, 'Well, okay. What did Nancy do? What did John do?' We concluded that there were three levels of contribution and rewarded the team members accordingly. I think it builds cooperation and makes them competitive, and the two are not necessarily mutually exclusive. I do want to foster individual excellence as well as team excellence."

He says that cooperative competition also applies among executives. "We actually have a fairly large percentage of our variable compensation dependent upon improvement in customer satisfaction," he says. "So it is driving the entire executive team to focus on making each other successful to make the customer satisfied. . . . What we really want to do is bring out the best in the individual and the best in the team. People are driven by different motivations, and I don't think focusing on either the individual or the team is right."

"We call it market-driven quality," Schwartz says, "because we have tied together the fact that we need to do things based on the needs and wants of our customers to excellence in everything we do across the whole business. So it's excellence in how we respond to customers, it's excellence in how we meet their requirements, it's excellence in how we perform all of our duties and work across the whole corporation. Quality is the way you significantly improve your cost and expenses in running a business."

As we've mentioned, "Federal Express," according to Fred Smith, its founder, "was designed from day one to meet customers' expectations. . . . Our philosophy is rather simple: Find out what customers want and give it to them." To make sure everyone understood that, Smith came up with a simple, direct statement of corporate philosophy that helped to win the first Baldrige service award — People, Service, Profit. "Three simple words," Smith says. "Easy to say, probably easy for you to remember. Very hard to do." He attributes part of the company's success to "the leadership theory of one of America's most famous philosophers, Pogo the possum" (the title character of Walt Kelly's popular cartoon strip that began in 1949). "Pogo, you might recall," Smith told a Baldrige Award audience, "suggested that in order to become a great leader, one need only look for a damn big parade and jump in front of it. And that's exactly what we believe happened with Federal Express."

Smith says that by the 1960s "it was clear that increased automation, mechanization, and computerization would require radically different logistics systems." That was the parade he jumped in front of, starting the air express industry in 1973. His company still holds about twice the market of his nearest competitor, but to maintain that dominance required a quality program that understood the importance of people. Federal Express handles 1.5 million shipments a day at 1,650 sites in 127 countries. Its air cargo fleet is the world's largest, and it has 90,000 employees.

Except for an army, no organization in history has ever sent so many people out to deal with strangers. Smith's employees do not necessarily have to charm all those strangers, but they cannot offend them. Smith tells his people that while a manufacturer can recall and perhaps correct a faulty part, Federal Express cannot recall or correct a bad personal encounter. Its employees are trained and given the power to do whatever has to be done to satisfy a customer — a considerable amount of individual authority and pressure. Federal Express is consistently on the list of best U.S. companies to work for.

If there is a single theme that runs through the Baldrige Award winners, it is employee participation. The small business winner in 1990 was Wallace Company, Inc., a family-owned distributor of pipes, valves, and fittings, primarily to the chemical and oil industries. It does most of its business in the Texas-Louisiana Gulf area, but it has international clients as well. The company has 280 employees, called associates, and since 1987, Wallace has spent more than $2 million on formal training programs for them. John W. Wallace, the chief executive, says the training does more than just train. "We personally conduct a lot of the training ourselves," he says. "When you interact with people at a day-long seminar [and] weekend retreats. . . . When you start listening to the suggestions or what your associates have to say . . . when you cease shooting the messenger . . . I think you have accomplished a lot toward driving out the fear within your organization."

Since 1987, the company's market share has almost but not quite doubled, sales volume went up 69 percent, and operating profits through 1989 increased more than seven times. The company cut the number of its suppliers from more than 2,000 to 325, and it has started a quality program to help train them. "We feel like this is one of the most important points of the quality movement," Wallace says, "getting down to the point where you are doing more business with a few superb suppliers." But the key to quality is people. "The only way we were successful," he says, "is that we were able to employ the resources of all 280 associates, and quality became an integral part of our daily operation."

Another point that Baldrige winners usually make is that you have to decide what is most important to work on, then attack the problems in order of importance. But, Osterwise warns, "sometimes top management tends to think those are the only five things that we can work on, and we don't recognize that in our case there are eight thousand people, and they can all work on five. As long as they're mutually supportive, you can work on a lot more things because they don't all work on the same five things I work on."

Schwartz is unusually candid about what prompted the Rochester facility to start a difficult, complex quality program. "It was one of the common motivations that you see with many companies," he says. "It was survival." A product line in 1985 failed, and if Rochester didn't get something out that customers wanted, and quickly, it could well disappear. "They had over 350,000 customers around the world," Schwartz says, "and those customers were wanting to see what the next product was going to be. If Rochester didn't produce one, they were going to lose their customer base to competitors all around the world. In that marketplace, there were over two hundred competitors who were more than willing to go out and take those customers away from IBM and away from Rochester."

Schwartz, who has been at IBM for more than thirty years, says one of the most significant developments "is the emergence of the Japanese computer manufacturers as very tough competitors. . . . there are now competitors in Europe. . . . Instead of a handful of companies in the United States making computers, which is what it was like thirty-four years ago, there are now thousands [of companies] around the world." Some of them, especially in Europe, may begin to get even more competitive for a reason that Schwartz and Wallace and Smith may appreciate. Kees van Ham of the European Foundation for Quality Management, talking about improvements the foundation hopes to make in Europe, says, "We have also started preparing for a European company [quality] award that is comparable to the American Malcolm Baldrige Award or the Japanese Deming Award."

For Osterwise, that threat of increased competition is somewhere down the road. He has one much closer. On a recent trip to Rochester, John Akers, IBM's chief executive, "referred to us," Osterwise says, "as 'the rabbit of IBM. You know, the rest of the dogs are chasing the rabbit. . . . I'm counting on you to continue to be the rabbit.' " It's almost enough to send a man back to his hot tub under a starry sky to wonder "What is the deal here?"

9

Government and Deficits

Samuel F. B. Morse, the nineteenth-century American artist and inventor, needed government funds to build the first experimental telegraph line between Washington and Baltimore for his "electromagnetic signaling system," the improved telegraph he had developed over seven years. He asked Congress for $30,000. A congressman from Tennessee, who hadn't a clue to what Morse was talking about, wanted half the money to support experiments in mesmerism (hypnotism), believed then to involve magnetic brain waves. Another congressman, from Alabama, thought the Millerites, a religious sect, ought to share in any government funds. Both suggestions were sarcastic, but the House chairman declined to dismiss the mesmer suggestion, ruling that "it would require a scientific analysis to determine how far the magnetism of mesmerism was analogous to the magnetism to be employed in telegraphs." Morse got his money on a vote of 89 to 83. Seventy congressmen did not vote, and many had walked out "to avoid spending the public money for a machine they could not understand."

A contemporary writer observed, "To those who thus ridiculed the telegraph it was a chimera, a visionary dream like mesmerism, rather to be a matter of merriment than seriously entertained. Men of character, men of erudition, men who, in ordinary affairs, had foresight, were wholly unable to forecast the future of the

191

telegraph. Other motions disparaging to the invention were made, such as propositions to appropriate part of the sum to a telegraph to the moon."

That was in 1842. Two years later, Morse sent his first telegraph message over the government-financed line. (That was also the year the Millerites had predicted the second coming of Christ. He didn't; the Millerites disappeared.) The telegraph is still with us, and the Congress is still not quite sure how to help American business and industry, either at home or abroad, nor is it sure what is wrong with the country's economy. At one time or another in recent memory, American leaders, individually or in groups, have blamed greedy businessmen, greedy unions, federal regulations, welfare mothers, the defense industry, social security, cheap labor abroad, other countries, federal borrowing, high taxes, low taxes, and lazy workers. Except in limited areas, the idea that quality may have something to do with America's economic problems seems not to exist in official Washington.

Myron Tribus, a Republican cabinet department appointee in the Nixon administration, believes it is a good thing that the federal government is not trying to lead what is now a grass-roots quality movement (see Chapter 7). He wrote, "We must not expect the people in government to lead in the establishment of TQM [total quality management]. They do not understand it and, in many ways, it threatens their positions." Talking of the changes that will be needed and the understanding that will be required by people in every community, he added, "No government is astute enough to understand how to deal with the complexities of the transformation and direct it centrally. No political system exists which will not attempt to turn this movement to its own advantage." Nonetheless, there is a role for the federal government to play because only it can solve the budget deficit; and while government cannot solve the international trade deficit, it can certainly make it worse.

Internationally, the United States buys more from its trading partners than it sells to them, giving it a trade deficit. Put another way, at the end of the trading day America pays more than it collects. That's not good in any business. To change that, the government can do three things. It can let companies work together to develop new and better products to sell abroad; it can help American producers get their products into foreign countries that are keeping them out; or, finally, it can keep other countries' goods out of the United States. Keeping goods out not only drives up costs domestically, it throws the world market into a dither.

Some nations need international trade to survive — not prosper, just survive. Japan, although it may be hard to believe, is in that category. Japanese schoolchildren are taught that theirs is a poor, crowded, island nation with no natural resources that must export to survive. Kenichi Ohmae, the Japanese consultant, says, "In Japan, we grow up with one textbook that basically says we are poor; we have no natural resources. So if we want to eat, we first have to work, but to work we have to import raw materials because we don't have any. We import raw materials, add value, export. That value added will give us the money to buy food. So if we don't work, no food; we starve." The Japanese see themselves struggling heroically and stoically against the odds — including Western racism and willful misunderstanding — to do what must be done for survival; their trading partners see Japan, Inc. — the people, the industry, the government, arm in arm — moving around the earth, rapaciously gobbling up markets with no regard for anyone's welfare save its own. Both views are wrong.

Pat Choate, the American political economist, says that Japan and the United States are "two varieties of capitalism," and each side discusses Japan in terms of its own variety. The United States criticizes Japan's closed domestic market, which limits international trade, but the Japanese point out that Japan has fewer laws than the United States regulating international trade. The Japanese count the number of measures to improve import trade their country has taken in recent years. Americans say that for all the measures taken, nothing has happened. From 1960 into the mid-'80s, imports to Europe and America, as a percentage of the total economy in each place, quadrupled. In the same period, imports to Japan as a percentage of the total economy increased so little, comparatively, as to be all but meaningless; the increase was less than 10 percent.

"The problem, by and large," Choate says, "resides with us [Americans] for not making legitimate demands on the Japanese. Instead, what we've done is we've nagged, and we have said, 'Be like us.' " Any number of competent observers, including Choate, have repeatedly pointed out that perhaps the last thing the Japanese would want to be is like Americans. What the Japanese do want, Choate says, is to find out what Americans want in trade concessions, specifically, from Japan. Choate says American officials keep telling the Japanese to be open and fair, and the Japanese keep asking what that means as a percentage of total trade; so while the Japanese talk about trade numbers, the Americans talk about trade ideals. "We wind up with both societies talking past each other," he says. "What the United States should do is quit being a free trade missionary. Go to the Japanese and say, 'Here are the results that we want. Let's make a deal. Let's have managed trade.' "

Howard D. Samuel, the head of the industrial division of the AFL-CIO, echoes the same idea when he dismisses American calls for "a level playing field," the accepted phrase for international fair and open trade. "Our competitors are not only playing by different rules," he says, "they are playing a different game. The idea of a level playing field is a fantasy; it can never happen."

Samuel wants to stop negotiating with our trading partners on products or markets, essentially a level-playing-field negotiation. "Instead," he says, "we should set some specific goals toward reducing the chronic U.S. trade deficit, looking ahead at least five years, and inform our trading partners that it is up to them how they wish to meet the goal — cutting their chronic trade surpluses either by reducing exports to us or by accepting more imports." The problem with that approach is that it assumes that all American trade problems are caused entirely by other countries' cheating, which is unrealistic but widely accepted, especially by America's political leaders, who then convince the people. According to a *Business Week*/Harris Poll survey, 55 percent of those questioned believed that "most of the problems of American business are the result of unfair foreign competition."

William N. Walker, a U.S. trade official from 1975 to 1977, wrote in an opinion piece for the *New York Times*, "Don't blame someone else for a series of problems that were brought about largely by our own actions and that we can solve only by ourselves." He also pointed out that if Americans really wanted a level playing field, the government would have to do away with import restrictions on "meat, sugar, rice, peanuts, tobacco, dairy products, textiles, apparel, motorcycles, automobiles, machine tools, semiconductors and steel."

Unfairness does exist. In 1989, Congressman Ron Wyden of Oregon awarded Korea the gold medal in the "innovative trade barriers" Olympics. That was based on a report, according to the *New York Times*, "that Korean movie distributors had freed snakes during the showing of American films in Seoul movie theaters as a way of frightening patrons away from made-in-the-United-States entertainment products." Some unfairness is not directed at the United States, but it winds up with the bill all the same. In the past decade, Samuel says, the United States has absorbed 60 percent of the exports from less developed countries while Europe, with a larger population, has accepted only 23 percent and Japan, with half the U.S. population, has taken only 7 percent. "Those who berate the United States for protectionist tendencies," Samuel says, "never seem to recite these numbers." Too little is made of it, but the only way for developing countries to get ahead is to export to the industrial nations, and the United States buys a wildly disproportionate share.

There are other international trade arguments involving several combinations of national or regional players, but the U.S.-Japan argument tends to get the most attention since the two countries have the world's two largest economies. From the popular American point of view, that trade argument can be stated rather simply: Japan cheats. As we've said before, all industrial nations do to some degree, but Japan does seem to hold the championship. From the popular Japanese point of view, which can be absorbed in the first thirty days any American lives there, Americans are lazy spendthrifts, too arrogant to learn, too shiftless to change, and too self-righteous to see their own faults. Americans often deeply resent and hotly deny these charges, as well they might since they are overstated but true.

The reason the Japanese don't buy American products, Japanese will tell you, is that except for airplanes, movies, television programs, and a very few products, Americans don't make anything the Japanese want. American goods cost too much, break down too often, and are all but impossible to repair. Americans do not make the kind of quality the Japanese want and can get from their own manufacturers. There is a story that Japanese tell to illustrate what they mean. A Japanese businessman stationed in the United States was transferring home. It is a Japanese social custom that a Japanese returning from overseas or a foreigner coming to visit take gifts to friends and associates. The gift should be thoughtfully chosen and beautifully wrapped; it is the care taken with it, not its cost, that matters. The businessman wanted something uniquely American and of superior quality. After an extensive search, he found the only item that met his two conditions. His friends and associates received handsomely wrapped containers of pure New England maple syrup. An American art dealer who often visits Japan on business says she takes well-decorated packages of American wild rice as gifts. In a post-industrial society, to two people at least, American quality is still represented by agricultural products.

In an increasingly acrimonious trade dispute, most Japanese and some Americans argue that the problem is primarily a lack of American quality; most Americans and some Japanese say the problem is primarily a closed Japanese market. It is a curiosity that these two arguments are rarely mentioned simultaneously. An American congressman, complaining of American goods being kept out of Asian markets, is not going to question whether those goods have sufficient quality to sell even if they were allowed in. A Japanese bureaucrat, insisting that Americans don't try hard enough to achieve success in Japan, doesn't mention a wholesale distribution system that seems specifically designed to keep outsiders outside, which in Japan is an honored historical objective.

Until Japan was forced by Commodore Matthew Perry and his U.S. Navy ships (and by implication, though not direct threat, their cannon) to open its ports and markets in 1854 — even under the gun, as it were, the Japanese showed a positive genius for obfuscation, dissimulation, and delay — Japan had been a totally closed society for three hundred years. That strict isolation did not end until nearly three years after the American Civil War, or to put it in sports terms, the Meiji Restoration and the Cincinnati Red Stockings, the first U.S. professional baseball team, started the same year. Keeping outsiders outside is one of the continuing complaints against Japan by American businessmen.

Another is *dumping*, which is, believe it or not, a technical term in international trade defined as "the sale of a commodity on a foreign market at a price below marginal cost." To put it more simply, dumping occurs when a product is sold in foreign trade for less than it costs to get it to market. The price at home, usually high, underwrites exports so that the producer can break into or capture a foreign market with an artificially low price. Dumping is international dirty pool since the object is often to drive domestic manufacturers out of business; then, if the foreign maker wants (and almost all do), it can raise the price substantially because there's no competition left. The General Agreement on Tariffs and Trade (GATT), the main group trying to regulate international trade since World War II, allows nations that can prove dumping to impose special taxes to get the import price back up to where it should be so that domestic producers can compete honestly. That's the theory, anyway. The practice can be something else again. *The Economist,* the British news magazine, reports that the European Community imposed antidumping duties on Japanese audiotape cassettes, not because they were driving European makers out of business, but because they, to quote the commission, "have forced the Community industry to undersell to hold its market share." That caused *The Economist* to wonder in print, "While Brussels bureaucrats are protecting less-efficient European manufacturers, who is protecting Europe's consumers?"

Samuel, the American labor official, dismisses that consumer protection argument because to him it ignores another point. "A few orthodox economists, and shortsighted manufacturers who benefit from low-cost imported components, will suggest that dumping benefits American consumers and should be encouraged," he writes. "They seem to forget that behind every consumer is a worker, and if dumping undermines our manufacturing sector, soon there will not be enough worker/consumers to sustain our economy." Samuel wants the laws against dumping to be enforced energetically. He insists that several American administrations have known that Japan, Korea, Taiwan, Singapore, and others have been dumping products in the United States, "but Republican or Democrat, no administration has been willing to do what is necessary to make dumping unprofitable for exporters."

However, the United States used antidumping taxes to help Motorola after it led an industry-wide fight in the early '80s against Japanese companies dumping pagers and cellular telephones in the American market. Motorola eventually got the American government to impose a 106 percent duty on the Japanese companies, but not before every other major American manufacturer had been hurt badly or driven out of business. The government appears to prefer to fight dumping by negotiation, not tariffs, even though tariffs are an internationally accepted remedy. A remedy that is not internationally accepted is protectionism.

American presidents who boast of their control over or understanding of foreign policy tend to be all but illiterate about the national economy. Inevitably, members of those administrations in Washington tend to see the national economy in its broadest global sense — trade and aid agreements, peaceful development, financial policy. Local politicians see it quite differently — jobs, grocery money, an education for the kids. That explains why there is always more support for protectionism in the Congress, whose members face essentially local elections, than in the White House, whose chief occupant may be the leader of the free world, but he can't pave your street, fix your sewer, or protect your job. Protectionism has a simplistic appeal, but it's not the answer.

C. Jackson Grayson, Jr., of the American Productivity and Quality Center, says the answer is quality. "If we pay attention only to protectionism," he says, "and try to level the supposedly very unlevel playing field — I don't think it's as unlevel as most people think it is — then we won't win. That is an effort, but it is not sufficient. It is something that attracts attention away from what we should be doing, which is working on the positive aspects of improving quality. In England in its downturn [at the end of the last century], the last thing they did was start protecting themselves against 'those unfair Americans and Germans.' It was the last act of a dying nation." Edwin L. Artzt of Procter & Gamble feels some protectionism, properly used, may be useful in limited situations for limited objectives. "Some of the protectionist attitudes are retaliatory," he says. "They don't let us in, why should we let them in? But I believe that our policy of supporting free trade as a principle is the only right policy for this country in the long run, and although a certain amount of retaliation as a temporary form of bringing other countries to the negotiating table is appropriate, the principle of protectionist antitrade policies is, I think, a wrong one."

Ohmae blames protectionism on politicians in both countries. "This is a situation," he says, "where politicians use nineteenth-century rhetoric because nationalism is one of the deepest-rooted sentiments. For a politician, the easiest way to get people's attention is to say, 'We have to work for the interest of Americans and the interest of our country.' . . . Therefore, when consumers vote with their wallets, they are voting a rational choice with the information [on quality and cost] available to them. But when the same person listens to the politician say that imports are really hurting your job, and we have to become protectionists, then the same people may vote for the protectionists' bills. The same is true with the Japanese. . . . The politicians can still get by with saying, 'Oh, we have to protect the Japanese interest.' What they're protecting is not the Japanese interest, certainly not the Japanese *people's* interest." Ohmae tells of arguing with Japanese politicians about their refusal to allow any rice to be imported, even though Japanese consumers pay two and a half times what Americans pay for rice. The government says it is necessary for national security to control the rice supply, so that the people can be fed in any emergency. Ohmae says he hopes all Japanese have good strong teeth, because on the 121st day of any emergency, they won't be able to cook the rice they've grown. The government stockpiles only 120 days' worth of fuel. What the rice policy is protecting is not the Japanese people but the agricultural vote for the ruling Liberal Democratic Party (LDP), some of whose members have vowed to stop even a single grain of foreign rice from entering Japan. That sounds absurd until you learn that in March 1991, officials of Japan's Ministry of Agriculture threatened to arrest Americans at the Foodex international exhibition in Tokyo unless they removed ten pounds of American rice on display in a glass case. Part of the ministry's official angst was caused by the Japanese newspapers, which had begun to report how much more Japanese consumers have to pay for rice to, essentially, buy votes for the LDP.

For global trade, it is important for the U.S. government to use whatever means it can to get American goods into foreign markets to compete for customers. Robert Galvin of Motorola says that the government has been helpful "assisting and gaining access to foreign marketplaces." Starting with the Carter administration, "there has been an openness to understand the needs to open marketplaces. I think more could be done, but considerable help has been given." It was government insistence that got Japan to open its domestic market to foreign pagers and cellular phones in 1982, and Motorola is doing well there. Artzt also mentions market access, but in a different way. "Our [American] investment base overseas," he says, "hasn't been growing as fast as the investment base of foreign companies in the United States. So our government has a commitment to help make U.S. business and industry more competitive on a worldwide basis, and that's a healthy thing. I think there's a very good rapport between U.S. business and U.S. government in pursuing this common interest."

American government officials, industrialists, educators, and labor leaders can occasionally agree on what ought to be done in specific areas of international trade, and in some other areas the disagreements are mild, more a matter of momentary or monetary preference than of economic or political belief. There is one area, however, where not only is there no agreement, the disagreement is often so bitter, personal, and political as to make reasonable discussion all but impossible. "It's almost," says Herbert

Striner of American University, "like a four-letter word in Washington: industrial policy."

Industrial policy in Japan dates in one way from the Meiji Restoration in the late nineteenth century, but in its modern form it began to take shape in the early twentieth century as something called industrial rationalization, briefly and inadequately explained as a sort of "okay, how do we make some sense of this competitive mess" policy that would let Japan concentrate its relatively limited economic resources. Think of it as a government effort to create the greatest good for the greatest number of Japanese. That industrial drive was interrupted briefly by World War II. Then, when quality production methods were introduced, some industries were encouraged, others discouraged. In electronics, computers, numerically controlled machine tools, and other high technology areas, the Japanese government at least partially financed industry-wide research efforts that would have been illegal under U.S. laws. Japan used the carrot-and-stick approach to move industries out of less profitable ventures and into more profitable ones. By the late '70s, the American people had wrongly come to believe that Japan's government bureaucrats decided which industries to keep alive and which to let die. It was the sort of imagined government control that sends America's freewheeling, independent entrepreneurs and industrial leaders into figurative fits.

Galvin of Motorola is representative in his attitude. "We are obliged," he says, "to work with policies of government affecting industry. . . . we must work together. I think there are more things that we can do together that are far short of any socialistic industrial policy class of effort, that have nothing to do with making choices of winners or losers in business. I would hope that there will be an enhanced amount of cooperation, but still with the private sector out competing and investing and risking on its own." Samuel represents many labor officials when he says that to keep the American economy strong, "we have to shed our nineteenth-century aversion to government support for specific industries." Since 1980, the White House has shunned industrial policy. "They overlook the fact," Roger Milliken says, "that every other nation in the world, in one form or another, has partnered with their manufacturing industry to help them grow, to help create high-paying jobs, and to build strength into their economies. And our leadership has just closed their eyes to that fact." That may be changing. By the spring of 1991, the White House was considering using federal funds to support twenty-two technologies considered critical in the future.

Clyde Prestowitz, a former American trade official, thinks Americans misunderstand the industrial policy that he (along with the financial consultant Steven Schlossstein) thinks played a major role in Japan's industrial success. "Among American observers," he writes, "the policy of government intervention has often been described as one of picking winners and losers. . . . In fact, they [Japanese officials] say their policy is not to pick winners, but, rather, to identify and back the winners the market has already picked, to ensure that Japan rides with the winners." The Korean government trade official Mangi Paik says, "Of course, in some sense, Japan has a managed economy, but one thing you should not forget is that even though the government's role in Japan is very big compared to the U.S., the Japanese bureaucrats respect competition very much. . . . While in Japan I looked at the Japanese electronics industry, for example. . . . Everyone wants to say that the Japanese government is better than the U.S. in fostering industry and giving it incentives, but it seems to me that the real source is the competition within the industry. It is very harsh."

Striner, who has probably studied industrial policy more than most Americans, thinks it developed out of necessity. "Beginning after World War II," he explains, "countries like Japan and most of the countries of Western Europe, which had their economies devastated and didn't have much time to argue theology about private market systems versus socialism, developed what I call the 'key player' model; that is, they said, 'If we're going to achieve a major restoration of our economy in the shortest period of time, who are the key people? Who are the key actors?' Well, government was key. Labor was key. Management was key. So that what began in the early '50s was the development of a completely new form of capitalism, a form of capitalism which doesn't start with the assumption that government is the enemy. Government is part of the solution. So these countries began to evolve a form of cooperation, a nonadversarial relationship between the public and the private sector, which has now produced a very, very effective form of competition. Japan, West Germany, France — these are not socialist countries."

Striner studied the eleven major industrial powers, including the United States and Japan, among the twenty-four member nations of the Organization for Economic Cooperation and Development (OECD), separating them into those who thought government was part of the problem and those who thought it part of the solution. He looked at their economies from 1970 to 1988, and in those countries where government was considered part of the solution, there was a productivity gain about 45 percent greater than the gain in those countries — Australia, Great Britain, and the United States — where government was seen as part of the problem. Remember that productivity is not just an economist's term; productivity drives standard of living. Quality drives productivity.

Striner says that "if we are to cope with the countries that are more successful in achieving quality of product, quality of service, we're going to have to change our perception of the role of government. . . . We really have an almost religious sense of revelation about the so-called free market system and the implication that every other system is anathema. . . . Now what's interesting about this whole argument of industrial policy is that the United States itself has utilized industrial policy and has achieved remarkable results, but we've managed to either forget or obscure that because it doesn't fit with our self-perception."

Striner says that during the Civil War, the U.S. government gave the states land for colleges that would train students in scientific agriculture so that American farms could produce the food that the rapidly growing country needed. Federal and state officials, county agricultural agents, and private farmers all worked together and, as Striner says, "produced the highest level of productivity in agriculture in the whole world." In a more recent example, he says, "the computers we now have were a result of industrial policy, which was a result of crisis." During World War II, the War Department needed a faster way to calculate the trajectory of new weapons systems, so the federal Department of Ordnance contracted with the Moore School of Engineering to build the first computer, because, according to Striner, "we didn't have any time to waste in terms of the free market system eventually producing an electronic computer."

Daniel Yankelovich says the argument against an American industrial policy is that "the government is the worst one to pick and choose winners and losers, and I think that's true. But I don't think that is necessarily the only form of industrial policy. . . . We should have a clear definition of the national interest on exporting jobs, on employing American workers, on import policy, and on other kinds of actions. Until we do, we're going to have our political system dominated by a squabble of *special* interests with no clarity about the *national* interest. . . . So I believe there will be an industrial policy in the future, but I don't think it's going to be the old bogeyman of picking winners and losers."

Whatever the policy is, Choate believes government must be involved. "Government cannot be a neutral bystander," he says, "when it comes to talking about the economic competitiveness of this country. It is a major player. It consumes a fifth of the gross national product. It sets the rules in which we operate. It does the negotiating with other governments. It cannot be a bystander."

There is another problem. Ronald Baker, the director of the Maryland Office of International Trade for Europe in Brussels, says that just when the United States needs it most, the government has cut back funding for trade promotion overseas. "The U.S. government," he says, "has failed to recognize the real benefits to the American taxpayer and the American community, in its widest sense, of promoting exports. Our export performance has been not very good the last fifteen years. . . . Now the states have got to step in. We just can't let the race be won by, perhaps, the Germans or even the Canadians, who do a much better job than we do on a per capita basis of promoting trade. . . . If the federal government can't do it, because of lack of resources, we states have to do it."

The states generally cooperate to promote American exports but compete for foreign investments — plants, for instance. Robert Reich thinks the United States should have a U.S. investment representative as well as the existing U.S. trade representative. While the government negotiates trade issues with a single voice, investment negotiations are left to each of the forty-three states that maintain permanent offices in foreign countries. The results are predictable. In 1980, Reich wrote, Tennessee attracted a Nissan plant to Smyrna and, through incentives, mainly tax concessions, paid $11,000 for each job that the plant created. "By 1986, Indiana had to spend $50,000 per job" to attract the Subaru-Isuzu plant to Lafayette. It doesn't end there. To keep plants, foreign or domestic, local governments have to make more tax concessions. In 1957, corporate tax payments amounted to 45 percent of local government revenues. By 1989, that had been cut to only 16 percent. Reich suggested that the United States look at the European model. "The European Commission," he said, "reviews local incentives offered by member nations in order to minimize bidding by one against the other. As a result, when Honda decided in 1989 to locate its first European plant in Britain, it did not receive a shilling of inducement."

Compared to the problem of international trade, states giving away tax revenue to compete for foreign industrial plants is an expensive but relatively minor problem. It certainly doesn't rank with the other four deficits that Joji Arai talks about: the federal budget deficit, the trade deficit, the capital deficit, and, the most important deficit to most Americans and the one least often mentioned as an economic or quality problem, the social deficit — education, crime, health care, drug abuse, violence. "All those things," Arai says, "which not many other countries have to suffer to the degree American society does, and those are having a negative impact on the competitiveness of the United States."

Ohmae says that it's obvious that the United States has been competitive in the global market in the past, so if it isn't now, "we have to really analyze what has happened to the United States corporate scene over the past twenty years. One thing has clearly to do with the greed of the American people." He says it starts with the federal government. "They were issuing deficit bonds year after year after year," he says, "and they really stimulated this kind of greedy tendency. . . . Everyone has become very greedy. So before working hard, before they think about global survival, global superiority, customer satisfaction, employee satisfaction, responsibility to vendors and subcontractors and dealers, they start talking about making money."

One need only read Alfred Sloan's autobiography, *My Life with General Motors,* to see where that may have started. Sloan headed a committee in 1921 to establish policy for the car company. He wrote, "The primary object of the corporation, therefore, we declared was to make money, not just to make motor cars." (Compare that to Collis Huntington's motto, quoted in Chapter 1, at Newport News Shipbuilding.) Eventually, in many American corporations, the chief executives would not care about the product at all but would care about the paper value — the stock price — of the corporation, a logical extension of Sloan's decision that the objective was to make money.

Ohmae thinks that what has happened is "in the United States, the basic value system has shifted from the Puritan days — hard work. If you worked hard, went through a very severe winter, and then planted some seed and cropped in the fall, you had Thanksgiving. I mean, this was the basic ethic of American life. Even in the days of Thomas Edison. . . . he said, 'One percent inspiration, 99 percent perspiration.' This means 99 percent hard work. . . . Not many Americans remember this, and I have to keep reminding my American colleagues that this was *your* country's founding philosophy."

Ohmae is slightly off. Hard work was not the founding philosophy of the United States, it was second. Something akin to classic communism — from each according to his ability, to each according to his need — was the founding philosophy at Jamestown Colony in Virginia in 1607 and at Plimoth Plantation in Massachusetts some years later. It failed at both places for the same reason: Since everyone would share no matter how hard each person worked, why work? In the fall of 1608, Captain John Smith took over at Jamestown and issued a new dictum: "He that will not worke, shall not eate." That's when hard work became the philosophy of what would become the United States, and it would remain the basic philosophy for 370 years or so. What became known as the Protestant work ethic was actually an achievement ethic and was not limited to Protestants. Anyone of any belief who worked hard would achieve something. After the Japanese learned from Deming and others how to work smarter, not harder, Americans also learned how to replace hard work. They replaced it with blue smoke and mirrors, pure financial illusion.

Reich says that American managers, faced for the first time with severe international competition, decided, in effect, that a facade was as good as a building. "Along about the late 1970s," he says, "a lot of American managers said, 'Wait a minute! Maybe what we really need to do is create the impression of dynamism and change, even if there's not very much dynamism and change underneath. How are we going to, in the short term, get our profits up? Why don't we engage in takeovers, friendly and unfriendly, leveraged buyouts, speculation in land, speculation in currencies, junk bonds? Why don't we create a dynamic financial structure that creates the appearance of a dynamic production structure but that is not nearly as expensive or hard and that can be done pretty quick?' And, thereupon, we spent the next twelve years, from the late '70s all the way through the '80s, manipulating money instead of investing in developing productive organizations." For a while that will work, he says, but not for long because "you've rearranged the slices of the pie, but the pie doesn't get any larger." Unless the pie gets larger — that is, unless productivity goes up — the standard of living stagnates. Productivity in the United States declined in 1989 and again in 1990.

Ohmae thinks the basic problems are deeply rooted and may go back to the educational and social system and what Americans teach their children. "You are no longer teaching young American kids as Puritan fathers and mothers taught their children," he says. "You have moved away from the work ethic. Society is first teaching what is your right, how you claim your right, and teaching independence, when interdependence is more important."

In a leading article (editorial), *The Economist,* noting that what America does soon becomes what the world does, said that the United States suffers from "an odd combination of ducking responsibility and telling everyone else what to do." It referred to what it called "a decadent puritanism"; one example said, "The decadence lies in too readily blaming others for problems, rather than accepting responsibility oneself." Neither *The Economist* nor Ohmae is the first social critic, foreign or domestic, to point out that the United States is among the world's best at teaching and defending individual rights and among the world's worst at teaching and demanding individual responsibility. Nowhere is that clearer than in the American handling of money.

The inability of Americans — government, corporate, and individual — to live within their means is frequently mentioned as the leading cause of America's decline. This is especially true in poorer countries that are pulling themselves into the modern world, often by making sacrifices. Staporn Kavitanon, the director of the Board of Investment, a Thai government agency, says, "The success of the Thai economy is not sheer luck. We have made an intensive effort to reach the point where we are now." Thailand is a profit-oriented, private-sector economy with an industrial policy. Starting in the mid-'80s, the Thai government focused on attracting tourists, encouraging exports, and looking for foreign investments. Tourism has increased 20 percent and exports 25 percent *each year* since, and when it comes to foreign investment, Staporn says it "has jumped by leaps and bounds. We are not talking percentage . . . we talk about times [multiples]." The key to economic success, he believes, was a severe belt-tightening by the Thai government to get its budget under control. Thailand used to pay 21 percent of its budget in interest on its debt. That has been cut to 12 percent. Staporn says that Thailand was willing "to swallow the bitter medicine" and now "we enjoy tremendously our economic expansion." Then, to amuse his American guests, Staporn adds, "Some people say, 'Well, why don't you guys send a guy to Washington to advise the American government how to reduce the debt?' "

It is the American government's unwillingness to eliminate the budget deficit — that is, to balance the federal budget — that continues to amaze officials in other countries. Staporn says he is always being asked how America could have been so big and so great with plenty of money for other nations to borrow just a few years ago, but now it has to look everywhere to borrow enough for itself. "So the difference is, I think," he says, "the affluent society consumes more than you can produce. This is very important for a country, just like a family. If you spend more than you can earn, then you are bound to be in debt, and you'll be in trouble."

The United States is in more trouble than the government's

budget deficit figures would indicate, because the figures are deliberately fudged. The cost of the savings and loan bailout, whatever it may eventually be — the figure $500 billion seems popular at the moment — will basically not show up in the budget. It is being done "off the budget." In effect, the government is keeping two sets of books — one that shows what it wants to be seen, the other that shows what is real. Keeping double books is sometimes illegal and always suspect, and the government fiddles with its money in ways that would put a business in bankruptcy and its accountants in jail. For instance, Congress does not advertise that all federal trust funds, including the one to finance social security, are routinely spent by the government as if those trust funds were intended for anything Congress cared to spend them on; the effect is to hide from the public how deeply in debt the country is. How much economic harm the deficit does or how much moral harm the deceit causes can be argued, but the truth is, Uncle Sam must now stand on the world corner, hat in hand, begging for money. It is a lousy position from which to negotiate international trade agreements.

How the United States went from the largest creditor nation to the largest debtor nation in the world is easy enough to analyze. It spent more than it had, and it did that because of politics, not economics.

Cutting spending is not politically popular; raising taxes is not politically popular. "The irony of this U.S. political comedy," Ohmae says, "is that people know it. . . . people know politicians are not telling them the truth, they are not focusing on the right issues. . . . But if they [the politicians] start talking about American educational problems and detailed studies of what it would take to regain America's industrial competitiveness, how to make people work harder and expect less, they don't want to face these issues because they're not going to be very popular."

The United States also has one of the world's lower rates of savings, which causes what Arai calls a capital deficit; that is, there

211

isn't enough money for private industry to borrow for investment at reasonable interest rates. It also means that the government, because of the budget deficit, is competing for that limited savings money, driving interest rates up. The figures change, but an American corporation borrowing money for new buildings or machines will have to pay considerably more interest than, say, a Japanese corporation. That raises the cost of American goods no matter how efficiently or with what quality they are made.

Artzt says, "When we have a federal deficit of the size that we have now, we are inevitably going to have a higher cost of capital than other countries, and that is an enormous competitive disadvantage. . . . We should be concerned about it [the deficit] not only because of the effect that it has on the cost of capital, but also because of the symptoms that it reflects; in other words, living beyond our means, spending more than we take in, excessive consumption, which is abetted by too easy credit." He says there is a trend in the United States now, caused by the collapse of some savings and loan institutions, to be more aware of what we owe and why we owe it. He feels that is "a profound change, and if we can continue to become more fiscally responsible, and if we can somehow educate the public to the importance of fiscal discipline on a national level, I think this country [America] is going to be in really good shape."

It may get to be in really good shape in the budget and capital deficits categories, and progress is already being made on the trade deficit, but in Arai's fourth category, the social deficit, the United States is going from bad to worse. The rich are getting richer; the poor are getting poorer. The mentally ill have been freed from dreadful institutions so that they can live on the streets with drunks, drug addicts, the unemployed, and the working poor — whole families in the world's wealthiest society with no place to call home. They are among the 31 to 37 million people with no health insurance who help to swamp emergency rooms in major

American hospitals where they join the victims of violent crime, AIDS sufferers, and the poor.

President Richard Nixon first declared a health care "crisis" in the United States more than twenty years ago. It has gotten much worse, but not for lack of money. In 1989, U.S. health care cost $600 billion, or roughly 12 percent of the total national economy. The United States spends more money on health care than any other nation, including those with some form of national health program, yet in infant mortality, a key measure of health, the United States ranks twenty-fifth among the world's nations, and it ranks sixteenth in life expectancy. Health care costs have become the leading cause of bankruptcy for individuals and small businesses, and in 1990, more than a quarter of the average company's net earnings went to health care. Auto company health care costs add about $500 to the sticker price of every car made in America. At the current rate of increase, the cost of health care for each employee, now at less than $4,000 a year, will reach $22,000 in the year 2000.

Nearly a third of America's preschool children have not had routine vaccinations. AIDS is approaching epidemic proportions, and no cure has yet been found. Doctors' incomes have increased much faster than the national average, driving up the cost of medical care. Lawyers file malpractice suits at the drop of a scalpel, so to protect themselves, doctors routinely do diagnostic tests that are expensive, unnecessary, and add to the misery of the patient and the protection of the doctor. Doctors pay enormous insurance bills, and some of them have been driven out of business by those costs. About 20 to 23 percent of a hospital's cost is usually for bureaucrats who keep records, bill patients, file insurance claims, fight with the federal government over payments, and generally try to make sense out of a needlessly complicated system that includes something like fifteen hundred different insurance schemes. People knowledgeable about health care in the United States no longer talk about a crisis or even a catastrophe; they now talk about the total collapse of the system. Imagine that: the richest nation on earth unable to afford medical care for its people.

Quality would help. Gregory S. Binns and John F. Early wrote about studies of several hospitals in the *Juran Report,* a Juran Institute publication. The *New York Times* summarized it: "The findings supported the argument that poor quality costs more, while high quality produces savings." On one type of operation, the two men discovered that it routinely cost about $6,000 in a high-quality hospital but about $9,000 in a low-quality facility. If you extend the one-third quality savings — which is, by the way, probably low — it would amount to an estimated $220 billion–plus in 1991, when Americans are expected to spend $661 billion on health care. That amount of money ought to be more than enough to provide adequate, even excellent, health care for 250 million people. It doesn't because without a quality system, the waste eats up as much as 40 percent. The answer is the same message that W. Edwards Deming took to Japan in 1950: driving quality up drives costs down, and it doesn't matter whether you're doing heart bypass surgery, designing a computer, or filing a malpractice suit. Everything is a system; all systems can be improved, and that includes the criminal justice system.

There is no more violent, crime-ridden society in the industrial world than the United States, and crime, too, is getting worse. The FBI's Uniform Crime Report indicated that violent crime in the United States increased 10 percent in 1990. "One of the fastest-growing occupational groups in the private sector in the United States right now," Reich says, "is security guards. There are more private security guards in the United States now than there are public police officers. The fastest growing public sector occupational group in the United States is correctional guards, prison guards."

Comparative criminal statistics are notoriously unreliable, but when car owners in New York City put signs in their windshields saying "No radio, no tools" so thieves won't bother to break in, criminals control the streets, no matter what the statistics say. That kind of smash-and-grab stealing is a nonviolent crime, and in that category, the crime rate in the United States is about twice that of Europe and four times that of Japan. In violent crime, the U.S. rate is far worse. The murder rate is at least four times that of Western Europe — some sources say as much as seven times — the rape rate seven times higher, and the robbery rate where force is involved as much as ten times higher. The leading cause of death among American male teenagers is murder. An American male of any age is twenty-two times more likely to be murdered than is a German male, forty-four times more likely than a Japanese. In 1989 (the last year for which figures are available), for every 100,000 residents, the United States had 429 people in jail or prison, more than any other nation on earth including South Africa and the Soviet Union; in Europe the rate was 35 to 120 and in Asian countries it was 21 to 140.

Whoever or whatever is to blame, crime in America is part of the social deficit that costs enormous amounts of money — $16 billion a year just to keep people locked up — and helps to destroy the quality of life that is part of the American standard of living. There may not be a single solution, but in Madison, Wisconsin, David Couper, the chief of police, has adopted the Deming quality method in his department as part of a citywide effort led by Joseph Sensenbrenner when he was the mayor. Couper created an experimental police district using the Deming method in one of the more crime-prone areas. From 1986 to 1989 burglaries in Madison went up 15 percent. In the experimental district, burglaries went down 28 percent. At the same time, police costs in the district went down, mainly through suggestions made by the officers themselves. That is only a tiny part of a highly successful program that is now being put into effect in four other police districts in Madison. Perhaps the most important improvement has been in the relations between the cops and the community; the people and the police now trust and like each other, allowing them to work together on the basic causes of crime.

As the social deficit exists now, if you have no hope of an education, no hope of job training, no hope of meaningful employment, no hope of reasonable health care, no hope of making a contribution, and no hope within society of improvement of any kind in your or your children's lifetimes, turning away from society and toward crime is a logical, if ultimately self-defeating, decision. What has kept the American dream alive over the years was the reasonable hope that things would get better. Without that reasonable hope, things inevitably get worse.

Underlying the entire social deficit is the largest single problem Americans face — education.

10

Students and Pipes

Adam Smith, the eighteenth-century Scottish philosopher and author of *The Wealth of Nations,* the greatest champion of free-market economics in history, believed that the government had three duties and only three: national defense, law and policing, and "certain public works and certain public institutions," like water pipes and schools.

Education is most worrisome to more Americans and is all but universally accepted as a legitimate function of government at all levels. The federal, state, and local governments in America recognize that responsibility; spending per pupil in the United States is second only to that in Switzerland, but that figure can be misleading. Herb Striner, a former university dean, says, "We like to think that the United States spends more money than any other country per capita on education. As a matter of fact, we don't." He says the money spent on higher education distorts the figures. "If you pull out the university end," he says, "the United States has one of the lowest per capita expenditures of all the major countries with regard to K through twelve education. Very low." Robert Reich agrees. In kindergarten through twelfth grade, he says, "we still trail behind seven other industrialized nations." He adds that since educational spending figures are all averages and wealthy suburban districts spend a great deal, then rural or poor urban districts are far worse than the average figures suggest. Nonetheless, the amount of money spent on education in America has been going up, and if money alone could have solved the problem, it would have been solved by now.

The U.S. government provides only 6 percent of the money spent on education in the fifty states, but there is a cabinet-level Department of Education, and both the Congress and the White House have probably made as many promises to improve education as they have to reduce the budget deficit. The budget deficit is worse, and the educational system, depending on whose multiple-choice test scores you believe, is either (a) not good enough, (b) bad, or (c) God-awful. Marvin Cetron, the author of *American Renaissance,* says, "We cannot compete in a world environment by using our brains and doing quality work the way we are right now. If we're going to produce quality goods, we have to have brighter people to work in the high technology areas, and we haven't. Fifty-three percent of all our people in the Ph.D. programs in the whole United States are foreigners, because our students can't qualify. . . . Second, our kids can't read. We are twentieth out of twenty industrialized countries in the education area. There is no one as bad off as we are. That's not the worst part. The worst part is our upper tenth — our brightest kids — don't measure up to the average of the other nineteen countries."

Striner quotes a 1984 New York Stock Exchange economic research report on productivity. "One of their observations," he says, "was that if you had to cite one factor which accounted for the much higher rates of productivity in Japan, it would be education."

In 1992 there will be a nationwide survey of adult literacy in the United States. A dry run of that test was done in Oregon in early 1991, and if the results there hold true for the nation, the need for immediate improvement in education will be even more obvious. In understanding basic numbers, the Oregon test showed that 82 percent of adults couldn't read a bus schedule and 65 percent couldn't determine how much medicine to give a child when the dosage was based on age and weight. Governor Barbara Roberts asked the obvious and painful questions: "How can an unemployed woman get to a job interview on time if she can't read the bus schedule? How can a father care for his sick daughter if he can't tell how much medicine to give her?" How well people could read depended on what you wanted them to understand, but fewer than 9 percent could read at a master level, and only 41 percent read well enough to be at an intermediate level. Nationally, things are no better; depending on who does the counting, 25 million to 70 million Americans are illiterate — and that's 10 percent to not quite 30 percent of the people. Literacy in Japan, by comparison, is 100 percent, or so close that the difference doesn't matter.

No government at any level in America is ignorant of the need to improve education, and there is no record of any official at any level saying he or she is satisfied with public education. The one thing on which all Americans seem to agree despite political affiliation, race, religion, gender, place of national origin, or any other category is that *education must be improved.* There have been as many schemes to get excellence in education as there have been to achieve quality in industry, and in education particularly, a few of those schemes have been so bizarre that they are evidence of the American people's desperation to find an answer, any answer. Part of that is frustration. The search for educational improvement has been going on for a long time. A national report in the late 1940s called public schools in America an "educational wasteland," and another in 1961 on the reading skills of American students was bluntly titled *Tomorrow's Illiterates.* The report in the early '80s was *Nation at Risk.*

In 1991, President Bush announced a four-part push to improve education in the United States. The basic outline was published by the Department of Education as *America 2000: An Education Strategy.* The plan says all 110,000 schools must be made "better and more accountable for results." The country has to develop "new schools to meet the demands of a new century," people already out of school must keep learning, and communities and families must support education. The program is long on goals, rankings, and exhortations but short on the specifics of how to accomplish any of it. One man who read the report commented, "Results are important, how they are obtained is not part of the discussion." Writing of the modern history of failing education in the United States, Myron Tribus said, "Political leaders, from the President down, have issued solemn pronouncements and 'goals.' Those who understand TQM have been unhappy and critical of these statements because they consist of goals, without plans to achieve them. These officials apply the managerial techniques which have already ruined much of American enterprise. We expect to have similar unsatisfactory results when they are applied in education."

In an article about attempted improvements in education in the 1980s, Denis P. Doyle and others wrote, "The federal, state, and local governments have poured millions of dollars into compensatory education, dropout prevention, drug education, and other schemes, most of which have failed. . . . In New York City, the Board of Education spent $68 million on dropout prevention, and the dropout rate rose 5 percent." The article cites a study of New York City that found that for every dollar spent in the classroom, two dollars is spent on overhead, including the salaries and costs of the four thousand employees of the Board of Education who are at headquarters, not at the schools. A similar study in Milwaukee had similar results. Doyle, a senior fellow at the Hudson Institute, and his colleagues, Bruce S. Cooper and Roberta Trachtman, both with the Fordham University Graduate School of Education, suggest spending less on the bureaucracy and more on the students: "States should consider allowing schools to become self-governing — with their own boards of trustees, like colleges — and then fund them directly rather than through the local school bureaucracy." They say that idea, "as simple as it is revolutionary," is being tested in Great Britain with enormous success. Under the British Education Reform Act of 1988, some schools in Britain are self-governing, compete for students just as companies compete for customers, and get money on the basis of how many students they can attract. The students are tested regularly on a national standard. So far, according to news reports, the experiment seems to be popular with everyone — except, of course, the British education bureaucrats who face a definite loss of power and a possible loss of jobs. "What parents seem to want," the article concluded, "is a good school, with a responsive, high-quality program, not a team of bureaucrats sitting at desks miles from the school."

The study does not mention what the students want; it is the students, not their parents, who are any school's principal customers and, simultaneously, its products, and it is, therefore, the students who define the quality of the school. The parents are the educational equivalent of stockholders, and they have a right to insist that their investment be treated well and wisely, but the students must be educated. To achieve that, schools have to adopt the same attitude toward quality that is now being adopted by leading American industries. Quality programs can be used in schools as well and as profitably as they can in factories, hospitals, and police stations. That is not the newest fanciful pedagogic theory; it is demonstrable fact.

Mount Edgecumbe High School in Sitka, Alaska, is the only public boarding school in the United States. It was run by the Bureau of Indian Affairs for Native American students from 1947 until 1983, when the state took it over as an alternative boarding school. About two hundred students come from all over Alaska, some 90 percent from rural areas, and the majority from homes that have problems, including alcoholism or abuse of some type. The students are not an elite corps, hand-picked to do well. Many of them are Native American; some do not speak English as a first language. They are neither smarter nor dumber, neither more nor less skilled, than American teenagers anywhere else. Native American students face the same basic problem faced by minority students everywhere. As a school official says, "[They] have extremely deep ties to their heritage and are struggling to keep the values and pride of the past while adjusting to a world dominated by another culture, another language and different social values."

Sitka, a port, is one of seven major cities in Alaska, but major is a relative term in the nation's largest and least populous state. Fewer than eight thousand people live in Sitka. The town was founded in 1799 and was the capital of Russian America. It was also the capital of Alaska from 1867, when the United States bought the territory from Russia, until 1900, when the capital was officially moved to Juneau (although nothing actually moved until six years later). The first college in Alaska was at Sitka, founded in 1878 by Sheldon Jackson, a missionary and educator, for whom it is named. A tourist brochure says Sitka's social and cultural life made it "the Paris of the Pacific" when San Francisco was still a gold rush settlement. Sitka now is a fishing, lumbering, and tourism center on Baranof Island, one of eleven hundred islands along the southeastern coast of the state. The town isn't especially cold in winter or hot in summer, but it's wet a lot; the knee-high rubber boots favored by fishermen are called "Sitka sneakers." On a clear day, however, you can stand on the Mount Edgecumbe campus on Japonski Island, connected by a bridge to Sitka, and watch eagles soaring in the clear, blue sky above the mountains across the inlet. And you can watch American high school students use the method taught by W. Edwards Deming to make themselves better, just as Ford Motor Company uses it to make better cars. The students call it Continuous Improvement Process.

Superintendent Larrae Rocheleau says, "Continuous Improvement Process does not cost anything. It is basically a change of attitude. Typically in education, what we've done in the past is throw money at problems rather than look at the management system of education. . . . Some people are not sure what quality education is. It's difficult to define. But in order to get the quality education, you have to get to the root of the problem. The root of the problem is the poor management system that most schools have in the United States." As enthusiastic as he is now, Rocheleau was not an immediate convert to the quality system. The first person at the school to think about education with quality was David Langford, a teacher, who says his interest started as "a fluke."

Burned out and fed up after seven years of teaching, he learned about quality from Jim Martin at McDonnell Douglas Helicopter in a ninety-minute meeting. "I came away from that thinking, 'This is it,' " Langford says, "and at that time, I didn't know quite what 'it' was, but I knew that what they had was a lot better than what we had." He began to study, reading everything that Deming had written or that had been written about him, watching video-tapes, talking to Myron Tribus and Joseph Juran, reading Kaoru Ishikawa to find out what was done in Japan, "and I came back and explained it to a lot of people, and they said, 'That's very interesting. Now let's get back to work.' " Rather than get discouraged, Langford began to use the Deming quality method with his computer club of twenty-one students. Langford took the club to Gilbert (Arizona) High School, where Dolores Christiansen had started teaching continuous improvement in her classes in business, entrepreneurship, and leadership management. The two groups of students visited companies around Phoenix that were using total quality management.

Back at Sitka, Langford's students began practicing continuous improvement, and in the spring of '89, they used an English project in persuasion to argue at a student-faculty assembly that changes should be made in the dormitory rules. The presentation was built around continuous improvement, and the factual information had been gathered exactly as it is in Deming's method. The English teacher, Kathleen McCrossin, became an enthusiastic supporter, as did the superintendent. "They were so excited,"

Rocheleau says, "had so many good things to say about the management process, and that's what sold me." In the quality program, students help make decisions. So far, the school dorm has been improved, the daily class schedule has been rewritten, and the traditional grading system is no longer used. Students, trained in statistics, keep track of their own performance using "grade calcs." Since nothing is considered finished until it's perfect, giving grades would be pointless or even harmful. "I found myself learning a lot more" without grades, says James Penemarl. "It's not the teacher having to check my progress, it's me having to check my progress. See, however much I learn is up to me, and if I want to learn, I'm going to go out and learn."

The experience getting quality started at Mount Edgecumbe is not unlike the experience at Motorola; no one was against it, but there were objections to the extra time it takes and the extra work it entails initially. One teacher said, "Possibly in the future, CIP will advance us to the state where it does save time or make things a lot more efficient, but at the present time, I find that it adds a lot of duties." Langford agrees that "it's not easier, but it's a lot more fun and a lot more rewarding. . . . If it was easy, everybody would be doing it, and we'd have great school systems, and everything would be changed around. But it's not easy. It takes hard work." It also takes cooperation and commitment, which traditional education does not. Rocheleau says no one felt a part of the old system. Students had no say at all, teachers had not much more control than their students, and even the school principal felt he was taking orders about his curriculum and how he ran his school. It was a system no one owned — or wanted to. "Now," Rocheleau says, "everyone is all into the process. We all work together to try and solve the problems for the good of our product, which is, in essence, the students." A student in an English class says, "It's made people work harder, and I think it's really practically done a miracle in this class." Another adds the endorsement, "Really, it smokes!"

The students have more control over their own lives — what they'll do and how they'll do it — but they have more responsibility as well. No one gets them up in the morning, no one cleans up after them, and no one makes them get to class on time. Under the old system, about thirty-five students were late to class each week and were punished for it. Under continuous improvement, students investigated the problem of tardiness, eliminated the causes built into the system that often made students late, got the administration to do away with punishment — which clearly wasn't working, anyway — and dropped the average weekly number of "tardies" from thirty-five to five. Imagine the time saved for teachers and administrators who do not have to listen to thirty-five earnest teenagers every week say how sorry they are, how they'll never do it again, and how it wasn't really their fault in the first place. That is a relatively mild example of the changes. Another that people find harder to accept is that the students help establish their own assignments and decide how they'll do them. Langford says, "We're continually trying to find more ways to involve the students in the decision-making processes here." That causes a minor problem. "New students that come into this system kind of go through a shock for a while," he says, "because they can't quite believe that we could trust people that much. They can't quite believe that we would want them to take that much more responsibility for their own education." It has made an enormous difference.

One student told Tribus, "We really didn't understand before. Then we just did what we were told, but didn't think about it." McCrossin says she's learned that her students can read books, and learn them well, that they couldn't handle before. "It wasn't that they couldn't do it," she says. "It was that I was keeping them from learning it before. Everybody needs to learn in their own way." (It is a point that Deming makes at his seminars: different people learn in different ways, and no way is superior to any other.) In a traditional school, students would read Homer's *Odys-*

sey, be given a quiz, often multiple-choice, and those who got a sufficient number of answers correct, even if they guessed, would pass whether they had learned anything about the ancient work or not.

In McCrossin's English class, students decided they would read the poem, write questions about what they did not understand, then meet in groups regularly to discuss the questions and raise related issues. To add to their learning, one student is studying Chinese mythology and another is studying Native American mythology to compare to the Greek. One student is writing a screenplay, others plan a Greek fashion show, and in a class we attended, there was a spirited discussion on the role of women in ancient Greece and modern America. There will be no examination. "They're all learning it," McCrossin says, "and they have a lot of energy and enthusiasm for what they're doing. That's what makes learning work. If it's somebody else forcing it down your throat, it's never going to work. You're never going to take it in." Her students agree. A young woman says, "Women's roles have changed a lot, but they haven't changed completely. And it [*The Odyssey*] is like history, practically. We can relate to them, and that's why we need to learn it. That's why we do learn it. And she's really stressed that to us."

Tribus, on his four-day visit, was impressed by what he saw in a biology class. He wrote in his report that the young students clearly had learned the facts, "but beyond that, they had learned how to organize their knowledge of facts [by logically relating them to each other]. In my own experiences as a teacher, I always found this the hardest to teach *at the college level*. Here I saw it happening with high school juniors." Tribus found another student who believed he was spending two hours each evening studying, but by keeping a simple statistical chart, he learned that his average was, in fact, thirty-five minutes. One key to quality education is student motivation. Langford finds that if he starts a new semester with a lengthy and detailed discussion — not a lecture, a two-way discussion — on what the class is about, what the students want to get out of it, what would prevent them from learning, and what it would mean to do the course with quality, students are forced to consider their own attitudes. "The student enthusiasm, drive, and efficiency so improved that they learned much more than they otherwise would have learned," Tribus reported. Jason Evans, a student, says, "I think continuous improvement is more of an attitude not to settle for doing the same thing every time, but to look at what you do and want to take it further the next time."

There is a conscious effort to get students to cooperate, to work together to learn rather than compete for grades. Rocheleau says that when new students arrive, they are dependent. "They look to *you* for guidance and support." An outdoor program at the beginning of school challenges them, and as each challenge is met and conquered, students become self-confident, even self-centered. Rocheleau says, "They say *I* a great deal." As the program goes on, students learn that even more can be done working together, and at that point they begin to say "*We* can do it." It is that *we* attitude that is most obvious at the school. Nickelle Cast, a student who had enrolled before CIP, says, "I think the whole atmosphere of the school has changed. Now people are working together, people get along better. . . . Like before, people didn't really care about school, but now everyone works together to do the best that they can do for everyone. People aren't just out for themselves."

At the school, you have to remind yourself that you are dealing with teenagers. There is an unexpected maturity, and students credit the quality program for that as well. "Well, CIP has helped me," Lisa Marie Polk says, "to hit — as Mr. Langford calls it — 'the big M,' maturity. I mean, it used to be where I didn't really care much about anything. I came here, and I started understanding CIP and understanding quality and productivity. All of a sudden, it just got kind of implanted in my mind. All of a sudden, I find myself adapting it to everything I do in schoolwork, and keeping my statistics, and my grade calcs, and everything. That's helped me grow up." That maturity may be forced by the demands of the students having to make decisions that at other schools would be made for them. For instance, the school has a statement of its mission, not written by the superintendent and imposed, but discussed, argued, written, and adopted by students, faculty, and administration together. Deming's fourteen points have been re-written by that same cooperative method to apply specifically to education.

There remains a long way to go. Told that we would be writing about the school, Langford asked only that we not make it sound as if Mount Edgecumbe is a complete and finished success. It is not. The school still has any number of problems to solve. Tribus agrees with that assessment, but "I came away enthusiastic over what I had seen." It is the only attempt of which he is aware to put a school completely into a quality program — everything from the dorm to the classroom to food service to administration. Tribus says the faculty must learn a great deal to improve the quality program, but he's optimistic because "they do not practice the self-delusion I encounter so often in my industrial visits. They know they do not know and are committed to doing something about it." The students appear to do well; about half the graduates have gone on to college, which is better than the national average. There is also a certain amount of pride among the students. One, talking about two major American corporations she had visited with classmates to study quality programs, says, "I realized that we knew just as much as they did, if not more in some cases. That really surprised me."

As much as the school has left to do, any success in American public education attracts attention, and requests for information are beginning to stack up. Students have been invited to other schools in "the lower 48" to talk about quality education, and as you would expect, they wrote their own presentation, called "Snow White and the New Management System." It starts when

King Deming is called to Japan to teach quality improvement, leaving Snow White in charge of the kingdom at home. The presentation stresses that students, teachers, and administrators must work together in mutual respect to achieve continuous improvement in education, because no one can do it individually. Snow White wants to put quality management into place when the kingdom starts to slip, but she's stopped by the Wicked Witch of Waste. Snow White escapes into the Forest of Opportunity, meets some characters who give her good advice, and winds up at the Seven Dwarf Mining Corporation. "Happy and Doc represent the willingness and organization of the new management system," the presentation says. "Grumpy and Dopey represent bad attitude and ignorance that interfere. Bashful, Sneezy, and Sleepy represent hesitation, distraction, and procrastination." Snow White teaches quality management to the Seven Dwarfs, improving their lives, but Waste finds her and gives her a poisoned apple. "As soon as Snow White took a bite of the apple, she fell into a deep sleep of status quo." If you know the fairy tale, you know that Snow White can be awakened only by a kiss from Prince Charming. Not this time. At Mount Edgecumbe, what awakens Snow White is a kiss from Commitment. He is, of course, a handsome prince who has been trained by Deming in continuous improvement. When he sees the sleeping Snow White, he knows that she is the quality he needs. "He then gave Quality the kiss of Commitment, and she immediately woke from her status quo sleep." Waste is banished, King Deming returns to the kingdom, "and because of the Prince's commitment and Snow White's quality, together they produced a beautiful daughter and named her Productivity. And the kingdom continually improved forever. However, the moral of the story is, as soon as you reach the point of success, don't get caught biting the apple of status quo."

Biting that apple is what Langford fears. "When I went back to my high school," he tells a student assembly, "after I'd been out for ten years, you know what I saw? The same thing. (Laughter.)

The same teachers teaching the same classes. I mean, it was just like I had never left. . . . Nothing had changed." In an interview, Langford explains what the students already knew. "Now, if you come back in three years or five years," he says, "I can guarantee you that you're going to see a school system here like none you've ever seen before. In fact, people that come into this system and see what's going on won't even know the right questions to ask. Because you'll see people operating on a whole other plane, working together, cooperating, making decisions, all those things that are part of this process will become just a natural way to work here." How close is he? "If I say we're 10 to 15 percent there, there is no such thing, because there is no there. Continuous improvement is continually revamping the system, changing it, and moving it toward ultimate perfection." Well, then, how long until he knows it was really worth the effort? "Oh, probably in about twenty-five to thirty years, and, see, that's the whole difference in thinking." Langford explains that when he goes to talk at other schools, everybody has a one-year plan, a three-year plan, even a five-year plan, but no one has ever produced a twenty-year plan. "But, see, that's part of the problem," he says. "By not having that long-term, pass-the-torch mentality, we're missing out on a lot of ways that we could improve the entire system."

The entire system desperately needs to be improved. Every spring in school districts across the United States, teenagers who cannot read, write, or make change for a dollar are awarded diplomas. Ninety percent of colleges and universities in the country must offer remedial basic education courses for their first-year students. American business and industry routinely spend billions on basic educational training. A Chicago bank, unable to find high school graduates to hire as secretaries, finally hired young graduates who wanted the jobs, then taught them English. During the earlier days of the Six Sigma program at Motorola, as it was about to make a high tech showcase out of one of its plants, it discovered that the majority of its employees there could not answer the question "What percentage of 100 is 10?" Lee Iacocca, Chrysler's chief executive, told a reporter, "I'm a big Detroit taxpayer. I paid so all these people could go to school. But wait a minute. Chrysler spends 11 percent of its $135 million training budget to teach hourly workers how to read and write." Remember, these are not people who cannot learn, because given remedial training at college or at work, they learned. In high school, for whatever reason, they either didn't learn or weren't taught. The fault is with the system. John Stepp, formerly at the Department of Labor, says, "Many American employers and union leaders are telling me that what we're getting out of the public school system often is, pardon the expression, scrap that has to be reworked, remade, at considerable expense."

"The first role of government," the consultant Michael Maccoby says, "is to make a healthy infrastructure to support global competition. The first thing in a healthy infrastructure are educated, healthy people. The problem of our [United States] government is not tariffs and all these other things; they're very secondary. I think free competition is great, but there have to be rules of the game. . . . But the point is we're not going to play unless we have people who are a lot more educated than they are in our society today, and we're not going to play in a society in which 37 million people have no health insurance, and where we are putting all the burden on companies, for example, to take care of the health costs, which are just out of sight, and we're asking them to take care of the education that is not done in the school system — not to speak of questions of the infrastructure of roads and airports, which are falling to pieces."

Not speaking of questions of America's physical infrastructure is what some American officials seem to do best. According to one report, $50 billion has to be spent soon to replace or repair 240,000 bridges in the United States. That is no secret — at least, not usually. In New York City, Mayor David Dinkins refused to give the City Council documents that include, according to a small newspaper item, "warnings that the city's bridges are so badly deteriorated that budget cuts would jeopardize public safety." A New York bridge official who argued against cutting funds for bridge maintenance was fired. That may be an extreme example, but every major city and every state in the United States has bridges that are no longer safe (one has already collapsed in New York State), highways with potholes the size of small cars, airports that are reminiscent of the earliest days of flight, and water pipes that leak.

Manford McNeil started Romac Industries more than twenty years ago and built it into an international success. The company makes huge clamps to repair water pipes and sells them world-wide. "The public doesn't think about water," McNeil says, "unless you turn on the faucet and nothing comes out. Then they think a whole bunch about it. . . . They have water mains that have been leaking for years, and the infrastructure in this country, as a matter of fact in this world, is really in tough shape. . . . God has a recapture clause: 'If you bury your pipe in His ground, He's going to turn it to dust.' And that's happening. . . . Older cities like Philadelphia or New York or those large cities are in terrible shape. . . . In Philadelphia . . . they buy hundreds of thousands of dollars of repair clamps a year. . . . The city of Cleveland can have five water main breaks a day every day. . . . The city of Seattle has one every other day, and that's not because we're smarter than Cleveland, we're just newer than Cleveland. . . . And as young as Australia is, they still have problems; we sell lots of repair clamps in Australia." One day the people will turn on the faucet and nothing will happen unless governments make repairs or replace pipes. That takes money, and we are back to the Tribus equation: quality produces productivity, which produces profits, which produces tax revenue.

In the meantime, Romac continues to make a profit by selling quality repair clamps in the United States, Europe, and Asia. "I think quality is like the practice of medicine," McNeil says. "You never quite perfect it. It's something that you are always striving for. We think that we have an obligation . . . to produce the best possible product that we can and market it for the benefit of the industry. Now that sounds . . . like we're not in business for a profit. That's not true." McNeil says he tries to make his employees see the importance of what they do to the man standing up to his waist in water trying to stop a leak. He says Romac is "good at quality," but he says the company has gotten better through its work in Japan. "The product is functional in this country [America]," he says, "but it also must be aesthetic in Japan — functional and aesthetic. This has made us very conscious of not only how it works, but how it looks. A label that's crooked on a box doesn't really make that much difference from a functional standpoint, but it looks like somebody doesn't care." He recalls that on a visit to Japan he noticed that the people handling his clamps put white gloves on. "That's kind of representative of the feeling that they have about product quality," he says. "They don't want to leave fingerprints unless it's necessary. . . . Function doesn't take a back seat to aesthetics, but there is nothing incompatible between function and aesthetic."

In the meantime, he says, "there isn't a perfect piping material. . . . it's subject to the trauma the earth goes through, it's subject to corrosion because of the hostile environment that it's in, and there really isn't a perfect answer to it. . . . Eventually, of course, the pipes will be replaced because we have gotten more and more people into smaller and smaller areas, and they need water. . . . If we made gold pipe, I'm sure it would last forever, but that's not economically feasible."

At the moment, neither is replacing the pipe or repairing the bridges or filling all the potholes. No government in the United States — local, state, or national — has the money it needs to repair its infrastructure or educate its children or provide adequate health care or protect its people from violent crime. Having blamed every possible villain, real or imagined, for a lack of money to do what needs to be done, only the barest handful of officials at any level seem to realize that the basic problem is a lack of quality, and until that problem is solved, none of the others can be. Joji Arai, the first to discuss the social deficit as an economic issue, says, "I still believe that if the United States really puts its mind to it, to overcome these deficits, and everyone works toward it, those problems can be solved."

11

The Global Marketplace

On June 18, 1812, President James Madison of the United States signed a declaration to start the War of 1812 against Great Britain. Two days earlier the British had repealed the maritime orders that had angered the Americans, but the war went on anyway for more than two years. On Christmas Eve, 1814, British and American negotiators concluded the Treaty of Ghent to end the war, but it ended as irrationally as it had begun. Two weeks later, the British attacked New Orleans, which was defended by a mixed bag of American regulars and volunteers commanded by General Andrew Jackson. The British suffered two thousand casualties and total defeat; the Americans had only a hundred casualties and complete victory, one of their few in the war. Jackson, widely and wildly cheered as a hero, eventually would win and serve two terms as president.

The reason the war started after the main grievance had been settled and continued after the peace treaty had been signed was communications. The only way for news to travel was by sea, and the fastest sailing ship could cross the Atlantic in two weeks, but three weeks was more normal and four weeks not unusual, so when the British attacked New Orleans, the peace treaty was still at sea.

In January 1991, a consolidated military force led by the United States attacked Iraq and Iraqi-occupied Kuwait with planes and missiles. Gary Shepard, a television reporter, saw the antiaircraft fire and bomb explosions from his hotel window in Baghdad and by telephone and satellite announced the beginning of hostilities to anyone watching *World News Tonight with Peter Jennings*. It was all but instantaneous. Until the Iraqi military stopped television broadcasts, American military leaders got bomb damage assessments from live Cable News Network (CNN) reports from Baghdad, just as the Iraqi leader Saddam Hussein had said earlier that he followed political developments in Washington and New York on CNN. Jim Hoagland, an American newspaper columnist, wrote the month before the war, "CNN is a technological and journalistic marvel that transmits not only news but an illusion of meaningful interdependence around the globe to plugged-in officials and travelers. . . . People everywhere know about the same thing at the same time. . . . anywhere is rapidly becoming everywhere."

Advances in communications technology have made as much difference to corporations as they have to countries and correspondents. Kenichi Ohmae, the managing director of McKinsey and Company in Japan, says, "One of the biggest changes that has taken place, over the last ten years particularly, is the proliferation of information. People in advanced countries receive information directly from the source through TV and [other] mass media." Thanks to satellites, fiber optics, and computers, geographical distance, so critical to communications in the War of 1812, is today inconsequential. For business purposes, every place is the same as every other place. Myron Tribus, the consultant, travels extensively and says, "Wherever you go in the world, you see Sony, you see Honda, you see Ford, you see producers distributing their things all over the world. This is an imperative because no nation can go it alone in the sense that no nation has all the resources required for survival, and in order to get the resources from others, you must trade with them." Ohmae says the old international trading rules that dated from the seventeenth-century British East India Company were that governments gave or sold private companies the right to produce and sell in their own countries; then, working together, the government and the company controlled information to consumers. No one knew what else at what price might be available somewhere else. "Now, it is completely different," he says. "People know what's best, cheapest, best quality, and, therefore, it is now the time for the consumers to choose products. . . . People have the information."

Rosabeth Moss Kanter, the Harvard professor and editor, says that information, the computer, and transportation advances caused the global market, and not only in manufacturing. "I mean," she asks, "what could be more local than the hospital down the street? Today, because of the ability to gather information, because of information technology, there are now hospitals that compete worldwide for the wealthy Arab heart patient or the wealthy European having discretionary surgery, because they can learn who those customers are, because they can spread their message, because the speed of transportation makes it easy for people to get there. There's practically nothing that's local anymore."

The "people matter, places don't" concept is one of four key elements in the modern economy faced by global companies. The others are that quality has replaced quantity as the way to measure manufacturing or service; that quality improvements are being made in some industries at a revolutionary rate, which the quality expert Joseph Juran says all firms must do if they don't want to fail; and that the economy is now customer-driven, as opposed to the days that Homer Sarasohn remembers when "the customer be damned" was a popular business opinion. "I love thinking about the consumer in the global marketplace," Kanter says, "because in essence, the consumer is what caused the political revolutions we're seeing all over the world. The falling away of the boundaries between Eastern Europe and Western Europe is all because people in Eastern Europe wanted to go shopping — they could see it on television, they could learn about it through mass media that don't respect national boundaries, and so they, too, wanted to participate." Ohmae agrees and refers to recent Russian disarmament agreements that he says were caused by "Bon Jovi and Levi Strauss, not the power of the Pentagons of this world. It's not the pressure of NATO and American military superiority that is really causing the Russian people to dismantle their hardware. I think it is the Russian people's awareness that their lifestyle . . . is not on a par with the rest of the world. . . . Ideology is not a central issue anymore. . . . people are not looking for nationalism. . . . people are looking for the good life." Power has passed to the consumer. "All over the world now," Kanter continues, "the customer has more power. Systematically, in industry after industry, power is shifting from the people who sell to the people who buy because they have more choices, because they can get it from anywhere, because there are more companies competing for their attention. . . . More competition, more choices, put more power in the hands of the customer, and that, of course, drives the need for quality."

Juergen Hubbert, a member of the Mercedes Board of Management and the head of its passenger car division, underlines that increasing competition. "It's becoming much harder," he says, "not only in the United States, where we have our competition, but even in Germany and Europe, all over the world. . . . I have a figure, which I remember, that in our field of activity [luxury automobiles], we had six competitors in 1980. In 1990, there are fifteen." The new competition came from companies in the United States, Japan, and other European countries. Even with the increased competition, Hubbert says, Mercedes still does well, even in Japan. "We had sales last year [1989] of thirty-five thousand cars," he says, "and this year we expect more than forty thousand. This means that we are number one among the imports. You can see that a high-quality and highly innovative car is even needed in Japan, in that very competitive market."

The competitive changes are all part of a natural progression of business that started with a tribal or village barter system and got increasingly complex. Two hundred years ago in the United States, there was a struggling national economy, but most of the trading that went on was local. Then, about a hundred years ago, the United States as a national economy became a region of the world economy, just as Europe did. At about the same time, Japan came out of three hundred years of isolation and the government started building a modern industrial economy to compete with the West. Robert Reich, the professor of political economics at Harvard, says, "Over the last fifty years, as transportation and communications costs have declined, the world economy has become, itself, globalized. Over the last ten years . . . you see the world economy shrinking even more. . . . Most large American companies, most large European and Japanese companies, have investments all over the world." The United States has $130 billion invested in Europe, and the twelve countries of the European Community have $190 billion in the United States. Some of that investment turns into jobs. Reich says that in 1989 "affiliates of foreign manufacturers created more jobs in the United States than American-owned manufacturing companies [and] American firms now employ 11 percent of the industrial work force in Northern Ireland." Foreign investments are not limited to the major national players.

It is likely that most Americans have never heard of a company named Unicord, but it is equally likely that those same Americans do know of Bumble Bee, the country's third-largest tuna canning company. In late 1989 Unicord, described as "an aggressive, young Thai company," bought Bumble Bee for more than the tuna company's assets were worth. Unicord is not the only Thai company with an interest in the United States. Saha-Union, a textile and footwear company, now makes thread at a factory it opened in Georgia early in 1990, and Siam Cement, in its first American investment, has joined an Italian firm in making ceramic tiles in Tennessee.

In all three cases, it made sense for the firms to locate in the United States because it put them in one of their larger markets, and being close to your customers is almost always desirable. It also put them inside the United States should the Congress pass legislation, as some members of Congress want, to protect American companies or jobs by keeping certain foreign goods out. Japanese auto makers are already under "voluntary restraints" and can ship only a limited number of cars from Japan to the United States, which is one reason that Japan has eleven relatively new auto assembly plants in North America; no one can keep you out if you're already there. Those plants do not build vehicles exclusively for sale in the United States. Honda makes cars and motorcycles in Ohio that it exports around the world, including back to Japan. According to Reich, "by the early 1990s, when Honda annually exports fifty thousand cars to Japan from its Ohio production base, it will actually be making more cars in the United States than in Japan."

Manuel Lujon, Jr., the American secretary of the interior, told reporters that he would not own a Japanese car or any foreign car, for that matter. Some other Americans feel the same way, and there are "Buy America" campaigns aimed at persuading American consumers to buy American products to help reduce the trade deficit. That is more difficult than it sounds. What, for example, is an American car? Is it a Honda assembled in Marysville, Ohio, by American men and women, or is it a Pontiac LeMans assembled at a highly automated Korean plant, based on a design by Opel in Germany, then sold under an American name? In the auto industry, American and foreign firms now routinely engage in joint ventures and are suppliers to and customers of each other, so an American car is, in all probability, an international product. The auto industry is fairly straightforward; in other industries, figuring out what belongs to whom can get much more complicated.

Peter J. Sprague, the chairman of the American National Semiconductor Corporation, has said, "We are using Russian engineers living in Israel to design chips that are made in America and then assembled in Asia." Deming, who often says he's fond of "stupid examples," is asked how he thinks of the global marketplace. He pulls a watch from his vest pocket and the battery-powered, lighted magnifying glass he always carries from inside his jacket; peering through the glass, he reads the small print on the watch case. "Assembled in China from Swiss parts, made in Hong Kong." As he tucks the glass and watch back in their respective pockets he says, "The global marketplace."

Paul Kreisberg of the Carnegie Endowment says, "Almost all large companies are now global companies — Japanese, American, European. It's very hard to go anywhere in the world and not find companies representing every [other] country in the world in that country and often merged together in complex interrelationships. . . . You find this less frequently with Japanese companies, but American and European companies have an enormous amount of interweaving of activities and interests." Daniel Yankelovich of the Public Agenda Foundation says, "The name of the game in the future for corporations is joint ventures. It's having your R&D capability maybe in East Germany and Hungary rather than in your plant in Philadelphia. So in human terms, we're living in each other's pockets. We are making partnerships and joint ventures across national lines. Corporations are losing their national identity. . . . Ten years ago, the world economy was nothing more than the sum of individual economies. There was no global economy."

To a good many people, there still isn't. Kreisberg says, "In one sense, it's all one big economy, but in terms of the entire structure of the American economy or the European economy, the global aspect of it remains a smaller part. If you take the total number of companies in the United States, many of the largest are these global companies. But if you look at all the business being done in the United States, the overwhelming proportion of the business is

241

being done by American companies. In Europe, the overwhelming proportion of business being done is by European companies, and in Japan, business is being done by Japanese companies." That has been true for a long time, but Yankelovich doesn't think it will continue to be true. "The integration, the cross-fertilization, the joint ventures, and the breakdown of lines of culture are creating a truly global market," he says.

If joint ventures are indeed the name of the future game, the United States may be at a disadvantage. Anand Panyarachun, the executive chairman of Saha-Union Corporation, says that when a Japanese firm sets up a factory in a foreign country, it works within the cultural and legal framework of that country. "But the others," he says, meaning Americans, "when they go to a foreign country, they still think they're setting up a factory in their own territory. They want to change the rules of the game. They want to level the playing field. They want to convert that into a part of their economy." Paron Israsena, the chief executive of Siam Cement, a conglomerate and the largest company in Thailand, is involved in several joint ventures, but he tends to avoid American companies in favor of the Japanese. "The big difference," he says, "in joining with the Japanese, they have fewer lawyers. We don't go through many, many stages of the legal process, and I think the Japanese are more practical. It's easier to talk to the Japanese than to the big American corporations, because in the American corporation, there are so many levels of control." Paron's one joint venture in Europe is with Michelin in France. He says it was difficult to reach them, but "after we contacted them once, and then we got the thing done fairly quickly, and we have become a very, very good partner of Michelin now in Paris."

Paron is not the only Asian who has noticed the incredible preponderance of lawyers in the United States. Jinnosuke Miyai, the president of the Japan Productivity Center in Tokyo, wrote a thoughtful article, comparing the two economies. "Another revealing difference between Japan and America," he said, "is the number of lawyers in each country. There is one lawyer for every 10,000 people in Japan. In America, the ratio is 1 to 700. This reflects how the Japanese prize harmony, avoid differences and seek consensus." He did not add, although he could have, that Americans are the most litigious people in the world, and he may have been generous in his statistics. According to *Parade* magazine, one person in every 360 Americans is a lawyer, except in Washington, D.C., where it's one in 22. Deming tells students at his seminars to try to arrange handshake deals with honest suppliers because a legal contract "is a piece of paper that any lawyer can wriggle out of." Lawyer-bashing has become something of a sport in the United States, but in international trade, America's lawyers and lawsuits are mentioned by others as part of the overall economic problem.

When a reporter asks Josh Hammond, the president of the American Quality Foundation, "If we [Americans] don't get better, what happens?" he answers, "The question is, who's the *we*? When you look at General Motors, they're all over the world. When you look at Germany, that was viewed as a closed industry, particularly in the automotive area, but they now have joint ventures with Japan. Why? Because the Japanese are coming to Europe, and it's better to be part of them, and it's natural to be part of them, and it's logical to be part of them. So all these joint ventures with Europe and with the Japanese, the *we* is not going to have capital letters. I think it's going to be smaller. The *we* is going to be all of us. There's a remarkable thing about quality in business that I've observed, that's the willingness to share the secrets. . . . That's because, I think, there's an understanding that the *we* is all of us."

Joint ventures and other modern production techniques have also created a relatively new trade problem. What is the nationality of anything? Thomas T. Niles, the U.S. ambassador to the European Community, says governments do have a responsibility to protect their citizens and companies from unfair trading practices, then he adds, "But I think it's also important that government recognize the reality of interdependence. . . . Inevitably, that's going to happen because the problems that we're going to be dealing with in the rest of this decade and into the next century are essentially global problems. They're the problems of dealing with the environmental issues that don't respect national borders, the extraordinary flows of investment capital around the world through new trading mechanisms, and the reality that when you buy something, you won't be able to tell where it was made or where its component parts were made. It's going to be an international product. That's an important reality."

What is, for example, an import into America or an export from America? The country buys more from other countries than it sells to them — or, at least, government statistics say so. Americans are told by their political, industrial, and labor leaders that the trade deficit exists because of trade barriers to American goods in Japan and other Asian countries and barriers to American agricultural products in the European Community. The perception, and sometimes the reality, of being treated unfairly by trading partners fuels the calls in the Congress and elsewhere for protection against foreign firms. Opponents of protectionist measures say that anything Congress does against Asia, for instance, would cause Asian countries to reciprocate. To which Roger Milliken, the chief executive of Milliken & Company, says, "All of those reciprocal actions are already in place today. They've taken them long ago. There's barrier after barrier after barrier to exporting into those [Asian] countries."

Still, global companies generally fear protectionism. Edwin Artzt of Procter & Gamble says, "I know it rankles people to see foreign countries have greater access to this market [America] than we have to theirs. But, inevitably, the way to solve this problem is to establish equal access principles through multilateral trade negotiations around the world. Protectionism is not going to strengthen this country. It's a Band-Aid." Hubbert, a German, agrees. "We as a company say there will be no Fortress Europe," he says, "because only if you can and will compete in a free market can you be strong and successful." He says that when the United States imposed "voluntary restraints" on the Japanese auto makers, the only thing that happened was that the Japanese opened assembly plants in the United States and car prices went up. The American consumer had to pay. "I think we should stay with free world trade," he says, "with free competition. We want to stay in this field because more than 50 percent of our cars are exported. We need the world market."

Most global companies of whatever nationality do need the world market. Therefore, the question of what is an import and what is an export is of a great deal more than statistical or academic interest.

The U.S. trade deficit does not mean only that foreign goods are flooding the American market. What helps to make the trade deficit higher for the United States is importing goods manufactured by American firms in other countries. What helps to make the American trade deficit lower are goods manufactured by foreign firms in the United States and exported to other countries. The American goods made overseas are American imports, driving the deficit higher; the foreign goods are American exports, pulling the deficit lower. As the American novelist Joseph Heller wrote in one of his books, "Go figure."

DeAnne Julius, the chief economist at Shell International Petroleum, did precisely that. America had a trade deficit in 1986, but Julius figured that if you took into account what American companies were doing overseas and what foreign firms were doing in the United States that year, the $144 billion deficit would become a $14 billion *surplus.* Those figures would not surprise Ohmae. In *The Borderless World,* he says that global companies "are helping to create a borderless economy where trade statistics are meaningless," but backward bureaucrats in the United States and Japan "miscount the trade figures and get them wrong month after month, and in the process they provide the weapons for economic war between nations."

Reich agrees. "We are entering into a new era," he says, "in which all of these companies are becoming global. They're doing everything all around the world, including their high value-added research, development, and fabrication. They're hiring people from all over the world. They're getting capital from all over the world, and, indeed, even at the highest management levels — except for the Japanese — you find people from all over the world. There is no such thing any longer as an American multinational; it's a global multinational. . . . Digital Equipment, IBM, Coca-Cola, GM, Ford, among many other companies, made more profits outside the United States in 1989 than they made inside the United States.

"There have been for the last 350 years," Reich continues, "companies that operated around the globe. What's new is that [the location of] corporate headquarters and the nationality of ownership now matter less and less because these global companies are exporting from every country. . . . Singapore's largest private employer is General Electric. . . . Taiwan [whose largest export market is the United States] counts AT&T, RCA, and Texas Instruments among its largest exporters." Ohmae says that U.S. figures show that America has an unfavorable trade balance with Mexico even though everyone recognizes that what causes it is American factories that have moved just across the border to take advantage of available Mexican labor. "So you have a trade deficit with Mexico," he says, "not because you have lost competitiveness with that country, but because you have migrated into Mexico for production." That is not a one-way street. Siemens, the German global giant, ships fuel injectors, antiskid brake solenoids, and transmission solenoids to almost every major industrial country from its factory in Newport News, Virginia. Sony and Sharp, both Japanese, export from the United States, as does Philips, a Dutch firm.

Michael E. Porter, also a Harvard professor, does not accept the Reich-Ohmae idea of a borderless world. He argued in *The Competitive Advantage of Nations* that the nationality of a company does, in fact, make a difference. "My theory," he wrote, "begins from individual industries and competitors and builds up to the economy as a whole. The particular industry . . . is where competitive advantage is either won or lost. The home nation influences the ability of its firms to succeed in particular industries. The outcome of thousands of struggles in individual industries determines the state of a nation's economy and its ability to progress."

The Economist concluded that the role of nations in the future would be about what it is today, but it used Julius's trade figures and other information to make an exception: "The one thing in which the nation-state's grip seems visibly to be loosening is the organisation of economic life." George Fisher of Motorola seems to agree, but not totally. "We have to differentiate," he says, "between companies and countries. . . . Does being a successful global company headquartered in a particular country mean that country will also be successful as an economic entity? Increasingly, the answer is no. . . . I don't want to argue that companies will prosper on a global basis independent of how their home countries prosper. But the separation will grow. In Motorola's case, I hope the separation never gets so serious that it weakens the link between this company and the United States."

Artzt of Procter & Gamble says that to a certain extent, the company has a commitment to the United States because "inevitably, every company, even though it is multinational in nature or global in its business operation, has to see itself in terms of its national roots, and in that sense, we're an American company. . . . We were founded in the United States. . . . We are citizens of a lot of countries, but our initial citizenship is here." Yankelovich says the nationality of corporations is confused by partnerships and joint ventures, "but they have responsibilities to their nations, and so in that fundamental respect, they are like citizens who may be diplomats and may have all kinds of entangling alliances outside the borders, but they still remain Japanese citizens or American citizens or British citizens."

Robert Galvin of Motorola does not think corporate nationality will disappear anytime soon. "In terms of the manner in which we are structurally organized and focused," he says, "there's a high quality of globalization in the larger companies. But it's not likely in the next couple of generations that we will lose the encultured, national-based makeup of most of us. I think Motorola will be an American-based company for a number of generations. I think the major Japanese companies will be looked upon as Japanese-based companies, and so for the Dutch, et cetera. But I think that we're also going to be more open-minded thinkers, individually, as we think about our roles in the other person's part of the world."

As opposed to the earlier American standard, especially in the 1960s and '70s, of insisting that all employees everywhere act like ersatz Americans, Motorola has adopted more appropriate policies. Galvin says, "We really put our feet in the shoes of the native. We try to populate our organizations with the natives to a substantial degree, and we genuinely try to understand the cultures and the tastes and the purposes of these people. There are a few things that we will not compromise, if, indeed, there happen to be varying standards, and one of those has to do with integrity. There are places in the world where standards of integrity are just different than the American standards on matters such as conflict of interest. But if you can get past that very important factor, the French or the Malaysians or the Scots or the Israelis all have much the same fundamental objectives of serving customer and having income for family. We respect the ways and means in those particular places."

That corporate attitude is no longer unusual in any country. Kunerth of Siemens says simply, "Our obligation to the different governments in the countries where we are is that in every country — and this is part of the corporate culture of Siemens — in every part of the world where we are, we want to be a good citizen of that country." Mangi Paik of the Korean Ministry of International Trade and Industry, says that global companies need to meet local needs for products around the world, and "we want the multinational firms to be more legitimate in society. They need to be good citizens, and they need to develop the local culture. At the same time, they can make money. The biggest question is how best can we harmonize those two goals." Paron of Siam Cement says that from the beginning, seventy-five years ago, the Thai company has had a four-part statement of philosophy. "And the last one," he says, "is concern for social responsibility. It is our responsibility to contribute to the society we live in, no matter if we live in Thailand or we live in Tennessee, United States. We would be a good citizen there and contribute to social responsibility, as we do a lot in Thailand. . . . We consider being a good corporate citizen a fundamental responsibility to our society. We have to be good or be useful to the community where we are operating." Tetsuo Chino, the president of Honda in North America, told the *New York Times*, "The bottom line of our company is to respect people. You have to respect the local community or you can't grow, and to do so, you have to become more American. We are trying to localize everywhere we operate. In Europe we are trying to be more European, in Brazil more Brazilian. This is a natural step for increasing business in the host country."

Artzt says that going back to the early days of this century, Procter & Gamble has operated the same way. "Our policy," he says, "has always been that we would operate as if we were citizens of the countries in which we're doing business, and that the interest of that country would be considered in all of the decisions we make. . . . At the same time, we think of ourselves as a guest in those countries. We're not in there to exploit. We're in there to develop a business, to help develop the economy of the country, to offer our employees the same kind of future that we offer our employees here [in the United States], and we do that to an extent in our own self-interest. It's a success model. We're proud of the fact that in many countries in the world, Procter & Gamble is thought of as a local company. . . . That's a direct reflection," he says, "of the way we conduct our affairs in these countries, and it's by design. . . . when a company like ours becomes thought of by the local consumers as a local company, the consumer feels more comfortable with our products."

Kanter uses Procter & Gamble as an example of one change the global marketplace has caused. "You may be doing R&D," she says, "as Procter & Gamble did for some new products jointly in Japan, Europe, and the United States, and attempting to integrate the best ideas from all of those parts of the world instead of the United States automatically dictating." She says that illustrates a critical difference between the old and new ways of doing business. "What it really means," she says, "is not that you're doing business in many countries; we've always done that. . . . What it means today to be a truly international corporation is that strategy can be set in many different parts of the world rather than just at headquarters, that there is a true local presence that takes advantage of the best of local talent, that finds a way to transfer the ideas or the output of production all over the world. . . . It's headquarters whose influence is diminishing."

The influence of American and European headquarters may be diminishing more rapidly than that of the Japanese. The Thai executive Anand says, "I think the Americans and Europeans have learned a lot in trying to train local people to take up positions of responsibility. The Japanese have a hang-up on this one. They are accused of feeling superior to local people. They will always say, 'Well, you know, the Japanese style of management is very complicated, very complex. It takes years to learn.' So when you talk about it to the Japanese, with thousands of years of culture and history, a span of ten years to them is very short. When you talk to an American, the Americans are in a hurry. They want to train people to take up managerial positions. Within five years they like to have, you know, number two man, number one man, a local man. A Japanese may talk about a generation or two."

Artzt says three things are critically important for international success, and one of them involves local people. "We have for years," he says, "been recruiting and developing and training people in countries all over the world, and in just exactly the same way that we did, and still do, here in our home base in the United States. You can't become a truly successful international company if you have to continuously export people in order to run your business. You've got to develop them." The other two ingredients for global success, he says, are "products that have a technology base that makes them appealing all over the world [and] a presence. We learned long ago that selling consumer products purely on an export basis was not a long-term recipe for success."

Tribus says that to compete in that world market takes invention, innovation, quality, and productivity. "Invention means getting the good ideas," he says, "and here we [Americans] have an advantage because of the heterogeneity of our population. . . . Innovation is the process of taking an idea and bringing it to the marketplace. . . . and the Japanese have recognized in the last ten years that innovation is the most important element for them because they already have achieved quality, and through quality you get productivity. We [Americans] had a White House Conference on Productivity. We never had a White House Conference on Quality [even though] the route to productivity is through quality."

Artzt says, "A very exciting development for us has been the realization that we don't need to alter the quality or the technology in our products from place to place in order to be successful. Consumers have very much the same value system around the world. . . . just as the world is shrinking in a lot of other ways, the evaluation of quality worldwide is coming together. . . . people everywhere have the same demand, the same grading system for evaluating quality. We tend to think in terms of electronic devices, or appliances, or automobiles, or high tech equipment, but it applies to a diaper, or a bar of soap, or a sanitary napkin, or a shampoo just as well, and that is now driving our business. . . . If the toughest market in the world in terms of judging the quality and performance of a disposable diaper is Japan, develop a product that is superior and more successful in the Japanese market and sell it all over the world."

In the old economy, a producer could please the customers in one country or even one region and be successful. For a major manufacturer, customers are now everywhere, with different backgrounds, different tastes, different demands, and the product has to please them all. That makes doing business in the global marketplace a lot tougher.

Siemens, the German firm, supplies about five hundred different systems to the world's automakers, all of whom are now demanding improved quality and reasonable costs. "They are demanding more and more quality," Kunerth says, "because they have to give their customers more and more of a very good and very reliable product." He says quality was part of the 150-year-old company's first statement of purpose, but how it produces quality has changed. Siemens, like Motorola, has studied the experts around the world and developed its own system of quality to satisfy, not only its customers in the global market, but its customers' customers as well. Talking about the environmental movement, particularly in Europe and North America, Tim Leuliette, the American on the management board, says, "We've got to change the way the vehicle operates, the way the vehicle interfaces with society. We've got technology; we need to apply it to a solution the customer can afford. That is a fundamental element of how we get our business. Technology drives us." The technology, much of it, comes from the aerospace industry. "We start to be able to tell the customer what technologies are available in the future, and he starts telling us his needs, and together we start predicting what our products need to be."

As soon as Siemens produces, say, a new fuel injector for one of its customers, all the other auto companies in the world learn about it almost at once. "And if it improves the product in a cost-benefit relationship," Leuliette says, "they want it too. . . . so it's customer-driven, and there's no one customer that's the toughest. These guys feed on each other quite well, and they keep moving the standard forward." To illustrate what that means to Siemens, Leuliette talks about the fuel injector plant at Newport News. "That's a unit that in 1985 produced 30,000 fuel injectors a month, and in 1987 produced 30,000 fuel injectors a week, and today produces 30,000 a day. And [by 1992] it will be producing 30,000 a shift twice a day." That has been and is being done through quality improvement. As Galvin once said, "Quality is quantity; quality is low cost."

Kees van Ham of the European Foundation for Quality Management sees that pressure for improvement on suppliers as a "powerful mechanism" to improve quality and to make more chief executives aware of it. In 1989, the five hundred chief executives of the most important companies in Europe were asked, "What priority does quality management have in your company today?" Van Ham says 15 percent answered "highest priority," and 60 percent said "one of the highest." He says had you asked the same people the same question ten years ago, no one would have rated quality as his company's highest priority.

Internationally, there is a new cooperative effort to make quality more important. The International Productivity Service (IPS) is sponsored by the U.S. Department of Labor; the Canadian Labor Market and Productivity Center; the European Association of National Productivity Centers, representing fourteen nations; and the Japan Productivity Center. The service, a clearinghouse for information, publishes a triannual productivity journal, sponsors an international symposium every two years (the next is scheduled in Oslo in 1992), and organizes smaller, more frequent conferences to keep up with the latest developments.

The IPS is headed by Joji Arai, who previously headed the Japanese Productivity Center in Washington, D.C. He has lived in the United States for many years, and his father was a Japanese cowboy in the old American West. In talking about Japanese and Americans, Arai uses *we* and *they* almost interchangeably — perhaps the only man in either country who does. He says that quality improvement worldwide is more important than who produces what where. "The final goal," he says, "is to generate new wealth by utilizing the resources available and coming up with new, added value. . . . and that generation of new value directly contributes toward improving the standard of living of people. [It] has to have this ultimate goal of improving the quality of human life. . . . The only way we can keep this world in peace is by generating more value out of limited resources so that people will be able to enjoy a better life."

12

What Now?

The sixteenth-century Polish astronomer Nicolaus Copernicus demonstrated that the model of the universe written by Ptolemy and accepted for fourteen hundred years was wrong. Astronomers already knew that the sun, moon, and planets never showed up where Ptolemy said they should, but, certain that Ptolemy was right because he was *the* accepted authority, those obvious mistakes of planetary movement were blamed on faulty translations of the original Greek manuscript or faulty mathematics. To put it in more modern terms, the problem was blamed on sloppy workmanship by later astronomers using Ptolemy's theory. Copernicus's contribution was to point out that those mistakes were not caused by bad translations or worse math but were *inherent in the system*. Ptolemy had the earth at the center of the universe, so his system could not be made to work. The sun did not revolve around the earth, and no amount of hard work, sophisticated technology, or clean living and constant prayer was going to make it do so.

Exactly the same thing is true of business and industry, manufacturing or service, government at all levels, education, health care — you name it — in the United States. The problem isn't in how the work is done, it's in the system. "You see," Myron Tribus says, "modern industry is a complex set of practices, protocols, procedures, policies, processes, that have to be linked and treated, all in one. If you follow the usual bad managerial practice of trying to divide the system up into independent pieces, and give everybody a job to do, then the system as a whole doesn't function together, and then it can't produce good products. It can't produce quality."

The American management and industrial systems in the years after World War II had a positive genius for producing quantity, and as long as quantity was the key, the United States ruled the economic world. Quantity doesn't sell anymore. Pat Choate can recite international trade figures from memory. "In the mid-'60s," he says, "we [Americans] had half the world's market share in basic industries; we're now at around 22 or 23 percent. In 1973, we had 15 percent of the world market share in business services, such as insurance, finance, travel, architectural service, and engineering service; we have less than 7 percent today. In the 1970s, we had these massive agricultural surpluses each year. They're gone; they'll never return. In the late '70s and early '80s, we had a high technology trade export surplus of over $28 billion a year. Since the mid-'80s, we're running a trade deficit. It really means that we're being pushed back across the board."

Herb Striner has his own set of domestic figures. "In 1970, 99 percent of all telephone sets sold in the United States were manufactured by U.S. companies," he says. "By 1988, this share was 25 percent. In 1970, 89 percent of all semiconductors sold in the United States were produced by U.S. companies. By 1988, this share was 64 percent. In 1970, almost 100 percent of all machine tools sold in the United States were produced by U.S. companies. By 1988, this share was 35 percent. In 1970, 98 percent of all color television sets sold in the United States were produced by U.S. companies. By 1988, this share was 10 percent. Finally, in 1970, 40 percent of all audiotape recorders sold in the United States were produced by U.S. companies. By 1988, this share was 1 percent."

"There is an awareness that we have a problem," Daniel Yankelovich says, "that it's a serious problem, that America is falling behind. And that seriousness of understanding is coupled with the fantasy-like view that it's going to be okay; that it's bad, it's serious, but 'they' will find a solution for it — sort of a magic-bullet mentality. . . . So what you have is public consciousness at a very peculiar stage of development, where there's awareness that there's a serious problem, but there's no real basic understanding of what needs to be done to come to grips with that, what the country has to do to come to grips with it. . . . It's a faith in America, it's a faith in the future, and it's also just a lack of realism in wrestling with the issues and a failure to understand them. If you feel your future is jeopardized and you don't have any conception of what to do about it. . . . you're either going to worry yourself sick or not think about it, and not thinking about it is a lot easier."

Not thinking about it *is* easier; it is also economically fatal. What needs to be done is not alchemy, not magical, and not impossible to understand. It *is* difficult to do, but considering the numbers of people in assorted companies and countries who have already learned how to produce quality, what needs to be learned in the United States is obviously not that difficult. A quality school in Alaska is being run by teachers, administrators, and students who have the same capacities and limitations as teachers, administrators, and students in other schools. There are quality hospitals; they are not staffed by geniuses. Quality programs within the federal government are run by the same types of bureaucrats and civil servants who are *not* running quality programs in other federal agencies. Quality products are now being profitably manufactured in American companies by adults who first had to be taught to read English and do simple arithmetic. A quality program, in short, is not intergalactic travel.

The easiest way to explain how a quality program works was given to us by Tribus. Imagine three concentric circles, the center one labeled *The Technical System*, the next labeled *The Social System*, and the outside labeled *The Management System*. Now, put all three in a box labeled *Education,* Tribus says, "because we're boxed in by what we know, what we think, our ways of looking at the world." Changing the whole system of concentric circles starts with the reeducation of the managers. "When Deming speaks of profound knowledge," Tribus says, "what he's talking about is the knowledge it takes to deal with all three levels and to understand the relationship between what you do and what's going to happen in those three systems." Obviously, if the management system decides to change the tools being used in the technical system, they're going to change how people react in the social system, whether they mean to or not. In a lumber camp, if management replaces axes with bucksaws, individual lumberjacks working alone must then work in two-man teams. The lumber camp's entire social system has just been changed. If you go from individual workers on an assembly line doing exactly what they're told over and over again to teams using statistical tools to improve quality, you have changed the social system within the plant, just as you do if you replace all the foremen with self-managing teams.

Where you are within those concentric circles dictates what you'll be asked to do. Generally, senior management is working on improving its own system and trying to guide the social system, but while they are aware of the tools in the technical system — charts, graphs, and other things — workers use those tools more often to improve quality production, while they also try to improve the social system that affects everyone in the company. However, workers lack the authority to change the management system. "So while we want everybody to be involved in improvement," Tribus says, "everybody's not doing the same thing. Each person has to make the contribution that's appropriate to that level."

Tribus says that everyone at every level can make a contribution if he or she thinks before doing any task: "What does it mean to do it with high quality?" That job, he says, will go smoother and better. He says there is a second series of rings, a sort of pecking order of possibilities. The center ring contains those things that can be improved individually, without any help or authorization. The next circle is those things that can be improved working with colleagues, and in the third ring are improvements that can be negotiated with the boss if you have collected enough good information to make your pitch. Then you hit a wall. In that final ring are those things that can only be improved by senior management. But imagining that you have arrived at that wall before you even start is a mistake. "Everybody's job is to identify those rings and get to work now," Tribus adds, "and not wait until President Bush decides that quality is the way we run the country. This is the thing people need to understand if they're going to get off dead center."

While the American quality experts say that quality must involve the most senior executives, that is a theoretical absolute; as a practical matter, they do not have to be involved from day one. Tribus says that lower-level personnel — by sending the boss copies of articles, or giving reports on quality program successes, or involving colleagues in a quality movement — can sometimes persuade an otherwise reluctant chief executive. Consider David Langford, the teacher who got quality started at Mount Edgecumbe High School in Sitka. "What Dr. Deming says is that quality needs to be implemented from the top down. Ideally," he says, "I agree with that. On a functional basis, I have some reservations, because if I had waited for quality to be implemented top down in this organization, I'd still be waiting. It would never have happened. But what I did recognize is exactly what he [Deming] says, that as soon as possible, top management has to be involved."

Langford also recognized another problem in getting a quality program started. "To implement a quality process, to me," he says, "is basically two areas: one is human relations; the second is statistical analysis. . . . When I first started this process, I thought the latter — statistical analysis — was 99 percent of the process, and human relations was 1 percent. Since we've been in it for two years, I'm now realizing it's just the opposite. We could teach anybody in a half-hour session how to do simple statistical analysis processing. . . . We can't in half an hour persuade people to use it." Persuading the American people — not just a few, but most of them — to adopt a quality culture is, as far as Yankelovich is concerned, essential.

"There's a whole set of principles," he says, "for developing standards of quality and an ethic of quality and a discipline of quality, but you don't see it very much here [in the United States]. Not enough. It's beginning; it's starting. In the last few years, there are companies that have made a lot of headway. There's a recognition of a concern, but it's now just a handful of leading companies rather than the thrust of the country. And for it to be the thrust of the country, it can't just be the initiative of a handful of managers. The whole culture has to support that point of view, and that's one of the reasons that people are important to this problem, not just technical experts. . . .

"The thing that's wrong with the debate on competitiveness [quality]," Yankelovich continues, "is that it's the property of the experts, the public is excluded from it." There are, essentially, three reasons for that, and all have to do with language. "I'm startled to realize, talking to some economists," he says, "that the word *quality* is not part of the economist's vocabulary. There is no concept of quality in traditional economic thinking." And if there were, that concept would not be called quality. That is far too simple a word; everyone could understand it, and that would not do. That is the second part of the problem. The experts speak the expert-technical-jargon language, as do lawyers and doctors, and each expert talks only about his limited area of expertise. It's the same as listening to the blind men describe the elephant — each describes the part he's feeling. "So what the public hears is a babble of voices, a cacophony," Yankelovich continues. "So long as that's the case, people can't sort it out by themselves; they're not experts, and they don't think it's their concern or their problem. They think it's something that the bankers and the econo-mists and the politicians are going to solve, and it's just not true."

He says the same thing happened once before in the United States in nuclear arms, when the experts were moving "toward an ever-escalating balance of terror" as each side upped the ante on mutual deterrence. That changed, he says, when a few experts started "to explain [to people] that the issue isn't that compli-cated, that it's fundamental, and that there's a need to grasp it. That hasn't happened yet with the competitiveness problem."

The third reason the public is excluded from the national debate on quality is corporate euphemisms. Things that would normally upset the American people are masked behind inten-tionally fuzzy words. No American corporation *fires* anybody any-more; companies are *restructured* or *downsized*, and unless you take the time to puzzle it out, no one knows that people are being laid off or fired or forced into early retirement. *Fired* is a harsh and understandable reality, and people know that a human being, perhaps a family, has been hurt. *Downsized* is a blurry image in "a kinder, gentler America," and people don't know what's going on or whether they should care. Another corporate nicety is "flatten-ing the corporate structure." What normal English-speaking man or woman not directly involved knows that "flattening," however necessary, means that whole layers of middle management are being wiped out? Chrysler used to have eleven management levels; it now has nine, and in four years nine thousand white-col-lar jobs have disappeared at the car company. Another three thousand may go this year. Not fired, flattened.

It probably will get worse in American industry. In a survey for *Fortune* magazine, the Wyatt Company found that among major American corporations, 41 percent expect that the number of managers will shrink in the next five years and 31 percent said the number of executives will shrink. And while 48 percent thought the number of executives would remain about as it is, only 29 percent thought there would be as many managers in five years as there are now. The bright spots were rather limited: 25 percent thought the number of managers would increase, 17 percent thought there would be more executives in the future. Which raises the question, What is the opposite of *flattening?* Or is it simply routine, growth-related *upsizing?*

To be fair, corporations are not alone in their efforts to be anything but clear. For years the government has found it completely impossible to communicate in simple English, and Americans in general have picked up the worst of their government's habits. The "reformed drunk" of our youths is the "recovering alcoholic" of our adult years. The comedian George Carlin begins a hilarious routine with the simple statement, "Sometime in my life, 'toilet paper' became 'bathroom tissue.' " Just when we need clarity, we get euphemistic mush; the people can't understand it and, therefore, can't help with the solution.

Without the involvement of people on all levels, nothing happens — not in a plant, not in a country. Using one or two quality techniques, Daisaku Harada of the Japan Productivity Center says, isn't what produces quality. Speaking of the Japanese experience, he says, "Quality is the way of thinking about the product or service we are going to provide. This means that top management of a corporation has to be deeply involved in the production of a quality product, and also each employee of that corporation has to be aware of the importance of making a quality product, and so it is a company-wide program which helps to produce a quality product." Or a quality government, quality school, quality hospital.

The Japanese have been saying that for years; in effect, they are trying to teach Americans what Americans taught them forty years ago. "The U.S. is a very, very good teacher," Kenichi Ohmae says. "The U.S. knows how to teach other countries. . . . but I think the U.S. is a very poor listener and learner. The U.S. does not learn very well."

But one thing Americans have learned from Japan: they don't want to live in a society where people suffer from *karoshi,* literally working themselves to death. If Americans believed *karoshi* and quality were synonymous, that would slow the quality movement just as it is beginning. What apparently is happening in Japan has nothing to do with the Japanese total quality system but a great deal to do with a Japanese social system that demands success — or, at a minimum, the appearance of success. Japanese managers will kill time in the equivalent of pinball parlors rather than go home immediately at the end of the day. They don't want their neighbors to think that they aren't important to their companies or that they don't work hard enough to achieve success. Industrial success is not, and certainly should not be, the only goal of an American quality movement.

"We shouldn't," Rosabeth Moss Kanter says, "try to get quality in America at the expense of the quality of life, because in this [quality] environment, there are more pressures on people, more demands, also more opportunities to contribute, and so the hours people work, one way or another, are going up at the same time that the interest in family life, the concerns of working parents, who are now prevalent in the workplace, are also very strong. How are we going to balance those conflicting demands? How are we going to keep the energies and the talents of people and, at the same time, acknowledge the fact that they have more to their lives than just work? If we don't acknowledge that, of course, we're not going to have anybody to do the work. . . . It is an economic issue, because getting the people to do the work is critical for success in this environment. What we're asking for is more brain power, which means more emotional energy at every level of the firm, and we're not going to get that unless people also feel reasonably comfortable that their personal lives are in control and that they have sufficient time to do what they need to do."

One of the great problems of the industrial revolution, which led to mass production, was that the machine was new and interesting so it attracted the attention, and there was less concern for the people running the machine than there was for the machine itself. "One of the most important events of the last hundred years," Donella Meadows told a symposium on quality, "has been the domination over the whole world of our . . . modern industrial culture. That culture is not very hospitable to either the concept or the creation of quality as experienced by individual human beings." Kanter does not believe Americans will accept that now. "We're not going to be blind conformists," she says, "who live in company towns and give our all for the great corporation. Americans are much too independent for that." Even if they weren't, blind conformists can't help a company think, improve, or get ideas. The quality movement is the first industrial change that is based on the importance of people thinking, where brains are more critical than machines.

Meadows, at the symposium, said, "The next frontiers . . . the only remaining ones, may be the far reaches of outer space or the depths of the ocean. . . . I think the next hundred years will be exploring the frontiers of quality of life, and the experience of quality of human beings. There are the far reaches of outer space where wonderful discoveries may be made; there are also the far reaches of the understanding of complex systems. We may make tremendous discoveries in the depths of the ocean, but I think we have far greater discoveries to make in the depths of the human soul." Kanter says, "I think, frankly, it has come down to what kind of lives we want to live, what kind of a society this is, and it's something ineffable, and companies, by the way, respond to that. Increasingly, American companies recognize that they need to be driven by values, not only economics." That's the reason Homer Sarasohn asked the Japanese, "Why are you in business?"

"We have grown to realize," Fred Smith of Fedex says, "that customer satisfaction must begin with employee satisfaction. All the more reason, therefore, to create a workplace that responds to the human desire to be part of a greater mission, one in which everyone can contribute and make a difference. But nothing can happen without total management commitment, and nothing will happen if that commitment isn't demonstrated on a daily basis. . . . We've tried to show our people in a variety of ways that our company's goals are very much in line with their personal goals . . . by answering a set of essential or fundamental questions. One, what's in this for me? Two, what do you expect of me? Three, where do I go if I need help? Where do I go to get justice if I have a problem involving my career? Four, is there an opportunity to grow, to be challenged, and to get ahead in this organization? When answers to these questions are reinforced by action, the next question most likely will be, 'How can I help?' "

None of that is new in American industrial history. Tribus says that when Henry Ford began his company he had just-in-time inventory delivery, he had worker participation, he had high pay for workers, and a concern, albeit paternalistic, for their health and well-being. In return, he got a superior car for its day. Then, Tribus says, the automobile industry was taken over by professional managers "who lost sight of the enterprise as a source of jobs and goods and began to think of it as a money pump." He refers to Alfred Sloan's comment that the purpose at GM was not just to make motor cars but to make money, and Tribus says, "Now if you have 100,000 or 200,000 or 400,000 people working for you, and you tell them, 'We're not in the business of making the best cars in the world, we're in the business of making money,' there is no way you get their hearts and minds to work on it." In a quality system, the hearts and minds are much more important than the arms and legs.

"One of the things," Stephen Schwartz of IBM says, "that we feel is terribly important to our market-driven quality thrust is the empowerment, the involvement, the participation of our employees, bringing them much more into the process of determining what the problems are, but more importantly, what the solutions are. So the role of the manager changes from one of managing, controlling, directing, and auditing to one of leading, empowering, coaching, facilitating. . . . So part of what you have to do is have your management team transformed from managers to leaders, and that's a challenge. The second part of the challenge is to convince your employees that you mean what you're saying, that you really do want them to become active, that you really have empowered them, that they really can take the lead."

Schwartz says there are three absolutely essential items from top management in a corporate quality program. "The first," he says, "is very strong leadership from the top so that everyone understands that this [quality program] is the most important. Second is our executive team must also change the way they operate with their management, and they must empower their management team, they must delegate much more power and authority to their management team, just like they're asking managers to do with employees. . . . Third is to make sure in everything they do, they walk like they talk. When there is a crunch of some kind, it is very easy . . . to revert to how you used to do it, because that was always considered successful in the past. So the toughest job is to continue to walk the talk."

IBM, Rochester, like Motorola, has built its own quality program. "We visited about fifty companies in the United States and elsewhere around the world," Schwartz says, "talked to a lot of quality gurus, and built our own strategy based on what we found. Or to quote Roger Milliken, 'We borrowed shamelessly from everywhere we could find.' " While the program is tailored to IBM, it has the same aim as Motorola or Federal Express. "The whole focus," Schwartz says, "is satisfying the customer, whether that be the internal customer or the external customer, because a lot of IBMers don't ever see our paying customers, they only service and support the other IBMers. But the focus is the customer, and we're driving everything that way." Notice the difference: IBM recognizes an internal customer; Motorola does not, and both are using similar Six Sigma programs.

As with most quality companies, IBM has drastically reduced the number of suppliers it uses and changed the way it does business with them. Instead of the typically American system of low-bid-wins, Schwartz says, "we formed a partnership with our suppliers. . . . and we share information back and forth. . . . and so I think the relationship with our suppliers is stronger today than it's ever been in our history." The relationship with customers has changed as well. Instead of building a computer, then taking it to the market and selling it, IBM now works with customers to find out what needs they have, develops the technology to meet or exceed those needs, and builds what the customers want. "By this time," Schwartz says, "it's presold, because what we're doing is providing something that they asked for. We are much more open with our customers about what we're doing. We bring them early into the development cycle of new products and solutions."

Laurence Osterwise likes to tell the story of the reception for the introduction of the AS-400 computer, the one that saved IBM's Rochester plant, which went on to win the Baldrige Award. A reporter asked an IBM customer admiring the machine how he liked it. The customer looked at him and said, "How do I *like* it? I *designed* it!"

Cadillac, which also won a Baldrige Award in 1990, got into trouble when it tried to anticipate needs that the customers never had. The car was made more fuel efficient in anticipation of $2.50 to $3 a gallon gasoline in the United States. "Well, we made it," says John O. Grettenberger, Cadillac's general manager. "Our cars were certainly more fuel efficient. But in the minds of the customers and the buyers out there, we had strayed way too far from historically what had made a Cadillac a Cadillac." Maryann Keller, the auto industry analyst, says potential buyers could not tell a once-luxurious Cadillac from any other GM car. It was clear that Cadillac had to change quickly or lose even more of the market to, principally, German and Japanese luxury car makers. Cadillac adopted simultaneous engineering, a technique to design a car and the process to make it at the same time. And everybody got in on the act.

"The old way of doing a vehicle," Grettenberger says, "was for the designers to come up with something that really appealed to the senses, and get excited about it, and ask the engineers to design a way that it could be built." Before the people who actually had to build the car were asked for an opinion, the standards for the car were locked in. Actually building the car became a series of compromises, and the customer got less than anyone had planned. "There are no hand-offs anymore," Grettenberger says; "nobody just does his part of the equation and gives it to the next guy for him to do his and pass it on down the line. It takes longer to get everybody together up front, but the final result is that you have a much greater appreciation for all the other pieces of the puzzle as you begin to work together. The bottom line is that you end up with something you can build without compromising the design. You get more productivity and efficiency at the same time you're answering the customer's needs. Really, the marketplace just pure and simple drove us to the simultaneous process, and it's really the way to go in the future."

There's another key change at Cadillac. "We've significantly changed the traditional adversarial relationship between management and labor at Cadillac," Grettenberger says. "We couldn't afford it anymore. . . . We realized that the union is not the enemy, we realized that management is not the enemy; the competition is the enemy, and the customer is the prize." Blue-collar workers now take part in staff meetings where decisions are made. White-collar designers and engineers sometimes work on the assembly line to see for themselves what the problems are.

All of that has made a substantial difference in the car. Cadillac has increased its warranty from one year or 12,000 miles in 1988 to four years or 50,000 miles in 1990 while its warranty costs dropped by 29 percent. Not to beat you over the head with it, but the fact remains that quality costs less.

Cadillac has been working with Deming for seven years. At least 1,600 employees have attended a four-day Deming seminar, and some of Cadillac's people have been to more than one. Deming's fourteen points are now part of Cadillac's business plan.

At IBM, Rochester, "I'd imagine that two thousand or more people have been through the Deming [video]tapes," Osterwise says, "and incorporated that in their approach. Most of our senior management in the early '80s attended Phil Crosby, so we've been there. We've been visited by Juran. We had an individual help us from Northwestern; we had an individual help us from Wharton, and then the Motorolas, the Xeroxes, and everybody else you could learn from, and sort of bring it all into the IBM culture and modify the IBM culture where necessary and make it work. People always ask, 'Do you have Feigenbaum, do you have Deming, do you have Juran? What system do you have?' None of those. . . . We're on the best of all systems." IBM built its own program specifically for IBM, but Osterwise quickly adds, "The 'wisdom' that we share on the vision [of quality], we didn't get it ourselves. We got it from reading about others, and talking with others, and we've benefited from the Baldrige process, and the outgrowth of Motorola, and Xerox, and Milliken, and Florida Power and Light, and many, many, many others. . . . It's almost hard to say what we borrowed, because we borrowed a lot. . . . What we've done is taken the best of them all."

Whichever quality program a company adopts, it will wind up with an immediate problem for management. "A person managing with these quality principles," Arv Mueller of GM says, "has to realize that he will be operating in two systems for quite a long time — the one that he's trying to serve, and the one that he's trying to create. And you get pushed and pulled a lot." You also get measured a lot. A quality company winds up using basic statistical techniques to monitor everything it does. When Federal Express first began to look into a systematic quality philosophy in the mid-'80s, the consultants began to talk about the use of statistics. FedEx officials couldn't imagine how statistical measurements could apply to their service business. Now, Smith says, "the ability to mathematically measure the quality of our service is fundamental to improving it. We measure every shipment that travels through our global service network on a real-time basis." Patrick Galvin, the vice-president of corporate systems development, says, "That's why at our company and at many others, you'll hear the maxim, 'You cannot manage what you cannot measure.' "

IBM's goal is six sigma quality by 1994 with specific and rigorous goals along the way. "What that gives you," Schwartz says, "is a disciplined way to measure your defect-elimination journey." He says everyone they talked to who was farther along in a quality program than IBM "said the thing they learned along the way is that if you didn't set aggressive targets that require change, if you set targets that you could get to by just working harder, or grunting harder, you weren't going to get the lasting change that you needed in the business, you weren't going to invent new ideas, new processes, new approaches."

Striner believes Americans have to invent new approaches to national leadership. Asked whether government, industry, or organized labor was the more likely American leader, Striner says, "What you're basically saying is that we must choose one of these as a leader. Not so. There's a different model. The model that has been so effective is a model where the Japanese don't see either government or industry or the unions as a leadership. The Germans don't see either government or the unions or industry as the leadership. What they've developed is a model where the key players, the individuals who have the most significance with regard to achieving a desirable social or economic objective, are brought together in a vehicle which permits the key people to work together to achieve the objective. . . . We've learned this in industry. Basically, when we moved in the direction of a participative management system . . . what we said was that the old hierarchical system of power just doesn't work." Striner says that's as true in government as it is in industry. Nonetheless, it flies in the face of the American tradition.

Historically, Americans have honored individuals more than groups. "It's often been said," Kanter says, "that Americans are intensely individualistic, and look who our heroes are: it's the cowboys out on the frontier." Among classic American motion pictures are those that feature the lone hero, like the lawman (Gary Cooper) in *High Noon* and the mysterious gunfighter (Alan Ladd) in *Shane*. But what works in the fiction of Old West movies doesn't work in the reality of modern management. "Cowboy management," Kanter says, "is a disaster for the company that seeks quality. . . . There are now a lot of revisionist histories being written about the West, where suddenly the cowboy doesn't look like a hero, and maybe the heroes are the townspeople who worked hard together to develop a particular area. I think we can look back and find threads in our past that are cooperative as well as individualistic, and that's what's important in today's emphasis and today's push." Actually, most Americans know that cooperation is the key to success, or they should know it, at least if they have seen *The Wizard of Oz*. If one thing is obvious in that film it is that Dorothy, the Tin Man, the Cowardly Lion, and the Scarecrow were completely dependent on each other. No one of them could have reached the Emerald City alone; together, they all made it.

Donald Petersen, the former chairman at Ford, says, "At any stage, wherever you are, however well you're doing, there's always someone, if you have good teamwork and cooperative effort going on, someone with good ideas of how you can improve further." Robert Reich adds, "You come to a realization that as an individual, yeah, you might have good ideas, but when you amalgamate those ideas with the ideas of other people, you have far better ideas, and you're far better able to accomplish what you really want." Deming is far more blunt. "People must learn to cooperate on problems of common interest . . . if we're going to survive."

But people can't cooperate unless they have the educational background to do it, and that starts in America's public schools.

Yankelovich says, "President Bush had, he said, a vision of being an education president, and part of that vision was that the United States would be number one again in the world by the year 2000 in high school achievements in math and science. Now, that's a vision that doesn't have a strategy attached to it. It's just rhetoric, empty words. . . . So you have a very sincere president presenting a vision, but it's a mockery because there is no real plan or strategy." What doesn't happen in America's public schools contributes to what doesn't happen in America's colleges and to what *does* happen in graduate programs for advanced degrees. "More than 50 percent of the doctorates awarded in engineering in American graduate schools last year," Reich says, "were not to Americans. . . . We are privileged to have some of the best institutes of higher education in the world. That's why we attract so many foreigners. But you have to worry. Why aren't Americans capable of doing that graduate work? What is there about our high schools and colleges that is not preparing that many qualified Americans to do engineering at that level, or science or mathematics?" In 1960, 13 percent of American college graduates were engineers. By 1988, it was 4 percent. "We are falling behind," Reich says, "partly because we're not thinking about quality and productivity in our classrooms, and partly because we're not willing to spend the money necessary to achieve that quality and productivity."

"We don't want to face up to the fact," Striner says, "that we [Americans] have to pay more taxes to do the things that we say that we want. . . . the real problem is that we're not willing to invest in order to achieve the objectives that we say we deserve." According to Choate, that must change. "Now the reality is," he says, "when we [Americans] go through the 1990s, it's going to be necessary for this to be a decade of investment. We're going to have to invest in our infrastructure, our education, our technology, and the retraining of our workers. Ultimately, this is going to require new taxes. There is still no free lunch. . . . Or if we don't do that, we must prepare ourselves to be the number three industrial power in the world in the year 2000. We're already the number two industrial power. We've had a massive slip. . . . Are we prepared to be number three?" C. Jackson Grayson, Jr., sees the same possible future. "If we don't make it on this one [quality improvement], then I think the United States will sink to a Third World power in the twenty-first century. I'm absolutely convinced of that." Choate says it may happen, but it isn't necessary. "We didn't build a $5 trillion economy because we're clunkers or because we're uncompetitive. What we need to do is just to put some things that are wrong right. What we need is to create an environment where we can think and act in the long term."

Meadows would agree. Talking about the successful, concentrated, American effort to put a man on the moon, she says, "This system can produce anything it wants; it just has to really want it, and be dedicated to it, and maintain that dedication. I think it can produce a culture of quality." She thinks that has to be done. We cannot continue with business as usual (see Chapter 4). "The two futures that I have come to believe in deeply as very possible," she says, "and in some senses almost inevitable, though there's still the choice between them as far as I can tell, are on the one hand, total destruction, and on the other hand, achievement of quality of life for all the people on this planet." The key to that choice is whether quality programs are adopted throughout American society.

Stephen Schwartz is talking about IBM, but his comment applies to everything else as well. "I would guess that the most important thing we have learned," he says, "is that you must integrate this [quality effort] into the business. Quality can't be a separate program, it can't be something that you delegate to a quality staff. It has to be everyone's business in the business." Or in the country.

In the presentation at Mount Edgecumbe High School, when Snow White escapes into the Forest of Opportunity, before she reaches the Seven Dwarfs Mining Company, she meets four wood-land animals in a clearing, Will, Belief, Wherewithal, and Doing. They explain to Snow White how you change an organization. Will tells Snow White that nothing happens until people want to change, and Belief says even that is not enough; they must also believe that change is possible. When people want to change and believe they can, Wherewithal says, they need the tools to make it possible. Doing speaks last: "My part's the easiest. Once the first three have been completed, things just simply need to be done."

In the United States, to solve the economic and social problems that are slowly crippling the most powerful, most productive, most democratic nation on earth, industrial, economic, social, and political leaders could do a lot worse than listen to these four forest creatures — Will, Belief, Wherewithal, and Doing — because things just simply need to be done.

Conclusion

Quality is a thoroughly pragmatic, dollars and cents approach to management that, done honestly and diligently, will increase productivity and lower costs. It is not some esoteric, philosophical debating subject like beauty and true justice, although too often it is treated as if it were. Skeptics sneer and say, "Quality, what does that mean?" It means larger business profits as you eliminate waste; it means schools and hospitals and government programs that run well and don't cost an arm and a leg; it means looking forward to going to work where you'll be proud of what you do. Quality also means a demanding, difficult, never-ending effort to improve. Some of the quality attempts that have failed did so because companies started their programs without realizing how incredibly demanding they would be. Because the parts of a quality program sound so logical and practical, it is assumed that if you put all the parts in place, you're home free. As David Langford, the teacher, said, if it were easy, everyone would have done it by now. It isn't easy; it *is* worthwhile.

Curt Reimann, the director of the Baldrige Award program, testified before a congressional committee. "It is noteworthy," he said, "that Japan's Deming Prize winners have demonstrated profit levels twice those of other Japanese companies. Studies in the United States have confirmed the linkage between quality, profits, and market share."

A quality program is not a recipe, it's a way of thinking, and the longer you work at it, the better you get. Instead of solving problems as they come up, a quality program lets you improve the system to prevent problems. Perhaps the most damaging belief in the United States is the comment Bert Lance, briefly President Jimmy Carter's director of the Office of Management and Budget, popularized: "If it ain't broke, don't fix it." As the consultant Peter Scholtes once said, "It sounds right, it has a facile surface logic, but it's wrong." Why do you want to wait for it, whatever it might be, to break? Why not continually improve the system so that not only does it not break, it actually gets better and less expensive? Besides, who told you that you'd be able to fix it if it did break? American elementary and high schools seem to have at least some broken parts, and they've been broken for a long time now. Why can't American public officials, educators, students, parents, and taxpayers even agree on what's broken? In those American industries where sales and profits and jobs have been disappearing for years now, aren't repairs past due? There's a lot breaking or broken in the United States; there's not much being fixed.

A quality program, at a minimum, lets you think about a great many seemingly disparate problems in a systematic way to see how they relate and how they could be improved without doing too much for one and making the others worse. The improvements you get are then built into the system so that other people can build increasingly sophisticated solutions on top; there's no need to reinvent the wheel every morning. Everyone gets to work toward improvement and makes a contribution. As Larry Osterwise said, it isn't just him working on the five most important problems at IBM, Rochester, it's eight thousand people working on five problems, and all the solutions are mutually supportive. George Fisher, at Motorola, doesn't think one person can run a major company by himself anymore; it's too complex. He wants every one of his hundred thousand employees thinking about improvements. With a quality program, the chief executive is still the chief executive, but he has a lot more help. As more employees are trained and educated, they need less supervision, so eventually they need less guidance to do a better job, solving problems rather than waiting for someone to tell them what to do.

Senior executives and managers sometimes resent the suggestion of a quality program because they see it as backhanded criticism, a snide insinuation that they have been wrong for all these years and are standing in the way of progress now. It is, to them, a personal affront. It shouldn't be. For nearly fifty years, senior American managers have been doing exactly what their customers asked them to do: make a ton of it, then make another ton faster. All that has happened is that their customers have changed their minds. Now they want quality. Just as American managers learned how to build a mass production system unrivaled in the world, they must now learn how to build a quality production system to compete in the global market. Of all the senior managers involved in quality we have interviewed since 1980, and there have been a lot of them, not one has ever said he wished he had not gotten involved with a quality system. To a man (regrettably, there were no women), each said it was the best and smartest thing he had ever done, and he only wished he'd done it sooner. *Not one* said it was easy.

With a quality program there is, undeniably, a threat to middle managers, but that threat exists without a quality program as well. With it, some middle management positions are eliminated (although at several companies, former middle managers are now teachers and facilitators). Without a quality program, companies will eventually be forced to fire people, and sooner or later every company runs out of people at the bottom to let go. Middle managers are next. The *Fortune* survey makes that clear (see Chapter 12).

Workers are sometimes reluctant because too often in the past various so-called quality programs have been little more than ill-concealed attempts to make the workers struggle harder to do a better job in the same failing system for the same pay. That reluctance can be overcome with honesty and success. Of the workers we have interviewed — more of them than managers — there have been varying levels of enthusiasm for a genuine quality program, but all of them have liked their jobs more, have been eager to come to work, and are proud of their ability to think, solve problems, and make improvements. We have lost count of the number who have told us that they are now allowed to do what they had always wanted to do — the best job they knew how. Langford was talking about students and teachers, but what he said applies everywhere: "I don't find anybody that says, 'I'm out to do poor work or do poor quality.' Every place I go everybody wants to do a good job. So the whole point is, how do we allow people to do that?"

Where organized labor fits in all this depends on organized labor. Union members and leaders will have to decide if their traditional us-against-them style makes sense in the modern world. Senior executives have to ask themselves that same question, not only about labor, but about government as well. Can the United States really afford three of its leadership groups — labor, industry, and government — fighting yesterday's battles? Political leaders have a contribution to make, but not if they continue to believe that their own reelections are more important than the nation's economic future. State political leaders may wonder if it makes sense to compete against one another to attract industry, in effect buying new plants with tax breaks and other incentives. Parents may consider finding the time to go to school board meetings, to get involved in school activities, to insist that math and statistics and logic and economics are suitable, even necessary subjects for young minds. And all of us may begin to think about each job we do and wonder what it would mean to do it with quality. We may ask ourselves, "Does this make sense, not only for me personally right now, but for the department, the company, the economy, the nation in the future; not only for me, but for my family, my colleagues?" As Donella Meadows suggests, if we insist on quality, if we practice quality, we will get quality. The history of the United States is that it can do anything it sets its mind to do. That is why an American first walked on the moon; America set its mind to it and stubbornly refused to consider anything but success.

Joji Arai thinks the *idea* of quality is already catching on in the United States, but that presents its own danger. "If you want to sponsor a seminar," he says, "and if you put 'Total Quality Management' as the title, you'll be assured of very enthusiastic participation on the part of American managers. If you ask the sponsors of the program what the definition of total quality management is, essentially what they come up with is nothing more than excellence in management, which American businessmen and academicians have been saying for so many years." It is not excellence in management, although excellence certainly wouldn't hurt. Total quality is an organized system that involves customers, suppliers, managers, workers, equipment, finance — literally, everything that goes into doing what you do. A quality program requires that you involve all of it, the *total*, in quality management. There is an occasional temptation just to do the parts of a quality program that you like, and you may get some improvement, but the effort won't sustain itself.

Fine, you'll do it all, you swear, but what do you *do?* How many steps are there? How long will it take? It took the Japanese twenty-five to forty years, but because they've written about it, because they are more than willing to share everything they have learned, it won't take nearly that long in the United States. Osterwise estimates that while it took Toyota twenty-five years, IBM, Rochester, will do it in ten years. Typically, a company (school, hospital, agency) sees some results rather quickly and good results in three to five years. Don't pay too much attention to those figures, however, because it really takes forever. Continual improvement never stops, but it's not drudgery. People who are doing it now say it's more fun than they've ever had. Now, what do you do?

There is a method used in quality programs that Walter Shewhart invented back in the 1920s and W. Edwards Deming taught the Japanese after World War II and teaches in his seminars now, so it's known as the Deming Cycle in Japan and either the Shewhart or the Deming Cycle in the United States. It's a circle, running clockwise, divided into quarters marked "Plan, Do, Study, Act." (Those who know the cycle are now yelling, "No, no; not 'study,' 'check.' Plan, Do, Check, Act." Sorry, Deming changed *check* to *study* in 1990, and it is his cycle. *Study* seems to be a more accurate word anyway. With only a check you might miss something.) He says *check* could mean to block, or pull up short, or rein in, and that's the last thing you want to do.) Essentially, you plan what you want to do, you do it (a small-scale test), you study the results, then you act; that is, you adopt, alter, or abort that plan. (Incidentally, if some of your plans don't fail sometimes, you are not taking risks that are big enough to pay off in big gains.) Since you are back at the top of the cycle, you start again. The Deming Cycle is a statistical device, and statisticians generally say that if you have ten days for the project, use five days for planning. Motorola did. As we explained in Chapter 6, the remark about Motorola's poor quality levels was made in 1979, but the Six Sigma program did not start until 1987, after it had been suggested in a test in one section of the company the year before.

We believe the Deming Cycle may be what you should do. Knowing all the quality programs, we have at least a working appreciation of their strengths and weaknesses. What we don't know is which one would appeal to you. Besides, wasn't it Osterwise who said that people would rather be led than managed? Why should we try to manage what you will have to do? We suggest that you get the Baldrige criteria, attend seminars on quality, read material by the experts, talk to people who are involved in quality programs, study videotapes, and study what the Baldrige winners have done. Look for a way to get continual improvement. One enormous caution, however: Don't try to copy what others have done unless you understand completely how and why they did it. Having studied and finally decided what you want to do, you've done the "Plan" part of the Deming Cycle.

The reason to try your plan on a small scale is to limit the cost of the failure if your plan happens to be faulty. For instance, the U.S. government, for a lot of acceptable, even excellent reasons, believed that a one-dollar coin would be a good idea, but instead of testing the coin in some limited way — say, citizen study groups around the country — it issued the coin, essentially testing it on a national basis. The Susan B. Anthony dollar failed, a nationwide flop. Another point is illustrated if you study why it failed. The customer didn't like it; Americans said it was too much like a quarter. Various government officials reacted badly and said, in effect, "No such thing! It's not like a quarter at all. It's a different shape, it's a different weight, it couldn't be more unlike a quarter. Now stop that silly fuss, be good citizens, and use the Susan B. Anthony dollar." And the American public, to paraphrase that famous *New Yorker* cartoon, answered, "We say it's a quarter, and we say the hell with it!" The moral of the story is, the *customer* defines quality, and arguing about his or her naiveté, crabbiness, or lack of taste and discernment won't change that definition.

Quality, remember, isn't just desirable, it's essential. The economy is real; it's not an abstraction. It's a trip to the grocery store, it's putting gas in your car, it's sending your child to college, it's keeping your job, it's health care or a movie or a taxi ride. The economy is not charts and graphs in a classroom or a Cabinet office. The economy is everything you do that involves money. It is, in short, how you live — or could live if things get better or worse. Quality drives productivity, productivity drives standard of living, and standard of living is the future. The question of America's future is of more than national interest. The United States has done a great deal for the world on social, economic, and political levels. Since World War II, it has been the free world's policeman, keeping international relationships more or less in order. That the country has botched one here and there is beyond question, but try to imagine the world over the last forty years without a strong, democratic America. It would have been a vastly different, far more unstable and unpleasant place. But now the country's ability to patrol its beat is limited by an economy turning sour. American forces went into the Persian Gulf crisis using the allies' money. U.S. economic problems are bad, and its social problems could become much worse. "When we are not competitive," Myron Tribus says, "the cost in our economy falls most harshly on the people near the bottom, and it creates a reason for social unrest. Unless we can create jobs and put quality back into education, put quality back into all the things we do, we will create a social situation which frightens me."

Joji Arai, the Japanese who uses *we* and *they* interchangeably for Japanese and Americans, believes the national and international possibilities are parts of the same problem, and the implications go well beyond the borders of the United States. The American budget, trade, financial, and social deficits (see Chapter 9) will determine the international status of the United States and, in large measure, how the world works in the twenty-first century. It is a penalty of world leadership that you cannot fail quietly or without consequences for others. Arai says world leadership requires military and economic power and an ideology that other countries respect. "The U.S.," he says, "is the only country that has those three items at the moment. Japan may have the economic [and the military] potential, but it has no ideological perception that other countries can really respect and follow. You have seen the collapse of communism, so they are out. Europe may become a united economy, a bloc economy, but. . . . you still will not see a United Europe as a sovereign state for a long time to come. So the U.S. is the only country that can lead the world into the twenty-first century." *Can* lead, but not necessarily *will* lead.

If the United States can't solve its problems with the four

deficits, then a loss of economic power will lead to a loss of military power, "and that will certainly upset the global balance of military power. Even though you may not have to worry about superpower confrontation anymore," Arai says, "there will be confrontation with somewhat smaller powers with strategic weapons that still require the superior military power that enables the United States to maintain peace throughout the world into the twenty-first century." Arai talked to us well before the Persian Gulf crisis, so his analysis now stands as prophesy, which makes the next part a bit more unsettling. The loss of military power, Arai says, because of the loss of economic power leads to the loss of ideological power. Welcome to the real world of dominoes.

"If you push this social deficit too far," he says, "it shows the negative side of freedom and democracy, and there will be a reactionary movement in the political arena." In this regard, Arai agrees with Daniel Yankelovich: when you create an expanding permanent underclass, you also create the demagogues who will exploit the fears of both the haves and the have-nots. "That," Arai says, "will have a negative impact on the future of the world. . . . I don't think Europe, or Russia, or Japan, for that matter, will be able to cope with those global issues. The U.S. alone will be able to, so what we'll see in the twenty-first century without the U.S. will be a terrible mess. . . . it's the disruption of order in the twenty-first century, and it's not desirable."

If you doubt that quality could have all those implications, think about the collapse of communism in Eastern Europe. Like Ptolemy's universe, communism revolved around the wrong core. Communism said workers were central, and the word *customer* doesn't appear in communist economic theory. The workers finally did not rise up against capitalist oppression, as Karl Marx said they would, they rebelled as customers whose needs were not being met by a state-run system. There were no chains to cast off, but there were no quality products to buy either. The worker, on the way to an inadequate home from a state-supported job, faced empty shelves or long lines and, in either case, surly clerks. Tribus talks of watching a Russian woman who worked for the new American McDonald's in Moscow being interviewed on television. What was the hardest thing for her to learn? "Being nice to customers." If those customers eventually turned their backs on communism, it does not mean that America's capitalist, democratic system is assured of success.

There are two theories developing simultaneously in the United States, and both argue that there's no reason for America to do anything about its economy, but for diametrically opposed reasons. One says that everything is just fine, the United States has merely hit a bad patch, and despite dreadfully negative reporting and nasty old naysayers, everything will be just swell any day now. Why do anything? To the best of our knowledge, that theory has no name, although the song title "Don't Worry, Be Happy" does spring to mind. The other theory has a name, the theory of the climacteric, first described in 1974 by a professor at MIT. Climacteric is from the Greek, a rung on a ladder, therefore, a critical point in life. The theory is entropy applied to economics; that is, economies, like birds, trees, people, stars, and universes, are born, live, mature, and die. The U.S. economy, the theory says, is dying and attempts to save it are futile. Why do anything?

We respectfully suggest that both theories are irrelevant. The first one we have heard before. In 1980, when we worked on *If Japan Can, Why Can't We?*, several otherwise intelligent people insisted that there was nothing wrong with the U.S. economy, but the way productivity was measured was flawed, so the economy looked as if it were sinking when it wasn't. The fault, they argued, was with the measurement, not the system. We argued that even if that were true, who would be hurt if productivity improved? Would it not, in fact, help everyone? We're still using the argument: even if the U.S. economy is, like Superman, about to leap over a tall building in a single bound, how could Americans be hurt if the economy leapt even higher? There is no penalty for making a good thing better.

The theory of the climacteric falls to a similar argument. We are both of an age when we are aware in the quiet moments just before dawn that we have lived more years than we have left. Does that mean we should stop living as best we can now? Even if the American economy is eventually doomed, why should Americans roll over and quit? If quality keeps the economy going for another two hundred years or so, isn't quality the thing to do? The Thai businessman Anand Panyarachun, who was appointed interim prime minister early in 1991, says, "I have great faith in our American friends. I think the fact that they have developed their country to the present level in just over two hundred years, there must be something inherently right, and there must be a sort of inherent strength within their own society that made them tick. So I would say that I have not given up hope, and I wish them well."

America certainly can't be hurt by good wishes, but it can't be helped by them either. The country's problems were not caused by outsiders, and outsiders cannot solve them. A solution exists, but it is difficult, it requires change and learning and upset, and it's never over. Still, it's preferable to the alternative. Which is to say that quality is very much like life.

Deming's 1950 diary shows that he was delighted when his lecture series to the Japanese students ended, and his students had helped him get through it: "They laughed heartily at my jokes all week." He held a dinner that night for his Japanese colleagues. Supplies were still short on the civilian market, so he bought "hors d'oeuvres" at the American post exchange on the Ginza — olives, tomato juice, and Ritz crackers. He did not record what the army's prepared meal was, but dessert was strawberry ice cream.

Deming used these informal dinners to urge the Japanese to improve the education of statisticians, but they talked of other things as well. "I often express the hope," he wrote in his diary, "that Japan would export four important products to America — beer, sake, Kabuki plays, and beautiful girls, and this pleases the Japanese very much." Japanese beer and sake are now readily available in America. There are beautiful Japanese women, particularly in Hawaii, California, and New York. However, the place of Kabuki plays seems to have been taken by automobiles, television sets, radios, tape recorders, VCRs, cameras, numerically controlled machine tools, optical fibers, telecommunications equipment, computers, and a good many other items that look good, work well, and make money.

Quality. Or else.

Appendix

Acknowledgments

Interview Subjects

Bibliography

Appendix

DEMING'S FOURTEEN POINTS

1. Create constancy of purpose.
2. Adopt the new philosophy.
3. Cease dependence on mass inspection to achieve quality.
4. End the practice of awarding business on price tag alone. Instead, minimize total cost, often accomplished by working with a single supplier.
5. Improve constantly the system of production and service.
6. Institute training on the job.
7. Institute leadership.
8. Drive out fear.
9. Break down barriers between departments.
10. Eliminate slogans, exhortations, and numerical targets.
11. Eliminate work standards (quotas) and management by objective.
12. Remove barriers that rob workers, engineers, and managers of their right to pride of workmanship.
13. Institute a vigorous program of education and self-improvement.
14. Put everyone in the company to work to accomplish the transformation.

CROSBY'S FOURTEEN POINTS

1. *Management Commitment.* To make it clear where management stands on quality.
2. *Quality Improvement Team.* To run the Quality Improvement Process.
3. *Measurement.* To provide a display of current and potential nonconformance problems in a manner that permits objective evaluation and corrective action.
4. *Cost of Quality.* To define the ingredients of the Cost of Quality (COQ) and explain its use as a management tool.
5. *Quality Awareness.* To provide a method of raising the personal concern felt by all employees toward the conformance of the product or service and the quality reputation of the company.
6. *Corrective Action.* To provide a systematic method of resolving forever the problems that are identified through the previous action steps.
7,9. *Zero Defects Planning and Zero Defects Day.* To examine the various activities that must be conducted in preparation for formally launching Zero Defects Day. To create an event that will let all employees realize, through a personal experience, that there has been a change.
8. *Employee Education.* To define the type of training all employees need in order to actively carry out their role in the Quality Improvement Process.
10. *Goal Setting.* To turn pledges and commitments into action by encouraging individuals to establish improvement goals for themselves and their groups.
11. *Error Cause Removal.* To give the individual employee a method of communicating to management the situations that make it difficult for the employee to meet the pledge to improve.
12. *Recognition.* To appreciate those who participate.
13. *Quality Councils.* To bring together the appropriate people to share quality management information on a regular basis.
14. *Do It All Over Again.* To emphasize that the Quality Improvement Process is continuous.

The Shewhart Cycle

Flow Chart

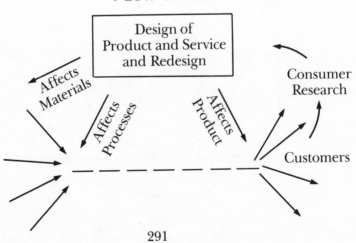

CONTROL CHART

Time of Arrival of School Bus
Patrick Nolan, Age 10

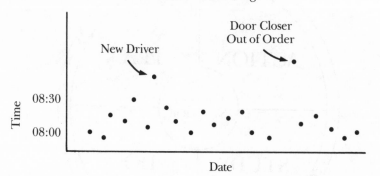

THE TAGUCHI LOSS FUNCTION

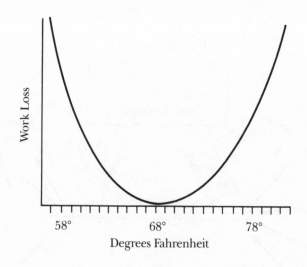

THE THREE SYSTEMS FOR WHICH MANAGERS ARE RESPONSIBLE

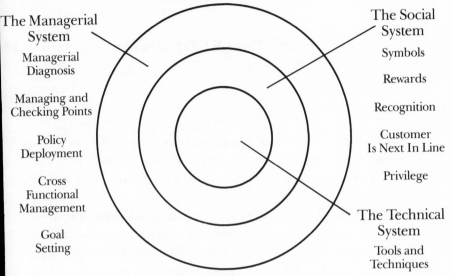

The Managerial
System

Managerial
Diagnosis

Managing and
Checking Points

Policy
Deployment

Cross
Functional
Management

Goal
Setting

The Social
System

Symbols

Rewards

Recognition

Customer
Is Next In Line

Privilege

The Technical
System

Tools and
Techniques

DOMAINS OF CONTROL

Beyond Control

Negotiable

Fix with
Colleagues

Fix with
Supervisor

Fix
Myself

Acknowledgments

This started in the same I've-got-it spirit that shows up in old movies when some young character (Mickey Rooney? Judy Garland?) says something like, "Hey, why don't we put on a show in the barn!"

We asked IBM to underwrite a 90-minute television documentary on quality, a tenth anniversary update of a program on productivity that we worked on in 1980. From there it just grew. IBM eventually financed three 60-minute documentaries, the research for which then went into this book. Because IBM underwrote the documentaries, it chose not to be mentioned in the programs. However, the company did not underwrite the book, so we are able to include some of the things IBM is doing in quality, which helps explain its interest in the subject. We hope that the people at IBM understand how much we sincerely appreciate their support. We want particularly to thank Michael Gury, Bill Harrison, and Arlene Wendt.

The number of people who interrupted their schedules to talk to us is amazing. Once they learned what we were trying to do, people in companies and countries around the world agreed to meet and answer our questions. We could not mention them all in the documentaries or the book, but we learned something from each of them, and we are grateful to all of them. We could not have done this without their help, and we hope they understand that. They are named in a separate list, which follows, and we apologize to anyone we inadvertently left out.

In Washington, the staff of CC-M Productions kept track of thousands of bits and pieces, assembled transcripts, did research, made calls and suggestions, and managed against the odds to maintain sufficient civility not to threaten either of our lives. The temptation must have existed, and may still. Our personal and professional thanks to Beth Bernstein, Ken Hall, Robert W. Mason, Michael H. Morton, Marie J. Nash, and Scott M. Stein.

In Garner, Marilyn Hankin was "first reader," making certain that we didn't get so carried away with our new knowledge that we forgot the need for clarity.

In New York, Elaine Markson, our agent, sold the idea of the book and got us started. Henry Ferris at Houghton Mifflin made the book better without once suggesting that it was anything less than letter perfect. That's a talent. Luise M. Erdmann insisted that we maintain a decent respect for the language. Good for her.

Patti Dobyns and Bob Mason and the adult children of the two families have put up with this in good humor, which could not have been all that easy. These projects have a way of supplanting normal family life.

Finally, John Noble and Ruth Prokop, our lawyers, resolved differences between IBM and Houghton Mifflin.

All these people deserve credit. None deserves blame. If we have somehow managed despite all the help and support to screw it up, we did that on our own.

INTERVIEW SUBJECTS

K. Aldingen, *Customer, Mercedes*
Blue Allen, *McDonnell Douglas*
Anand Panyarachun, *Saha-Union*
Joji Arai, *International Productivity Service*
Peter Armstrong, *State of Arkansas*
Edwin L. Artzt, *Procter & Gamble*
Martin N. Baily, *University of Maryland*
Ronald E. Baker, *State of Maryland*
Esther Barnett, *McDonnell Douglas*
Klemens Barth, *Mercedes*
J. A. Bauer, *Gee & Jensen*
Glenn Behrman, *Roses Plus*
Carla Bensen, *Hines VA Hospital*
Sherry Bleuel, *McDonnell Douglas*
Connie Boucher, *Determined Productions*
James L. Broadhead, *FP&L Group*
Laurie Broedling, *Department of Defense*
Andy Brophy, *Signetics*
Roberta J. Burish, *FP&L*
Carolyn Burstein, *Federal Quality Institute*
D. E. Butler, *VEDA*
John Capellupo, *Douglas Aircraft*
Ben Carlson, *Vernay Laboratories*

Marvin Cetron, *Forecasting International*
Pat Choate, *Political Economist*
Jean Choi, *Determined Productions*
Kristella Coleman, *Training, Inc.*
Wendy Coles, *General Motors*
Earl C. Conway, *Procter & Gamble*
Sam Coverdale, *McDonnell Douglas*
Philip B. Crosby, *Philip B. Crosby Associates*
Joan Cummings, M.D., *Hines VA Hospital*
Hank Dangerfield, *Gee & Jensen*
Al Daniels, *Motorola*
Len DeBarras, *Motorola*
Keith R. Decker, *FP&L*
W. Edwards Deming, *Consultant*
Neil Dial, *Motorola*
J. W. Dickey, *FP&L*
Do Won-Han, *Samsung*
Richard Dobbins, *FP&L*
Jim Dykes, *Signetics*
Ken Easterling, *FP&L*
Jim Erwin, *FP&L*
Geraldine Evans, *Hines VA Hospital*
Goldie Evans, *Hines VA Hospital*

296

Faculty, *Mount Edgecumbe High School*

Maribel Fajardo, *Motorola*

John R. Fears, *Hines VA Hospital*

Armand V. Feigenbaum, *General Systems Company*

Paul Feisthamel, *Signetics*

Lance Felker, *Department of Commerce*

George Fisher, *Motorola*

Jim Fix, *McDonnell Douglas*

Paula Foreman, *Saatchi & Saatchi*

Jay Forrester, *MIT*

Ronald Galarza, *Training, Inc.*

Robert W. Galvin, *Motorola*

Jacque Gensler, *The Analytic Sciences Corp.*

Denny George, *FP&L*

Jean-Marie Gogue, *MAST*

John Gonzales, *Roses Plus*

Milt Gossett, *Saatchi & Saatchi*

Alan K. Graham, *MIT*

I. J. Grandes del Mazo, *Consultant*

C. Jackson Grayson, Jr., *American Productivity & Quality Center*

Carol Griffin, *Motorola*

Carol Hall, *Hines VA Hospital*

Kurt Hamann, *Siemens*

Joshua Hammond, *American Quality Foundation*

Han Chul Wang, *Daewoo Electronics*

Daisaku Harada, *Japan Productivity Center*

Walter Lee Harris, *Hines VA Hospital*

Christopher Hart, *TQM Group*

Lewis Hatala, *AT&T*

John Hawkins, *Hines VA Hospital*

Robert Hayes, *Harvard Business School*

Thomas M. Heller, *Incentive Management Group*

William J. Hensler, *FP&L*

Mat Heyman, *National Institute of Standards & Technology*

Jack Hillerich, *Hillerich and Bradsby Co.*

Robert Holbrook, *FP&L*

Kenneth Hopper, *Consultant*

Osamu Hoshino, *Utah Travel Council*

Juergen Hubbert, *Mercedes*

Alberta Irby, *Hines VA Hospital*

Freddye Jackson, *Brown Lincoln Mercury*

Jerry Jasinkowski, *National Association of Manufacturers*

Jin Hee Ma, *Determined Productions*

Brian Joiner, *Joiner Associates*

James Jones, *Hines VA Hospital*

Melissa Jones, *Signetics*

Joong Nam Yoon, *Determined Productions*

Debra Joseph, *Training, Inc.*

Joseph M. Juran, *Juran Institute*

Rosabeth Moss Kanter, *Harvard*

Maryann Keller, *Furman Selz Mager Dietz & Birney*

Gé Kester, *Kester Wholesale Flower Company*

Antoinette L. Keys, *Training, Inc.*

Choong S. Kim, *Daewoo Electronics*

Hans Klauss, *Siemens*

Renate Kortel, *Benetton*

Paul Kreisberg, *Carnegie Endowment*

Norbert Kubts, *Modesalon*

Norbert Kühe, *Mercedes*

Walter Kunerth, *Siemens*

David Langford, *Mount Edgecumbe High School*

Interview Subjects

Bernard Lapple, *Mercedes*

Lee Jae Sung, *Seoul Metropolitan Police*

Thomas H. Lee, *Center for Quality Management*

Dan Lehman, *Hines VA Hospital*

Tim Leuliette, *Siemens*

Steve R. Levy, *Bolt, Beranek, Newman, Inc.*

Rainer List, *Mercedes*

Karin A. Luro, *Gee & Jensen*

Michael Maccoby, *The Maccoby Group*

Mangi Paik, *Ministry of Trade & Industry, Korea*

Nancy Mann, *Quality Enhancement Seminars*

Jerry Mark, *Bureau of Labor Statistics*

Kathleen McCrossin, *Mount Edgecumbe High School*

Manford McNeil, *Romac Industries*

Donella H. Meadows, *Dartmouth College*

Carol Anne Mears, *Department of Commerce*

Alan Mendelowitz, *General Accounting Office*

Richard M. Miller, *Gee & Jensen*

Roger Milliken, *Milliken & Company*

Janey Mobley, *Hines VA Hospital*

Ronald D. Moen, *Consultant*

Mike Morely, *Hines VA Hospital*

Susan Moulton, *Bay State Skills Corp.*

W. G. Mulder, *Romac Industries*

Tom Murin, *Department of Commerce*

Brian G. Nelson, *Training, Inc.*

Dave Nelson, *Honda of America*

Thomas T. Niles, *U.S. Foreign Service*

Ann Richards Nitze, *Art dealer*

Kelly Ochoa, *Douglas Aircraft*

Kenichi Ohmae, *McKinsey & Company*

Jan Ooms, *Roses Only*

Tony Paretino, *General Motors*

Laurence Osterwise, *IBM*

John M. Parisi, *Gee & Jensen*

Paron Israsena, *The Siam Cement Company*

Maggie Perkins, *Saatchi & Saatchi*

Verline Perry, *Training, Inc.*

Donald Petersen, *Ford Motor Co., ret.*

J. B. Pfizer, *Hines VA Hospital*

Eileen Pierce, *Hines VA Hospital*

Jackie Ramsdell, *Signetics*

Gipsie Ranney, *Consultant*

Gilbert Rapaille, *Arcuetype Studies*

Cline Reese, *Romac Industries*

Robert B. Reich, *Harvard*

Curt Reimann, *Malcolm Baldrige National Quality Award*

Stan Renteria, *Motorola*

Thomas Resch, *Mercedes*

Larrae Rocheleau, *Mount Edgecumbe High School*

Jerome Rosow, *Work in America Institute*

Stefan Ruzic, *Mercedes*

H. Saito, *Fuji Photo Film Company*

Howard Samuel, *AFL-CIO*

Sangbum Hyun, *Determined Productions*

Homer M. Sarasohn, *IBM, ret.*

Peter Schadel, *Mercedes*

William Scherkenbach, *General Motors*

Lynn Schermerhorn, *McDonnell Douglas*

Steve Schlossberg, *International Labor Organization*

Peter Scholtes, *Joiner Associates*

Louis E. Schultz, *PMI*

Bertrand Schwartz, *Modernization Association*

Stephen Schwartz, *IBM*

Carveth Scott, *McDonnell Douglas*

Edward M. Sears, *Palm Beach Post*

Akio Sekiguchi, *Nippon Oil Company*

Nat Semple, *Committee for Economic Development*

Marie Sharp, *Training, Inc.*

Shoji Shiba, *MIT*

Bill Smith, *Motorola*

Edna M. Smith, *Motorola*

Joel Smith, *McDonnell Douglas*

Blanche Snow, *Bama Pie*

Robert Solow, *MIT*

Pat Sparks, *Honda of America*

Richard J. Srednicki, *Citibank*

Ben Staley, *Romac Industries*

Staporn Kavitanon, *Office of the Board of Investment, Thailand*

Ray Stata, *Analog Devices, Inc.*

John R. Stepp, *Bill Usery & Associates*

John Stewart, *McKinsey & Company*

Herbert Striner, *American University*

Students, *Mount Edgecumbe High School*

William Tappe, *UTTA*

Arne Thirup, *Pajaro Valley Greenhouses*

Alan Thompson, *Romac Industries*

Myron Tribus, *Exergy, Inc.*

William Usery, Jr., *Bill Usery & Associates*

Kees J. van Ham, *European Foundation for Quality Management*

Bart Walker, *Romac Industries*

Minnie Warner, *Training, Inc.*

Frank Wilfing, *McDonnell Douglas*

Ericka Witnauer, *Saatchi & Saatchi*

John Wolf, *McDonnell Douglas*

Daniel Yankelovich, *Public Agenda Foundation*

Alan Young, *Bureau of Economic Analysis*

Katrin Zörner, *Benetton*

Marilyn Zuckerman, *AT&T*

BIBLIOGRAPHY

BOOKS

Auld, Douglas A. L., Graham Bannock, R. E. Baxter, and Ray Rees. *The American Dictionary of Economics*. New York: Facts on File, 1983.

Barsh, Russel Lawrence, and James Youngblood Henderson. *The Road: Indian Tribes and Political Liberty*. Berkeley: University of California Press, 1980.

Bhagwati, Jagdish. *Protectionism*. Cambridge, Mass.: MIT Press, 1988.

Braddon, Russell. *The Other 100 Years War: Japan's Bid for Supremacy, 1941–2041*. London: Collins, 1983.

Brinkley, David. *Washington Goes to War*. New York: Knopf, 1988.

Bryson, Bill. *The Mother Tongue: English and How It Got That Way*. New York: William Morrow, 1990.

Carnegie, Andrew. *Autobiography of Andrew Carnegie*. Cambridge, Mass.: Riverside Press, 1920; Boston: Houghton Mifflin, 1948.

Chancellor, John. *Peril and Promise: A Commentary on America*. New York: Harper & Row, 1990.

Choate, Pat. *Agents of Influence: How Japan's Lobbyists in the United States Manipulate America's Political and Economic System*. New York: Knopf, 1990.

Christopher, Robert C. *Second to None: American Companies in Japan*. New York: Fawcett Columbine Books, 1986.

———. *The Japanese Mind: The Goliath Explained*. New York: Simon & Schuster, 1983.

Crosby, Philip B. *Quality Is Free: The Art of Making Quality Certain*. New York: McGraw-Hill, 1979.

Cussler, Clive. *Dragon*. New York: Simon & Schuster, 1990.

Dabney, Virginius. *Virginia: The New Dominion*. Garden City, N.Y.: Doubleday, 1971.

Bibliography

Deming, W. Edwards. *Out of the Crisis,* 2nd ed. Cambridge, Mass.: MIT Center for Advanced Engineering Study, 1986.

Dertouzos, Michael, Richard Lester, Robert Solow, et al. *Made in America: Regaining the Productive Edge.* Cambridge, Mass.: MIT Press, 1989.

Diggins, John Patrick. *The Proud Decades: America in War and Peace, 1941–1960.* New York: Norton, 1988.

Drucker, Peter F. *The New Realities.* New York: Harper & Row, 1989.

Ferris, Timothy. *Coming of Age in the Milky Way.* New York: William Morrow, 1988.

Fields, George. *From Bonsai to Levi's.* New York: Macmillan, 1983.

Gabor, Andrea. *The Man Who Discovered Quality.* New York: Times Books, 1990.

Gibney, Frank. *Japan: The Fragile Super Power,* rev. ed. New York: New American Library, 1979.

Gleick, James. *Chaos: Making a New Science.* New York: Viking, 1987.

Grayson, C. Jackson, Jr., and Carla O'Dell. *American Business: A Two Minute Warning.* New York: The Free Press, 1988.

Halberstam, David. *The Reckoning.* New York: William Morrow, 1986.

Heller, Joseph. *God Knows.* New York: Knopf, 1984.

Ishikawa, Kaoru. *What Is Total Quality Control?: The Japanese Way,* translated by David J. Lu. Englewood Cliffs, N.J.: Prentice-Hall, 1985.

Juran, J. M. *Juran on Leadership for Quality: An Executive Handbook.* New York: The Free Press, 1989.

Kennedy, Paul. *The Rise and Fall of the Great Powers: Economic Change and Military Conflict from 1500 to 2000.* New York: Random House, 1987.

Kilian, Cecelia S. *The World of W. Edwards Deming.* Washington, D.C.: CeePress Books, 1988.

McPherson, James M. *Battle Cry of Freedom: The Civil War Era.* New York: Oxford University Press, 1988.

Manchester, William. *American Caesar: Douglas MacArthur, 1880–1964.* New York: Dell, 1978.

Mant, Alistair. *The Rise and Fall of the British Manager.* London: Pan Books, 1979.

Morita, Akio, Edwin M. Reingold, and Mitsuko Shimomura. *Made in Japan: Akio Morita and Sony.* New York: Dutton, 1986.

Ohmae, Kenichi. *The Borderless World: Power and Strategy in the Interlinked Economy.* New York: Harper Business, 1990.

Owen, Mal. *SPC and Continuous Improvement.* London: IFS Publications, 1989.

Pirsig, Robert M. *Zen and the Art of Motorcycle Maintenance.* New York: William Morrow, 1976.

Poore, Ben Perley. *Perley's Reminiscences,* vol. 1. Philadelphia: Hubbard Brothers, 1886.

Porter, Michael E. *The Competitive Advantage of Nations.* New York: The Free Press, 1990.

Prestowitz, Clyde V., Jr. *Trading Places: How We Allowed Japan to Take the Lead.* New York: Basic Books, 1988.

Reich, Robert B. *Tales of a New America.* New York: Times Books, 1987.

Reischauer, Edwin O. *The Japanese Today: Change and Continuity.* Cambridge, Mass.: Harvard University Press, 1988.

Sansom, George. *A History of Japan, 1615–1867.* Tokyo: Charles E. Tuttle, 1963.

Scherkenbach, William W. *The Deming Route to Quality and Productivity: Road Maps and Roadblocks.* Washington, D.C.: CeePress Books, 1986.

Schlossstein, Steven. *Trade War: Greed, Power, and Industrial Policy on Opposite Sides of the Pacific.* New York: Congdon & Weed, 1984.

Sloan, Alfred P., Jr. *My Years with General Motors,* edited by John McDonald with Catharine Stevens. Garden City, N.Y.: Doubleday, 1964.

Smith, Adam. *An Inquiry into the Nature and Causes of the Wealth of Nations.* London, 1776; New York: The Modern Library, Cannan Edition, 1965.

Striner, Herbert E. *Regaining the Lead: Policies for Economic Growth.* New York: Praeger, 1984.

Tazewell, William L. *Newport News Shipbuilding: The First Century.* Newport News, Va.: The Mariners' Museum, 1986.

Thompson, Robert Luther. *Wiring a Continent: The History of the Telegraph Industry in the United States, 1832–1866.* Princeton, N.J.: Princeton University Press, 1947; New York: Arno Press, 1972.

van Wolferen, Karel. *The Enigma of Japanese Power.* New York: Knopf, 1989.

Vogel, Ezra F. *Japan as Number One: Lessons for America.* Cambridge, Mass.: Harvard University Press, 1979.

Walton, Mary. *Deming Management at Work.* New York: Putnam's, 1990.

Wolf, Marvin J. *The Japanese Conspiracy: The Plot to Dominate Industry World Wide — and How to Deal with It.* New York: Empire Books, 1983.

ARTICLES

"America 2000: An Education Strategy." U.S. Department of Education, Apr. 18, 1991.

"America's Decadent Puritans." *The Economist,* July 28, 1990, pp. 11–12.

Arai, Joji. "Productivity Experience in Japan." *International Productivity Journal,* Spring 1990, pp. 59–65.

Associated Press. "Productivity of U.S. Workers Declines 0.8 Percent in 1990." Raleigh, N.C., *News and Observer,* Mar. 7, 1991, p. 10C.

———. "Rate of Imprisonment in U.S. Is Cited as Highest in World." *New York Times,* Jan. 7, 1991, p. A14.

Avishai, Bernard, and William Taylor. "Customers Drive a Technology-Driven Company: An Interview with George Fisher." *Harvard Business Review,* November–December 1989, pp. 107–14.

Barnett, Jim. "Workers Manage to Make the Decisions." Raleigh, N.C., *News and Observer,* Mar. 8, 1991, p. 6C.

"Be Bold, Be British." *The Economist,* Mar. 23, 1991, p. 19.

Birnbaum, Jeffrey H. "White House to Name 22 Technologies It Says Are Crucial to Prosperity, Security." *Wall Street Journal,* Apr. 25, 1991, p. A2.

Bolte, Gisela. "Interview: Will Americans Work for $5 a Day?" *Time,* July 25, 1990, pp. 12–14.

Bradsher, Keith. "Building a Dream on Wireless Gear." *New York Times,* Oct. 16, 1990, p. C2.

Byrne, John A., and William C. Symonds. "The Best Bosses Avoid the Pitfalls of Power." *Business Week,* Apr. 1, 1991, p. 59.

Carnevale, Anthony Patrick. "Train America's Workforce." American Society for Training and Development, 1990.

Choate, Pat. "Japan and the Big Squeeze." *Washington Post,* Sept. 30, 1990, p. D1.

Clark, James C. "Trivial Pursuits: What We Do and Don't Know Is Up for Grabs." *Washington Post,* July 2, 1990, p. D5.

Cole, Robert E. "Large-Scale Change and the Quality Revolution." In *Large-Scale Organizational Change.* Mohrman, Mohrman, Ledford, Cummings, Lawler, and Associates. New York: Jossey-Bass, 1989, chap. 11.

———. "What Was Deming's Real Influence?" *Across the Board,* February 1987, pp. 49–51.

Council on Competitiveness. "Mixed News on Quality Efforts in US." *Challenges,* November 1990, p. 5.

———. "Commission: U.S. Needs Skills to Grow On." *Challenges,* July 1990, p. 1.

"Crime in America." *The Economist,* Dec. 22, 1990, pp. 29–32.

Crosby, Philip B. "Criticism and Support for the Baldrige Award cont." *Quality Progress,* May 1991, pp. 42–43.

———. "The Pragmatic Philosophy of Phil Crosby." *Reflections,* No. 8.

Bibliography

Cutler, Blayne. "Health Scare." *American Demographics,* July 1990, p. 11.

Dentzer, Susan. "America's Scandalous Health Care." *U.S. News & World Report,* Mar. 12, 1990, pp. 25–30.

Dobyns, Lloyd. "Ed Deming Wants Big Changes, and He Wants Them Fast." *Smithsonian,* August 1990, pp. 74–83.

Dowd, Ann Reilly. "Help for Would-Be Exporters." *Fortune,* Apr. 8, 1991, p. 13.

Doyle, Denis P., Bruce S. Cooper, and Roberta Trachtman. "Education Ideas and Strategies for the 1990s." *American Enterprise,* March–April 1991, pp. 25–33.

Egan, Timothy. "Oregon Literacy Test Shows Many Lag in Basics." *New York Times,* Apr. 24, 1991, p. A23.

Ehrenreich, Barbara. "Our Health-Care Disgrace." *Time,* Dec. 10, 1990, p. 112.

Farnham, Alan. "The Trust Gap." *Fortune,* Dec. 4, 1989, pp. 56–76.

Farrell, Christopher, et al. "Why We Should Invest in Human Capital." *Business Week,* Dec. 17, 1990, pp. 88–90.

Feigenbaum, Armand V. "America on the Threshold of Quality." *Quality,* January 1990, pp. 16–18.

"Flight to the Bumble Bee." *The Economist,* Dec. 22, 1990, p. 89.

Frendenheim, Milt. "Health-Care Costs Grew Sharply for Employers." Raleigh, N.C., *News and Observer,* Jan. 29, 1991, p. D1.

Gabor, Andrea. "The Front Lines of Quality." *U.S. News & World Report,* Nov. 27, 1989, pp. 57–59.

———. "The Leading Light of Quality." *U.S. News & World Report,* Nov. 28, 1988, pp. 53–56.

Garvin, David A. "Quality on the Line." *Harvard Business Review,* September–October 1983, pp. 65–75.

Gill, Mark Stuart. "Stalking Six Sigma." *Business Month,* January 1990, pp. 42–46.

Godfrey, A. Blanton. "The History and Evolution of Quality in AT&T." *AT&T Technical Journal,* March/April 1986, pp. 8–20.

Gordon, Suzanne. "A National Care Agenda." *The Atlantic,* January 1991, pp. 64–68.

Gwynne, S. C. "The Right Stuff." *Time,* Oct. 29, 1990, pp. 74–84.

Hayes, Robert H., and William J. Abernathy. "Managing Our Way to Economic Decline." *Harvard Business Review,* July–August 1980, pp. 67–77.

Henkoff, Ronald. "What Motorola Learns from Japan." *Fortune,* Apr. 24, 1989, pp. 157ff.

Hoagland, Jim. "Awake and Plugged In at 4 a.m." *Washington Post,* Dec. 13, 1990, p. A23.

Hoerr, John. "Sharpening Minds for a Competitive Edge." *Business Week,* Dec. 17, 1990, pp. 72–78.

———. "With Job Training, a Little Dab Won't Do Ya." *Business Week,* Sept. 24, 1990, p. 95.

Holusha, John. "The Baldrige Badge of Courage — and Quality." *New York Times,* Oct. 21, 1990, p. 12F.

———. "Business and Health." *New York Times,* Dec. 19, 1989, p. 32.

Hopper, Kenneth. "Creating Japan's New Industrial Management: The Americans as Teachers." *Human Resources Management,* Summer 1982, pp. 13–34.

"How Companies Handle Layoffs." *Fortune,* Apr. 8, 1991, p. 39.

Ishihara, Shintaro. "Warning from Japan: Trust Yourselves, Not Your Leaders." *Washington Post,* Oct. 7, 1990, p. D6.

Johnson, Julie, and Robert D. Hershey, Jr. "Of Vines and Snakes." *New York Times,* Mar. 7, 1989.

Juran, J. M. "A Tale of the Twentieth Century." *Juran Report,* Number 10, Autumn 1989, pp. 4–13.

Karabatsos, Nancy. "Absolutely, Positively Quality." *Manager's Pak* (American Society for Quality Control), July 1990.

Katz, Donald R. "Coming Home." *Business Month,* October 1988, pp. 56–62.

Kindleberger, Charles P. "An American Economic Climacteric?" *Challenge,* January–February, 1974, pp. 35–44.

Kogure, Masao. "The Origin of Quality Contorol [sic] in Japan: The Birth of TQC." *Societas Qualitas* 4 (3), July/August 1990, JUSE. Translated from "Total Quality Control," 41 (7), July 1990, JUSE, pp. 58–65.

Koretz, Gene. "The Unions Thrive Abroad — But Wither in the U.S." *Business Week,* Sept. 10, 1990, p. 26.

Kurtzman, Joel. "Japan's Mythical Trade Surplus." *New York Times,* Dec. 9, 1990, p. F13.

"A Larger Crowd at the Finish." *U.S. News & World Report,* June 12, 1989.

Levin, Donald P. "The Campaign to Be 'American.' " *New York Times,* Feb. 14, 1989, p. D2.

Lieberman, Ernest D. "Rebuild America by Rebuilding Labor." *New York Times,* Jan. 8, 1989.

Lippert, John. "Cadillac Sets Sights on Quality Reputation." Raleigh, N.C., *News and Observer,* Nov. 29, 1990, p. D1.

Meadows, Donella. "Quality of Life." In *Earth '88: Changing Geographic Perspectives,*" edited by Harm J. De Blij. Washington, D.C.: National Geographic Society, 1988, pp. 332–49.

"Memos Withheld by Dinkins Cite Bridge Safety Hazards." *New York Times,* Jan. 31, 1991, p. A13.

Mitgang, Lee. "Panel's Report Urges Overhaul of Job Training." Raleigh, N.C., *News and Observer,* June 19, 1990, p. 2D.

Miyai, Jinnosuke. "Human Resources: Japan's Sole Natural Wealth." *International Productivity Journal,* Spring 1990, pp. 45–52.

"The Modern Adam Smith." *The Economist,* July 14, 1990, pp. 11–12.

Mullen, Jim. "Owners Need Not Apply." *Inc.,* August 1990, pp. 76–78.

"Murder America." *Newsweek,* July 9, 1990.

Oberle, Joseph. "Quality Gurus: The Men and Their Message." *Training,* January 1990, pp. 47–52.

"Oil Equals Power." *The Economist,* Jan. 12, 1991, pp. 83–84.

Pennar, Karen. "Yes, We're Down. No, We're Not Out." *Business Week,* Dec. 17, 1990, pp. 62–63.

Postel, Sandra, and Christopher Flavin. "Reshaping the Global Economy." In *State of the World, 1991.* Worldwatch Institute, project director Lester R. Brown. New York: Norton, 1991, pp. 170–88.

"The Public Is Willing to Take Business On." *Business Week,* May 29, 1989, p. 29.

Reich, Robert B. "Who Is Them?" *Harvard Business Review,* March–April 1991, pp. 77–88.

———. "The Real Economy." *The Atlantic,* February 1991, pp. 35–52.

———. "Who Is Us?" *Harvard Business Review,* January–February 1990, pp. 53–64.

Rice, Marc. "Medical Assistants, Prison Guards to Be in Demand, Study Says." Raleigh, N.C., *News and Observer,* Apr. 10, 1991, p. 10C.

Rifkin, Glenn. "Pursuing Zero Defects Under the Six Sygma [sic] Banner." *New York Times,* Jan. 13, 1991, p. F9.

Rosecrance, Richard. "Too Many Bosses, Too Few Workers." *New York Times,* July 15, 1990, p. F11.

Rosenthal, Harry F. "FBI Says Violent Crime Up in U.S." Raleigh, N.C., *News and Observer,* Apr. 29, 1991, p. 1A.

Rowen, Hobart. "Japanese Market Strength Is Detroit's Own Fault." Raleigh, N.C., *News and Observer,* Nov. 9, 1990, p. 19A.

Samuelson, Robert J. "What Good Are B-Schools?" *Washington Post,* May 9, 1990, p. 27.

Sanger, David E. "Japan Shuts U.S. Rice Exhibition." *New York Times,* Mar. 18, 1991, p. C1.

———. "U.S. Suppliers Get a Toyota Lecture." *New York Times,* Nov. 1, 1990, p. C1.

Sawhill, Isabel V. "Taxes, Benefits, Choices." *Washington Post,* Nov. 5, 1990, p. A15.

Schmidt, William E. "Hard Work Can't Stop Hard Times." *New York Times,* Nov. 25, 1990, p. 1.

Sensenbrenner, Joseph. "Quality Comes to City Hall." *Harvard Business Review,* March–April 1991, pp. 4–10.

Shearer, Lloyd. "From the Fact File, Intelligence Report." *Parade,* Feb. 25, 1990.

Shiba, Shoji. "Quality Knows No Bounds." *Look Japan,* May 1989, pp. 30–31.

———. "Managers of Quality." *Look Japan,* April 1989, pp. 30–31.

Simmons, Tim. "Proposal Would Cut Teachers, School Jobs." Raleigh, N.C., *News and Observer,* Mar. 28, 1991, p. 1B.

"The State of the Nation-State: With All Her Faults, She Is My Country Still." *The Economist,* Dec. 22, 1990, pp. 43–46.

"A Story So Short, Even Kids Who Take the SATs Can Read It." *Newsweek,* Sept. 10, 1990, p. 33.

Taguchi, Genichi, and Don Clausing. "Robust Quality." *Harvard Business Review,* January–February 1990, pp. 65–75.

Taylor, Alex, III. "Can Iacocca Fix Chrysler — Again?" *Fortune,* Apr. 8, 1991, pp. 50–54.

"Turn of the Screw." *The Economist,* Jan. 19, 1991, p. 64.

Uchitelle, Louis. "No Recession for Executive Pay." *New York Times,* Mar. 18, 1991, p. C1.

———. "Business Scene: The True Roots of U.S. Decline." *New York Times,* Oct. 22, 1990, p. C2.

"The Value of an Education." *New York Times,* Nov. 8, 1989.

Wade, Nicholas. "Editorial Notebook: America's Last Robot?" *New York Times,* Sept. 29, 1990, p. 22.

Waldrop, Judith. "You'll Know It's the 21st Century When . . ." *American Demographics,* December 1990, pp. 23–27.

———. "The Dropout Myth." *American Demographics,* October 1990, pp. 17–18.

Walker, William N. "Trade Doesn't Need Scapegoats." *New York Times,* Jan. 6, 1987.

Wareham, Ralph E. "Supplement 1.2: History of Statistical Quality Control." In *Handbook on Statistical Quality Control,* c. 1945, pp. 1.2a–1.2e.

Wicker, Tom. "U.S. Should Attack the Real Deficit." Raleigh, N.C., *News and Observer,* Nov. 10, 1990, p. 15A.

Wiggenhorn, William. "Motorola U: When Training Becomes an Education." *Harvard Business Review,* July–August 1990, pp. 71–83.

Wood, Robert Chapman. "The Prophets of Quality." *Quality Review,* Winter 1988, pp. 18–25.

Woodruff, David, et al. "A New Era for Auto Quality." *Business Week,* Oct. 22, 1990, pp. 84–96.

Zeman, Ned, Lucy Howard, et al. "Pessimism." *Newsweek,* Dec. 24, 1990, p. 6.

TELEVISION AND MOTION PICTURE

Cacoyannis, Michael. *Zorba the Greek.* Based on the novel by Nikos Kazantzakis. Great Britain: Rockley Productions, 1964.

Dobyns, Lloyd. *The Deming Library,* vols. 1–18. Washington, D.C.: CC-M Productions, 1987–91.

———. *Work Worth Doing, Parts 1 & 2.* Washington, D.C. (U.S. Dept. of Labor): CC-M Productions, 1988.

———. *The Japan They Don't Talk About.* New York: NBC News, April 22, 1986.

———. *Japan vs. USA: The Hi-Tech Shoot-Out.* New York: NBC News, Aug. 14, 1982.

Dobyns, Lloyd, and Reuven Frank. *If Japan Can, Why Can't We?* New York: NBC News, June 24, 1980.

UNPUBLISHED DOCUMENTS

Arai, Joji. "Quality World-Wide Perspective." Lecture, National Productivity Network, Mexico City, Mexico, Nov. 26, 1990.

Crosby, Philip B. Letter to the author. Aug. 6, 1990.

Deming, W. Edwards. "A System of Profound Knowledge for Industry, Education, and Government." Typewritten, Oct. 5, 1990.

———. "Quality." Lecture, Ohio Quality and Productivity Forum, King's Island Conference Center, Cincinnati, August 1989.

———. "Quality, Productivity and Competitive Position." Seminar, Quality Enhancement Seminars, Inc., Dallas, Sept. 27–30, 1988.

———. "My Sixth Trip to Japan, June, 1960." Mimeographed. Washington, D.C., 1960.

———. "My Fifth Trip to Japan, November 1955–January 1956." Mimeographed. Washington, D.C., 1956.

————. "Japan 1950." Mimeographed. Washington, D.C., 1950.

Feigenbaum, Armand. "A Judgment on the National Quality Award." Testimony, House Committee on Science, Space, and Technology, Mar. 20, 1990.

Galvin, Robert. Untitled remarks. Malcolm Baldrige National Quality Award ceremony, Washington, D.C., Feb. 22, 1989.

Hart, Christopher. Testimony, House Committee on Science, Space, and Technology, Apr. 20, 1989.

Joiner, Brian. "Learning How to Learn Faster." Lecture, Ohio Quality and Productivity Forum, King's Island Conference Center, Cincinnati, August 1988.

Koyanagi, Kenichi. "The Deming Prize." Pamphlet, The Union of Japanese Science and Engineering, Tokyo, 1955, revised 1960.

Mount Edgecumbe High School. "Snow White and the New Management System." Presentation, Sitka, Alaska, 1990.

Osterwise, Laurence. Untitled remarks. Malcolm Baldrige National Quality Award ceremony, Washington, D.C., Feb. 13, 1990.

Reimann, Curt W. "Quality in the United States." Testimony, House Committee on Science, Space, and Technology, Mar. 20, 1990.

Samuel, Howard D. "Is a Level Playing Field a Fantasy?" Undelivered lecture.

Sarasohn, Homer M. Letter to the author. Oct. 11, 1990.

Smith, Frederick W. Untitled remarks. Malcolm Baldrige National Quality Award ceremony, Washington, D.C., Feb. 13, 1990.

Stepp, John R. "Global Competition: The Role of Industrial Relations." Presentation, U.S. Department of Labor, Washington, D.C., June 2, 1987.

Tribus, Myron. "TQM at the Grass Roots." Preliminary discussion paper. Undated (Spring 1991).

————. "The Application of Quality Management Principles in Education, at Mt. Edgecumbe High School, Sitka, Alaska." Report for presentation. November 1990.

For the three-part video series
Quality . . . Or Else
and
companion Course of Study,
please contact:

CC-M Productions
8510 Cedar Street
Silver Spring, MD 20910

■ 800-453-6280